What people are saying about *Leading from the Heart* ...

"Kay Gilley's new book directly addresses the most dearly-needed personal characteristic we need in the world at this crucial time in human evolution: courage. **Leading from the Heart** is a prescription for transformation. It offers a road map for those who can summon the spiritual courage to be absolutely authentic—to know and love themselves, be willing to change, and lead from the heart with power and conviction."—**John E. Renesch**, editor/publisher, *The New Leaders*

"Kay Gilley has written a book that profoundly and persuasively reminds us that 'who we are' is the more basic consideration that requires our attention before we consider issues of management and organization. And, she offers some very practical advice and exercises to help us pursue a 'path of courage and heart.' This is a tough minded, open hearted, exhilarating book that will be appreciated by organizational leaders who are open to changing themselves as well as their organizations."—**Winston Franklin**, CEO & Executive Vice President, Institute of Noetic Sciences

"**Leading from the Heart** is a personal, insightful, and passionate story about holistic healing in the workplace. I heartily recommend it to everyone seeking the courage to be more productive and fulfilled at work."—**Joan Borysenko, Ph.D.**, author, *Minding the Body, Mending the Mind*

"Kay's questions are faced honestly and her ideas considered seriously. This thought provoking book provides a very encouraging framework to both know what it means and to actually find one's own way to lead from the heart."—**John Davis**, Director of Business Development, MEMC Electronic Materials, Inc.

"A compelling guide for leaders who dare to make their personal values and business spirit more congruent."—**Dr. Patricia A. Fishkoff**, Austin Family Business Program, Oregon State University

"This book represents an outstanding explanation of what we must all go through as leaders to achieve the best leadership we can. It is a must read for any manager responsible for taking their organization through major change. Congratulations, Kay Gilley. You've hit a home run."—**Ed Oakley**, co-author, *Enlightened Leadership—Getting to the Heart of Change*

Leading from the Heart

LEADING FROM THE HEART

Choosing Courage over Fear in the Workplace

KAY GILLEY, M.S., PHR

Butterworth–Heinemann

Boston Oxford Johannesburg Melbourne New Delhi Singapore

Butterworth–Heinemann

A member of the Reed Elsevier group

Recognizing the importance of preserving what has been written, Butterworth–Heinemann prints its books on acid-free paper whenever possible.

Library of Congress Cataloging-in-Publication Data
Gilley, Kay.
    Leading from the heart : choosing courage over fear in the
    workplace / Kay Gilley.
        p.   cm.
    Includes bibliographical references and index.
    ISBN 0-7506-9835-7 (pbk. : alk. paper)
    1. Leadership.   2. Employee motivation.   I. Title.
HD57.7.G55   1996
658.3'14—dc20   96-26132
                                                CIP

British Library Catalouging-in-Publication Data
A catalogue record for this book is available from the British Library.

The publisher offers special discounts on bulk orders of this book.
For information, please contact:

Manager of Special Sales
Butterworth–Heinemann
313 Washington Street
Newton, MA 02158–1626
Tel: 617-928-2500
Fax: 617-928-2620

For information on all Business publications available, contact our World Wide Web home page at: http:/www.bh.com/bb

10 9 8 7 6 5 4 3 2 1

Printed in the United States of America

To my father and Jim Hargreaves,
with love and gratitude.

Table of Contents

Acknowledgments

Even before I sat down to start this book, I knew that writing it had to be a collaborative effort. I could not write about working collaboratively and learning to learn together without reflecting those practices in every step of the project. Although I put my soul into the project and shepherded it, the book belongs to many people. I cannot list everyone who has supported me on my own journey to the Path of Courage and in the development of my ideas, but I would like to publicly thank those people who were most important to me in this work.

Dave Peck, my special friend and professional associate, has supported me with words of encouragement and with suggestions. When I was ready to give up in the proposal-writing and marketing phases, he nudged me along and kept me on the Path of Courage. Forty-plus people read various versions of the manuscript. A handful went beyond the call of duty, sometimes reading multiple versions, to give me the detailed feedback that significantly shaped the book: Ben Bonner, Dan Desler, John Harelson, Kent Jennings, Kar Lazarus, Marshal McReal, and Michael Scott Rankin.

My friend and colleague Maggie Moore made many contributions not only to the book but also to the development of my consulting practice: When I started my business shortly after graduate school, she began mentoring me and has been instrumental in helping me develop my own ideas. At one point during the writing of this book when I faced completing a rewrite in very little time, Maggie dropped everything and spent most of a vacation proofreading and editing my manuscript.

Lysle Betts, Janna Knittel, and Amy Winkelman are proof that my angels have been watching over me and over this project. Each came into my life just when I needed help with the technical editing of the book, and each "just coincidentally" had a gap in her own career which made space for my project.

My agent, Sheryl Fullerton, lent her expertise, patience, sympathy, and encouragement to artfully guiding me through the proposal-writing process and then worked determinedly to find a publisher. Wink Franklin and Willis Harman at the Institute of Noetic Sciences (Sausalito, California) helped bring Sheryl and me together.

Finally, I want to mention those people who contributed to this book by enriching my life: Paul Frishkoff, accounting professor at the University of Oregon, who helped me to develop my own ideas through his course, Creativity in Business; Meg Wheatley, who wrote *Leadership and the New Science*, inspired me to think in a new way about organizations, and provided Berkana Institute for exploring these new ways of thinking; the people in my client companies, who allowed me to receive as well as give in my work; Kathryn Ralston, whose friendship and encouragement have been critical to me.

I owe special acknowledgment to Mary Jeanne Jacobsen, who has been my partner in growth; to Kay Porter, without whom there would have been no journey; to my father, who taught me about leadership by the way he lived his life; and to Jim Hargreaves, who helped me find the courage to do almost everything.

Introduction

This is a story of love, truth, courage, and growth for leaders and for organizations. It is a personal, sometimes deeply personal, story about my passion: guiding people and organizations to achieve their potential, working in community with one another. I fervently believe that people cannot achieve their full potential in an organization that is not achieving its own potential. By the same token, the organization cannot achieve its potential without the individuals within them achieving their own. None of us can hope to elicit from others qualities by which we ourselves are unwilling to live and work.

At the doorstep of the twenty-first century, organizations of all kinds—nonprofits, business, industry, and governments—face turbulence unlike any they have ever known. As chaos and confusion become more and more common and the pace of change accelerates dramatically, leaders must be able to work in conditions of increasing and continuing ambiguity: stable conditions simply don't exist any more. Leaders must display a deep, centered courage and authenticity that *en-courages* those around them to learn to deal with uncertainty, to keep the organization on course, and to be open to change. If organizations are to survive and thrive—indeed if our society is to survive and thrive—leaders must find new perspectives on leading.

A missing piece in most businesses has inhibited organizational unity—a phenomenon that holds people and organizations together, inspires them, and gives the resilience and responsiveness necessary to grow and develop in increasingly complex environments. This missing component isn't linear, logical, rational, or even explainable: it just happens when the "magicians"—the leaders—create the right conditions. Then, although the workplace experience may swing from exciting to peaceful and satisfying, people feel happy and energized. This "magic" generates the capacity to do the seemingly undoable.

Many traditional, hierarchical organizations have failed or faltered in the past two decades. Others hope for the easy, quick fix and hang on through a desperate and accelerating cycle of organizational change efforts. Although efforts at workplace democracy, employee involvement, and high performance work systems generally improve results and increase satisfaction, they often leave the people in them feeling over-worked and burned out. Leaders at all levels of all organizations must reevaluate their perspectives on work and begin to find ways to work which energize and renew the people within them.

Joe is a client of mine. He is fifty, and his current company is the largest of several largely successful ventures he has started during his career. Joe's present company is very promising. Applying innovative approaches to standard ways of delivering his service, he has developed a model that is drawing industry recognition and investment interest nationally. His other ventures were "small potatoes" compared to this company's potential, and the work I have done with him has helped him identify his fears about moving forward. He is now committed to building the company to its potential.

Some time ago I attended a meeting in which Joe talked to a group of his managers about the future of his young and rapidly growing company. He shares his hopes and dreams, and he shares his fears about continuing to grow the company. Even as his voice breaks and a tear comes to his eye, he shares with the managers both his sense of responsibility to the employees and the company's clients and his faith that the team that helped bring the company this far will continue to keep it healthy and prosperous. He asks for their commitment to take the company to its full potential. There is great enthusiasm: as one manager later put it, "I'm really jazzed to make this happen!" And the growth is happening.

In the same city just a few miles away, Ted, the leader of a similar organization gives a similar speech, but Ted lacks the courage to name and address his fears. He tries to make all the managers happy by telling them what he thinks they want to hear, but this approach makes the managers question his integrity. His past exaggerations have led to skepticism and cynicism among his employees. People listen dutifully as Ted fidgets and then recites his remarks despite his feelings of unease. When he is finished, his audience asks itself one question: "Will it *really* happen?" Then, a manager asks whether they have to go back to work; after all, it is 3:30 P.M. on Friday. Ted, feeling let down, goes back to his office.

Why is this "magic" present in some organizations and not in others? In this book I discuss the nonquantifiable, intangible aspects of organizations that can emanate from the leadership at all levels to produce this magic and explain what allows Joe to accomplish incredible growth with dynamic flexibility while Ted and his company trudge along and just survive from one day to the other.

I would not have been open to reading, much less writing, this book just a few years ago, when I thought that any worthwhile concepts should be reducible to a set of defined parameters and cause-effect actions. Many readers of this book may share the same opinion. I ask those readers to have faith, while I acknowledge that I once would not have mustered such faith myself.

Although I have written extensively over the years, in the early stages of this project I spent several days wrestling with words in a new way. After the words began to flow, the solution to a puzzle which I had been seeking for four years began unfolding on the computer screen. This experience reminded me of a line from Meg Wheatley's book *Leadership and the New Science*: "Disorder can play a critical role in giving birth to new, higher forms of order." Earlier I had looked for surface order and had looked at *things*, at what people were *doing*: behaviors, practices, approaches, training. The solution to my puzzle, however, was not to be found in *doing*. The answer was in a higher form of order.

We must look at the ways we run organizations as we approach the twenty-first century. We must stop focusing on what we *do* and begin to consider who we *are* as human beings in community with each other. The doing and the being in our organizations are both important for accomplishing our purposes, but we must balance our focus in the workplace. In this book I emphasize *being*, because traditionally we have only been concerned with the *doing*.

When we experience people as machines or as stagnant entities, we experience organizations in the same way. Neither we nor our organizations are mechanistic or static. Organizations are living systems of human beings. The intangible missing pieces that machine models lack are the very things living systems have: joy and vitality, which work can and should bring to people.

Ignoring the personal integrity that people bring to their work and how they have been in relationship to that work can cause *doing* to fail partly or completely. Leaders wrongly expect *doing* to equal *results*.

What we do ≠ Results we get

Instead the invisible factor of *who we are* is integral to the results.

What we do + Who we are = Results we get

Our quantitative minds have tried and tried to retain equilibrium while ignoring the critical *who we are* component. When we take *who we are* out of one side of the equation, forces bent on equilibrium subtract it from the results. Yet we fail to understand why the results we get never seem to be what we expect, at least not over the long term.

What we do = Results we get (who we are)

We always seem to get something less than the results we expect or hope we will get. As managers tinker and tinker with *what we do*, the failure to acknowledge the *who we are* factor creates greater and greater disequilibrium, weakness, awkwardness, and the inability to flex and change on a dime as conditions require. Tinkering with what we do can produce moderate improvements and even significant short-term improvements; but tinkering burns people out and leaves them sapped of creativity in the workplace and sapped of energy for the rest of life. By itself, changing what we do hasn't produced the results we want over the long run, and it never will until who we are is taken into account.

My inner wisdom tells me that as I write, there are leaders across this country who are beginning to feel, intuitively, that something has been neglected. They are beginning to feel that it is time to do something different, and they also believe it begins with them. They have a sense, but they don't really know what it is all about.

More than doing, this *something different* isn't easily described, and it is frightening. They know they must *be* different, but they don't know what being different means. It's a different way of *being* in our workplaces, and it's a different way of *being* on this earth. Sadly for many of us, our being out of the context of our doing is a foreign concept indeed.

Being different requires us to view the organization from a new perspective. This book integrates four concepts that are critical to the new organization perspective for the twenty-first century. This new perspective says that organizations don't change, people do, and until we are willing to be different in our leadership roles, real organizational transformation will not occur.

The first of the four concepts that make up the new perspective says that there are two paths in life and in work. There is the Path of Fear, which is taken by most leaders in the United States today, and there is the Path of Courage and Heart, which connects people with spirit, joy, and passion in their work. The new perspective requires us to consciously choose the Path of Courage and Heart and then to be purposeful about reflecting that decision in all that we do. Our traditional, analytical, control-driven systems of management (a word that shares the root, the Latin *manus*, "hand," with the word *manipulation*) have so indoctrinated most of us to a fear-driven reality that many have lost touch with the courage that is part of every one of us by nature.

Leaders on the Path of Courage know that twenty-first-century responsiveness demands all the resources of a company: the whole person—the body, mind, and spirit—of every person, including the leaders themselves. On the Path of Courage, leaders create an environment of respect for people and for the process of involving people. They know it is more important to listen than to talk. It is more important to ask questions that increase awareness and consciousness than to have answers. Leaders on the Path of Courage are purposeful about outcomes, but they are open and flexible about how to accomplish them. The ability to live and work on the Path of Courage comes from a strong sense of inner being.

The second concept in the new organizational perspective comes in because leaders need to do their own internal growth work before they will have the courage to accomplish significant transformations within their companies. Real organizational transformation requires a complete change in our belief systems; it requires negating virtually all our old assumptions and certainties about how things are and replacing those assumptions with a new worldview. This change requires literally giving up the world as we have known it in exchange for a world in which the old rules do not work. Not only don't the old rules work, there simply are no rules about what to do in the new world because it is changing too rapidly. The only rules that work are those about being—those in which we examine our relationships to self, work, each other, and our larger environment. The new world demands that we do not and cannot know what will happen. People in a company cannot be asked to go through that free fall unless their leader has been there and has survived to tell about it enthusiastically.

Many "enlightened" leaders turn to gurus, the Bible, Confucius, Buddha, the *I Ching*, great philosophers, and other sources of enlightenment to aid them in their manipulation of the future, but few of these leaders have personally grown. They have intellectualized the concepts of spirit, spirituality, and soul but haven't truly experienced a change in their being or their core belief systems when it comes to leading people. This book offers the next step. It guides leaders through the *experience* of personal growth.

The third concept in the new perspective is that we must focus our efforts at change on the *being* of people rather than on their *doing*. Most organizational change only tinkers with the surface of the old system by focusing on changing how we do things. Increasingly it has become clear that the answer does not lie in what managers or leaders do. Fundamental change can be made only by focusing on being, how we should be rather than what we should do. This is not another how-to-*do*-it book: It is a nonprescriptive how-to-*be*-it book, which invites readers to discover their own unique personal journey to a new way of being.

In the fourth concept, the new perspective invites readers to begin to see work differently. When our relationship with our work is filled with energy, vitality, creativity, and enthusiasm, work becomes an integral part of life, and being whole is an important part of the new way of being. Spirit and creativity and the need for a productive outlet for them in community with others are as much parts of our humanness as are our bodies and our minds. When creativity is stifled, people become sick, and companies become stagnant. We need a new perspective in our organizations, not just so that we can feel better, although we will feel better. We need a new perspective because the future belongs to leaders who are self-aware, conscious, committed, and courageous from the inside out. These are the magical qualities that allow organizations and the people in them to come to life.

I am a seasoned manager. I have worked in traditional and conservative organizations since the mid-1960s. I have lived in conservative parts of the country. I have a graduate degree in business from a very traditional university. I understand bottom lines and profit margins. I understand investment incentive and return on investment. Talking about magical qualities in the workplace and the personal role of leaders in producing the magic is fearsome to me. Yet the evidence has become too overwhelming to ignore. If the bottom lines of organizations are to be strong, if there is to be a healthy return on investment that provides the incentive for putting money into American business instead of following the flood of investment into foreign markets, and if U.S. products are to be competitive with foreign products in quality, price, availability, and innovation, the need for a new way of working can no longer be ignored.

The book is divided into three major parts. Part One, "Searching for a New Path," details my search to define that magical quality that some workplaces seem to have and that others lack. The "path" is the journey that a leader must take to come to peace with his or her inner being, in order to choose the Path of Courage. Part Two, "Exploring the Path to Leading from the Heart," takes the reader along on my journey of discovering my own spirit and shares the soul searching and the lessons I learned along the way, as well as offering examples of similar learning by others. Part Three, "Buying the Ticket," explores the price that must be paid for commitment to this way of working; describes work as the only tangible manifestation of spirit-borne qualities such as creativity, community, expansiveness, aspiration, and inspiration that many people have in life; and finally invites readers to find the courage to join me in a commitment to make a difference in our workplaces.

Because some of the ideas that I introduce may be new or may seem abstract to the reader, I have included features to assist readers to become acquainted with the new concepts of leadership. First is the tool kit. Most of us can generate volumes of the things we should *do* as managers, but for many of us the shift to leadership and *being* leaves us in a vacuum. What now? Parts Two and Three are designed to acquaint readers with the new concepts of being. "Tools for Being on the Path of Courage" are provided at the ends of the chapters in each of those parts. These tools are designed to incorporate some of the concepts explored in the chapter into a list of things to remember about being. Each chapter also includes one or more introspective activities to guide readers' personal explorations. Early readers of this manuscript thought that working through some of these simple exercises not only helped them understand the suggested changes but also helped them integrate the new ways of being into their daily work and personal lives. One reader even said she came to understand the dynamics of her organization for the first time.

Leading from the Heart is not a book for skimming or speed-reading. Several readers of the manuscript said that they spent a great deal of time on the book. Some mentioned reading particular chapters over and over again. One said he became "hyper-connected," and he sometimes spent a full week on a single chapter, reading, rereading, doing the activities, and processing the ideas presented. Still another used the book as a "business-person's meditation guide." After he finished his initial reading of the manuscript, he would let the book fall open each day, and then he would read that section. He related that often it provided him with exactly the advice he needed for the events of the day.

This is not the book that I set out to write, although I believe I have actually been working on it for years. It is not at all what I expected. It is a work from my own place of wisdom that knows everything my brain does and much more than my brain can comprehend. What a change that was for me! I was accustomed to deciding what I would do, determining how to do it, and then *making* it happen. This time something stronger than my intellectual, analytical self guided my work. My subconscious began solving puzzles I had been tinkering with for years. At times I wrote with such fervor and passion that I lost track of other things and discovered parts of me I hadn't known before: the poet, the musician, the dancer, the artist, and the playful child. I knew peace, joy, acceptance, and understanding, the likes of which I have never known. Such a connection to, and trust in, this inner wisdom, I believe, the leaders in our organizations desperately need in order to provide the courage required for increasingly turbulent times. As leaders discover and integrate parts of themselves they have never considered to be part of their business or professional personas, they bring life to their workplaces in ways they have never imagined possible.

Writing this book has been a gift to myself and to others—a gift of love, a gift from my heart. Sharing it with you brings deep, heartfelt, and peaceful meaning and connection to my life. I hope you consider the ideas my gift to you.

Part 1

Searching for a New Path

Chapter 1

Accepting Our Silent Earthquakes

In the winter of 1989–1990, the world began to change. A slow, silent earthquake began to crumble physical structures as great as the Berlin Wall and symbolic structures of monolithic bureaucracy like the statue of Lenin in Red Square. The new leaders included poets and playwrights who had struggled to keep the spirits of whole nations of people alive amid systems that sought to stifle the individual spirit. After generations of struggle for survival within confining structures, millions were "liberated" into a life of chaos. They had broken from the yoke of totalitarianism without having any structure or order to put in its place. They found themselves in the midst of the pain, confusion, and struggle that chaos inevitably brings. Chaos is a creative incubator from which a higher order can emerge, but chaos can be frightening. It can be frightening for the people plunged into the midst of it, for those charged to lead them, and for those who watch and wait and feel powerless to help. Fear can breed protective measures, violence aimed at ensuring the survival of one's own family, friends, and kind. At its extreme, fear can breed genocide.

Many of those propelled into the chaos are angry. Some expected a painless metamorphosis—new birth without the gestation period or the pains of labor. Others feel angry and victimized because they didn't choose this quiet revolution. Who will take care of them now? Still others are angry because quiet revolution hasn't been so quiet after all. They feel cheated because nations they believed would protect them did little but watch the decay, the war, and the genocide. The people who started the earthquake instinctively knew that there had to be a better way to live—a life in which they could not only survive but could thrive. They cleared the way to make it happen. Yet generations of programming left their native instincts about how to live in a different way anesthetized.

Anyone who has gone through any of life's transitions probably recognizes the signs. The large-scale social transition in Eastern Europe was not unlike the death of a parent or spouse, a divorce, the birth of a child, or a midlife crisis. In each there is the possibility for a better life, and in each there is a sense of loss. In each there are anger, fear, and often guilt and resentment. In each, when times are rough, there is wishing, maybe even trying, to go back, yet people know that it would never work. In each there is a chaotic time of gathering courage, patience, faith, and the commitment to move forward; a period of reassessment, exploration, discovery, and decisions about where life will lead us. To survive any of these personal transitions and thrive, we need a clear sense of direction, strong values, and a belief in our own ability to weather the storm and to have a better life because of our experience.

AN INVISIBLE EARTHQUAKE AT HOME

The slow, silent earthquake of Eastern Europe is not unlike the silent, invisible earthquake occurring in our U. S. workplaces. I often hear employers lament, "People just don't care anymore" or "You just can't get good help." Their complaints may vary. They talk about halfhearted performance. They deplore that employees don't think about what they're doing. They bemoan lack of commitment and "punching the clock" attitudes. They mourn a "lack of respect." They anguish about how careful and guarded they must be and how laws have tied their hands. And when the finger of blame is pointed, they blame everyone. The state and federal governments are blamed for excessive legislation and regulation; then they are blamed for not doing something. Managers, employees, schools, and parents are blamed for ineptness or indifference. International competition is blamed. Labor unions are blamed. The blame goes on and on.

At the same time, employees who have grown accustomed to secure employment if they "just do their jobs" have been thrust into roles that force them to give more of themselves—their creativity, teamwork, and problem-solving skills. Others downsized out of midmanagement jobs after many years are disillusioned because "After all those years, this is what I get!" People know instinctively that there has to be a better way. Yet the better way is not readily apparent. New management models have toyed with different forms, but little has really changed.

What is it that the employers want? They want energetic employees. They want enthusiasm, excitement, and initiative. They want employees who love their work—who put their heart into what they are doing. They want employees who care about the company, who see that everyone has to work together for the company to succeed. They want commitment and a spirited work force. They want trust. They want love. The employers want from employees what they often unknowingly are unable or unwilling to give: *themselves.* Employers have been unwilling or unable to give the people that work for them the benefit of the doubt, the trust, the faith, the risk taking and the commitment that they want and expect workers to give them.

Companies across America have turned to legions of consultants and management gurus to learn new ways of managing people, but many managers are discovering that their companies are not unlike a house without a foundation. It is hard to stabilize a company without a strong foundation so that it can be functional over time, especially amid chaos. These transitions are like personal ones. We need courage, patience, faith, and commitment to move forward. To survive and thrive, companies need a clear sense of direction, strong values, and a belief in their ability to weather the storm. When we weather personal crises, even though we often depend upon a support system of friends and family to provide encouragement, we ourselves make the changes and adaptations.

When an organization moves through a transition, leaders at all levels are called to elicit commitment, faith, patience, and courage. Leaders can exemplify a clear sense of vision for everyone, can embody the values and belief in the organization's ability to weather the storm. Leaders as individuals can make changes in their being that enable them to play the important roles in the transition.

Sam is a good example of a leader who has made that personal transformation. Sam is just over forty. He's a determined service entrepreneur who has taken a business from two employees to about two hundred in just over ten years by consciously choosing to "take the high road." His business has succeeded because it challenges the assumptions about how people should be treated—both inside the company and outside. When he first came to me, Sam's fast-growing company, that had a service-coverage area of about 60 miles square, was failing to keep pace with its growth, largely because Sam and other managers in the company were blocked by a host of fears in their relationships with each other and their relationships with themselves. I attended a meeting with Sam and several of his staff after he and I had spent months in coaching sessions exploring his new role as a leader who can transform his organization. A change that had been building for some time seemed to take place in an instant as he started talking softly but definitively:

> It occurs to me that we have been running this company on 50 percent, and 50 percent just isn't good enough anymore. I have done 50 percent of what I should have. I have failed to do the 50 percent that I didn't want to do, and no one has held me accountable. In an unspoken quid pro quo, I have let the rest of the management team get by with failing to do the 50 percent of their jobs that they don't like. I haven't held them accountable, and they haven't held me accountable.
>
> Then they have done the same thing with people who reported to them. At the end of this lack-of-accountability chain, there has been the person on the frontline trying to do a job. We haven't done our job in training, counseling, or following up on the counseling, and then we wonder why the employee isn't doing the job.
>
> I've gotten by with doing the 50 percent that I am comfortable with, and so has everybody else. Fifty percent just isn't good enough for this company any more.

Sam's speech could have become the opening salvo for a war of intimidation if he hadn't done the inner work to ensure the shift he was making was in alignment with his personal integrity and values, values that included a deeply held faith in people, a faith that had allowed him to build his business. Sam knew his company couldn't change until he personally changed. He had to change his relationship with himself before he could change his relationships with others and before he could ask them to change their relationships with him, with each other, and with their work. In the months that followed, an evolution began. Conflicts were resolved. Performance problems were addressed. Policies and procedures were developed. Uncomfortable situations that had been ignored were acknowledged and addressed. Things that had been put off "till we have more time" began to get attention. Accountability eased its way into Sam's company.

Courageous leadership is conscious leadership, and conscious leadership is hard because leaders begin to see how they have created what they have blamed others for and how they have created what they wanted to avoid. Conscious leadership is hard because it requires us to give up our illusions. Yet it is the only way to develop intentionality. It is the only way to achieve the vision, values, mission, and goals that we have worked so hard to develop in recent years and to make these things take on life and meaning for people everywhere in our organizations.

Insulated from their own hearts and their own core values, many managers have looked to employees for what they may have sensed, but not acknowledged, they themselves lacked. They have lacked caring, commitment, complete involvement, trust, courage. With a void in their sense of being, they have turned to learning to *do* things that generate in employees what the leaders themselves lack: new management techniques—Management-of-the-Month Club. These managers use new management techniques like an addictive drug to fill in the void in what they *are* with new things to *do*.

Just as a house needs a firm foundation to endure, for a company to be a spirited workplace over time the leadership must be courageous, patient, faithful, and committed at its very core of being. Then the company is leading from the heart. Often when I talk about leading from the heart, people think that I am talking about letting employees push management around. That is not my idea of leading from the heart. That isn't leadership of any kind. It is cowardice. Leading from the heart requires courage. The English word *courage* actually derives from the Latin word for "heart." As the physical heart enables us to have physical life, heart courage gives us life in another sense. We put our whole heart into the endeavor. We see the endeavor as a matter of life. Courage gives life to our work as leaders and to the relationships that are so important in workplaces alive with learning, growth, and improvement.

Over two thousand years ago, the Chinese philosopher Lao-tzu talked about *t'zu*, which he described as his "first treasure." *T'zu* in Chinese means caring or compassion, and the Chinese character for *t'zu* is rooted in the character for "heart." Lao-tzu wrote about *t'zu* as the source of courage. A company cannot be a spirited workplace over time without leadership that courageously brings life to the vision and values the company holds and embodies them in every act and in every decision. A company cannot be a spirited workplace over time without leadership that knows that every person in the organization has a critical role in its success as well as an unabashed belief in helping each person succeed. Ultimately a company cannot be a spirited workplace over time without individual leaders who have the courage to look inside and develop a loving relationship with themselves so they can stop needing to get from others what they most need to give themselves.

LEADERS: REAL HUMAN BEINGS LEADING REAL PEOPLE

Leaders who lead from the heart have a high level of self-awareness. They know who they really are at their core—the good, the bad, and the ugly. They don't crave new things to do like a drug that keeps parts of themselves compartmentalized. Some leaders are naturally able to lead. Many have spent years peeling away layers of insulation, unlearning the ways they have kept spirit distant from and uninvolved in their work and in their lives. They have spent years unlearning the habit of doing more and more to fill the void inside them and relearning the peace of just being present, open, and flexible. They have spent years unlearning ways of appearing to be superhuman to make room for a real human being to lead real people in an organizational quest. They have spent years unlearning that employees are robots without emotions and relearning that each person is a real human being with hopes, dreams, fears, hurts, and pains.

It is virtually impossible for real people to find the courage to exercise initiative to try new things, to make mistakes, and to learn from those mistakes in the presence of a perfect, superhuman being. In early meetings with executives and executive teams, I often bring a head of broccoli with me. This vegetable does get raised eyebrows and sometimes vegetable humor as people query what we are going to do with the broccoli. I then proceed to explain that I am about to explain the most important leadership lesson they may ever receive. I point out the general shape and configuration of the broccoli. Then I pull off the next largest division of the vegetable and note that it has the same shape and configuration. I break off each successively smaller unit of broccoli and demonstrate how each unit reflects the size and shape of the whole. Finally, I tell them that if we were to look at a single cell of broccoli, we would discover that, even on the cellular level, the plant retains the same shape and configuration as the whole.

Companies are a lot like broccoli. The leadership of a company is its "broccoli seed." What occurs at the top will be recreated again and again in successively larger business units until it encompasses the whole enterprise. So it is critical that the executive team understand exactly what it reflects into the organization. Self-awareness work is the work of discovering the broccoli seed of the company. It is about learning how everything that occurs is the result of the seed that has been planted by our actions, what we say, and either the consistencies or the incongruities between our words and actions. Just as Sam had unwittingly created broccoli seed for his organization that said, "Fifty percent is OK, as long as I don't have to do the things I don't like." When he said, "Fifty percent is *not* good enough," he planted a different kind of seed, the seed of accountability. When he walked his talk and began being accountable himself, he fertilized the seed. As he started holding others accountable, the seed began to replicate itself.

Work on self-awareness reveals to individuals and groups what is being created and what is needed for change. Groups that have done this work can consciously choose to plant seeds of learning, risk taking, social responsibility, respect for the environment, respect for the whole person in the company, or excellent customer service. It takes a lot of courage to erase our illusions and objectively see ourselves, both individually and collectively, but it is the only way that a company will discover what seeds it has planted. Sam is passing the courage test, one day at a time, and he is planting seeds of courage and accountability as he does.

When leaders get in touch with, and live as, the real human beings they are every minute of every day, then and only then can others be free to soar to greatness in the leader's presence. Joe, the client I mentioned in the Introduction who is growing a dynamic and innovative company, is beginning to get in touch with his greatness. For the first time, he sees the company he has created as his life's work. For the first time, he is able to feel a sense of purpose and to share his hopes and dreams (and even fears) with his whole team. He shares his need to work with people as a team and to help each of them achieve greatness so the company can achieve its potential. His approach is not theatrics; theatrics would be transparent. He speaks to people from the depths of his heart, from having taken a hard look at himself and accepted himself exactly as he is. He is frightened, and despite his fear, he is choosing the Path of Courage rather than the Path of Fear that, ironically, appears easier and safer. This exposure of human frailty has had an incredible impact on his company. Employees talk about feeling important and making a difference. They have spirit. Joe is learning to lead from the heart by peeling away layers of insulation. He is demonstrating the courage of heart leadership by looking within and doing his self-awareness work first.

EACH LEADER AND EACH INDIVIDUAL ARE UNIQUE

Before we can become leaders each of us must recognize that every human being is unique. To be a leader means seeing individuals, not monolithic groups of people. To be a leader means discovering what works for us personally when we are living from spirit, not following a how-to-do-it prescription in a book, and it means discovering and respecting that same place in each and every individual with whom we come in contact. To be a leader means actively seeking to guide people to find and work from the place where the company's broccoli seed and each person's individuality overlap, rather than forcing everyone to work in lockstep with the way we may personally prefer.

Categories and labels are mindless ways to avoid listening, to avoid thinking, to avoid personal decision making, and to avoid connection. When groups of people are categorized, the manager doesn't have to take time to think about the individual who is present. Categorization prevents even considering that an employee may be a hard-working, skilled person who is proud of consistently top-quality work, is active in his church, and leads a Scout troop. When a manager says, "He's union!" he avoids seeing the individual. It is much easier to hate a label than it is to hate a skilled craftsman who works hard, takes pride in his work, and is active in church and scouting.

When a union steward labels a woman "management," the single mother working full time, raising three kids on her own, and taking care of an aging father can be overlooked. We don't have to consider that she does volunteer work for the United Way campaign and works with her kids at the local food bank on Saturdays. Hate is much easier when we don't know those things. It's easy to hate "management," but much harder to hate a single mom who takes care of her father and takes her kids to volunteer at the food bank.

Categories and labels are easy ways to stop connection and to separate us. They cause us to focus on one part of an individual and by so doing to miss the whole person, to forget that the "union guy" and the "manager" are living, breathing human beings with feelings, a family, hopes and dreams, and a spirit just itching to soar. The leader who leads from the heart looks carefully at individuals, so the uniqueness and value of each are appreciated. Whenever generalization slips into our thinking, we must work at being conscious of it and at recognizing it for exactly what it is—a way to separate and disconnect us.

Everyone who works with us and for us is a human being with a heart, a mind, feelings, and a spirit. Traditional management structures have treated people as compartmentalized beings. The message has clearly been, "Bring your body and the part of your brain that thinks like we think and leave the rest at home." We cannot expect that we can sever an employee's arm and tell him or her to leave it at home. The bleeding from the severed arm makes the person weak and unproductive. But we sever people from their minds, spirits, and souls and expect them to perform at 100 percent. Traditional managers who have held such expectations have accepted neither their own spirits and souls nor the needs of those aspects of themselves, so they haven't been able to accept those aspects of others.

Acceptance of our authentic selves frees the energy that so many of us have diverted to keeping the person we truly are stuffed down inside where no one will see him or her. Acceptance frees the energy needed to bring ourselves completely to whatever it is we do. We don't need artificial symbols that reinforce our egos by telling us we are worthy and valuable. When we have self-confidence, confidence in our true, authentic self, we are able to be connected to the rest of the team. We believe in people, and that belief inspires others to give 100 percent and then some. We accept people just as they are and value differences as a gift of perspective and a step toward wholeness for the team. Although we often don't know what the growth will look like, leaders are learners and teachers who trust that change will bring exciting advancement. Leaders have courage, for their achievements take courage.

WHO ARE HEART LEADERS?

As I struggled to make the concepts in this book understandable, I thought about writing for my father, a longtime tool and die maker who retired from a low-level management position for an automobile manufacturer. How would I make these concepts understandable to him? Wrestling with this question, I realized that my father had been a natural at leading from the heart. After years of formal and informal educational research, I have now become aware that it was the leadership qualities that he embodied that I am talking about. This simple man with little formal education was a natural leader of people.

I can talk about what he *did*, but it was the person inside and his comfort with that person that enabled him to lead people so naturally. Always bringing infectious laughter with him, he had a zeal for living. Anything he took on, he did 100 percent, and it seemed natural for those around him to do the same. He was truly a team player, jumping in to help others without being asked. (One of his greatest challenges in making the transition to a position as manager in a union work environment was not being able to jump in and help when there was a deadline to be met.) My father was absolutely unconditional in his love and support for people and encouraged them to try new things and to do their very best. He inspired me, trusted me, and always the patient teacher, helped me learn from my mistakes. He always accepted me exactly as I was, but he wanted me to put 100 percent into being the person I was.

Although he worked very hard, he brought balance to his life by putting his all into everything that he did when he was doing it, whether it was dancing, fishing, gardening, reading voraciously, leading a community project, coaching a Little League baseball team, or supporting a child in a project. A lifelong student, he loved to learn, loved to help others learn, and was exhilarated by advancement and change. He truly cared about people, and he cared about helping them accomplish what they wanted for themselves. The way he lived brought energy to his life and to those around him. The qualities I had observed in my father as I was growing up were many of the ones I'd spent nearly thirty years trying to identify in effective leaders.

Although a few people who lead from the heart are naturals like my father, most have spent considerable time and energy unlearning the things that insulate them from spirit. They have often been crippled with years of management training, that teaches them how to keep others and ourselves "in control."

As the Latin root of the word suggests, traditional *management* training has often focused on manipulating people to the company's ends in the belief that the company can prosper when the individual cannot. Courageous leaders know that a company can never prosper over the long term unless those who make it up also prosper.

Those who lead from the heart have learned courage. They may often feel like the leader of a group of revolutionaries when they lead a group of people who have just discovered spirit for the first time. Not unlike the people of Eastern Europe, some of their employees may feel fear, guilt, anger, or resentment as they try to achieve their potential. Yet without workplace spirit, an organization is destined to mediocrity or failure. If the leader has the courage to lead from the heart, the payoffs are significant.

WHAT DOES HEART LEADERSHIP LOOK LIKE?

A friend of mine was recently involved in the creation of a work unit to manufacture a new product at her Fortune 100 company. The core team that developed the new unit wanted to build a team that tapped individual spirit. They did. A lengthy selection process incorporated criteria that were largely based upon the human qualities the individuals brought to the job: their leadership abilities.

Even though the workers, mostly production workers, had demonstrated significant personal leadership qualities before selection, more time was spent peeling away layers as a group. They spent five days as a group, learning more about themselves and what it means to be a member of a team—learning to help, to care about, and to respect their teammates. Leadership was developed at all levels in the team.

Although the team is still fairly young, the results have been extraordinary. Team members have taken "ownership" of the product line, and each feels accountable for getting the job done. Members actively seek and give feedback. The team has either met or beaten every scheduled milestone along the road to generating the new product, a highly unusual accomplishment within the company. Other production lines have required twelve individuals to do the work, but this team has accomplished a similar assignment with seven.

My friend, a manager from another department who attended part of a team meeting, observed what seemed more reminiscent of a football pep rally than of a work meeting. People exuded enthusiasm. "They cheered each other or the team five times while I was there!" This enthusiasm occurs when people are tuned into each other and share a belief in what they are doing together.

THE DOLLARS AND CENTS OF HEART LEADERSHIP

Although I am repeatedly told by businesspeople, "We don't have time for that stuff" or "We can't afford that touchy-feely stuff," study after study of companies learning to balance consciousness with their focus on the bottom line indicate that this approach is a financially winning formula that makes the world a better place in that to live and work. The rapid startup of the team at my friend's workplace initially saved the company the thousands of dollars often associated with delinquent starts, and the team continues to save with its enhanced quality and productivity. These are ways that heart leadership pays off for employers.

When I was explaining the premise of my book to a former department store detective, her eyes instantly lit up. With much animation, she began talking about a store in that she had once worked. For the first time, she recognized a pattern. Certain managers had consistently experienced higher theft rates than others had. When a manager changed, often the theft rate in a department changed.

Thinking over some of the managers involved, she believed that the ones who had treated employees with trust and respect and who had encouraged employees to be creative and innovative were the ones that had lower theft rates. Those who were most controlling had the highest theft rates. "Those employees whose managers treated them with respect and gave them the opportunity to grow didn't need *things* to fill their lives. Those who didn't get that opportunity from the job took *things* to fill their personal needs!"

"More than 35 percent of workers surveyed in a 1993 "fax poll" by *Inc.* magazine reported that a sense of mission and purpose is their single most important long-term motivator. Fewer than half that number were motivated by money."[1] When leaders intentionally plant broccoli

---

1. Margaret Kaeter, "Mission: Impossible?" *Business Ethics*, January–February, 1995, p. 24.

seed that enables people to experience consciousness, the sense of commitment, motivation, satisfaction, and purpose they feel becomes a financial asset.

Published in 1993, an eight-year study of companies profiled in the *100 Best Companies to Work For in America* revealed a 19 1/2 percent annual return for those companies during a period in that the three thousand largest companies in the United States averaged a 12 percent annual return.[2] Covenant Investment Management interviewed seven thousand government, business, and labor leaders to develop a 36-category index on social responsibility, that includes measures of employee, consumer, and community relations as well as responses to environmental problems.

Using this index, the firm rated the Business Week 1000 on performance. The business stocks that scored in the top 200 of this index had increased in value by 100 percent over the last five years while the Standard and Poor's index of 500 stocks had increased only by 85.4 percent. Even the middle 600 of this rating had experienced 92 percent growth that still outperformed the Standard and Poor's index by 6.6 percent.[3]

Kotter and Haskett studied corporate culture and performance and discovered that "over an 11-year period net profits grew 756 percent in companies that had an ethic of 'multiple stakeholder satisfaction and involvement,' compared to a 1 percent increase in a comparable set of companies that kept to traditional management practices."[4]

Although for at least fifteen years the rising cost of medical coverage to employers has been a recurring theme and cost-containment programs have become standard operating procedures, these very people have failed to their own accountability in creating an environment that fosters poor health. In the United States, heart attacks most frequently occur at 9:00 A.M. on Monday mornings, and the most common reason given by those who have heart attacks is "job dissatisfaction."[5] The stress created in our bodies when we are not working from spirit is a well-documented cause of a host of maladies that take their toll in medical costs.

---

2. Gary Hirschberg, "Is Corporate Responsibility Good for the Bottom Line?" Keynote address at the Transforming the Soul of Business conference, sponsored by the National Institute for New Corporate Vision, Hilton Head Island, SC, 8 February 1995.

3. See note 2 above.

4. Juanita Brown and David Isaacs, "Building Corporations as Communities: The Best of Both Worlds," in *Community Building: Renewing Spirit and Learning in Business*, ed. Kazimierz Gozdz. San Francisco, CA: New Leaders Press, 1995, p. 78.

5. Deepak Chopra, "Magical Body, Magical Mind," Nightingale-Conant Corporation, audiotape set.

Dr. Redford Williams has spent years researching the relationship between the emotional assumptions that people bring to life and their likelihood of having a heart attack. According to Williams, individuals exhibiting cynicism, a mistrusting attitude toward others, anger, aggressive treatment of others, time urgency, and free-floating hostility are extremely likely to have a heart attack.[6] Yet despite managers' feigning concern over health care and insurance costs, most companies manage their workers in a way that creates, or at least allows, these very characteristics not only to prevail but often to be rewarded.

Daniel Goleman, a psychologist and author of *Emotional Intelligence*, studies how our emotions either enable or impede our effectiveness. He reports on other research supporting Williams's findings:

> Howard Friedman, psychologist at the University of California at Irvine, analyzed more than 100 studies of personality and illness and found that chronic emotional distress—being constantly hostile, anxious, pessimistic or depressed—doubles a person's chances of serious disease. That makes incessant emotional distress a stronger risk factor than smoking. To the degree that we learn to control a hot temper or find more effective ways to relax, we lower our odds of illness and bolster the effectiveness of our immune and cardiovascular systems."[7]

People in spirit-respecting workplaces take time to know, and come to peace with, themselves. They understand why they have a "hot temper," and they work from a more relaxed place in themselves. When we ask people to "sell their souls to the company store" as the old song goes, whether consciously or not, the employees *will* extract more than a paycheck in return. The cost to the company may include increased theft, diminished quality, faltering customer service, or escalating insurance rates. When we lead from the heart and champion the development of the unique individual in every worker, the payback is greater than just a good feeling. When we provide an environment in which people can discover spirit, feel important, feel a part, and know they make a difference, we are rewarded with increased quality, service, safety, innovation, and countless other competitive edges.

---

6. Redford Williams, M.D., *The Trusting Heart: Great News about Type A Behavior* (New York: Time Books, 1989).

7. Daniel Goleman, "The New Thinking on Smarts," adapted from D. Goleman, *Emotional Intelligence, USA Weekend*, 8–10 September 1995, p. 6.

LEADING FROM THE HEART DOESN'T MEAN BEING A PUSHOVER

There are two paths in life, and there are two paths in leadership. There is the Path of Fear, which is taken by most managers today, where control and manipulation reign supreme, and there is the Path of Courage and Heart, where people are connected through spirit, joy, and passion in their work. At best, fear produces stagnation. At worst, fear courts negativity and paralyzes a company's ability to compete effectively. Our traditional, analytical, control-driven systems of management have so indoctrinated most of us to a fear-driven reality that many have lost touch with the courage that is by nature part of every one of us.

When we take the Path of Fear, we inevitably create what we fear the most. Explosive, creative energy is unpredictable and uncontrollable and frightening to many, if not most. People may say that creativity and involvement are what they want, yet most leaders are afraid of "losing control." Fear of uncertainty and potential loss of market position often fuels the desire for control. When we try to harness spirit that is by nature wild and free, we cripple it and invite fear where none need exist. Controlling measures, and the fear that are their source and by-product, dampen creativity, rob a company of its edge, and make it vulnerable to competition—exactly what the controlling managers feared when they began trying to control workplace spirit.

Demonstrating the leadership that creates and sustains an environment for untapped and unlimited sources of energy takes tremendous courage. Leaders on the Path of Courage know that twenty-first-century responsiveness demands all of a company's resources: the body, mind, and spirit of every person. The ability to survive and thrive in perpetual chaos lies in the ability to live with ambiguity, to challenge perceptions of reality, and constantly to reassess and create new options for responding to change.

On the Path of Courage, leaders create an environment that respects people and the process of involving people. They know it is more important to listen than to talk, more important to ask questions that increase awareness and consciousness than to have answers. Leaders on the Path of Courage are intentional about outcomes but open and flexible about how to accomplish them. On the Path of Courage, leadership doesn't depend on old assumptions about events, outcomes, or people for an easy but reactive answer. Such leadership cannot depend *only* upon what is quantifiable because the very act of measurement creates distortion.

On the Path of Courage, we challenge old assumptions that may keep us from discovering new possibilities; we look at similar situations and explore with others how it will be different this time. We balance the quantifiable with the intuitive, with vision and values, and with our belief in our ability to produce a positive result. In a world of rapid change, secure and flexible leadership gives us the resilience to thrive when others, locked into old ways of seeing and doing, struggle to make things happen the way they did in a world that no longer exists.

On the Path of Courage, we define our purpose and how we will operate—our values, operating principles, standards of excellence, and accountability—and we cannot know where we are going. We no longer limit our tomorrows with goals and action plans inevitably based on yesterday's or today's reality. We have the courage to set the course for greatness. We know we will never know exactly how things turn out, and we know we will find meaning and growth from whatever emerges as long as we consciously learn and focus on our purpose and values.

On the Path of Fear, legions of executives have built careers based upon delivering predictability. Yet in order to guarantee a predicted outcome, those same executives have had to severely restrict their companies' potential. In thirty years in business, it has been my experience that most managers' actions are driven by fear—fear to risk being great. They restrict input to what agrees with their thinking; hiring and socializing newcomers into "how we think" and "what we say." Occasionally, someone suggests that some new thinking may be useful, and someone from a different background or with a different personality type is hired. Inevitably that person is at once urged to "become like us." The newcomer eventually gives up and either quits or becomes part of the organizational groupthink.

I was brought into an organization after a study indicating that people at all levels were so locked into dysfunctional relationships that they were unable to respond to significant changes in their organizational environment. At our third, multi-day session, one of the longer-term employees observed that the study and subsequent report that resulted in my work was quite similar to one done five years earlier . . . and another done ten years earlier . . . and another done fifteen years earlier. What was interesting, he said, is that few of the people who were in the organization fifteen years ago were still employed, but "We continue to behave in the same way. It's almost as if it's contagious," he said. "People 'catch it' when they come to work here." Newcomers concurred. They seemed to notice it immediately just before they were sucked into the culture.

As was the case with this organization, people on the Path of Fear may say they want other opinions or increased participation or committee action, but they want such things only within a limited range and based upon the company's accepted view of reality. In my work I frequently do a multi-day process, called Focused Intent, with groups of executives. This process helps leaders learn the intricate details and linkages required for the success of a project, of a business unit, or of the whole organization.

One of the most important things I do as I guide the group quest is to ask questions that challenge the current view of reality. It is rare in any group that at least one individual does not cling desperately to the Path of Fear. That person does almost anything to keep the rest of the group from discovering that reality may be different from what they'd assumed in the past. It takes courage to leave what we have believed to be true to venture down an unknown path, but only by taking new paths can we really come to learn what the potential of ourselves or our organizations is. Courage isn't courage if we don't continue to look fear in the face, to accept that fear is with us, and to move forward. When we try to circumvent fear, overpower it, run from it, deny it, or hide behind reactive courses of action born of cowardice, our responses are always crippled. It takes incredible courage to put aside judgment, to look at each situation, and to greet it anew.

Some may be intimidated and fear they won't have the stamina for courageous leadership. Such leadership does demand more of us than does traditional management, and many of us may already feel we are giving too much. When we talk about the time and energy we are giving to our jobs now, we neglect to look at all the energy we spend running fear-based strategies—vast amounts of energy can be expended trying to control actions and outcomes—trying to force what cannot be forced. More important, we overlook the invigoration that comes with renewing ourselves daily in the rewarding work of leading people and organizations to higher and higher levels of achievement and meaning.

I believe that everyone has the potential to develop the courage to lead from the heart. Willingness, desire, and expressed intention to be a leader are important ingredients, but there is more. If we are going to lead from the heart, we must know our hearts. To know our hearts, we must listen to them and accept what they provide.

We must have the courage to do our personal work first, to become aware of our own fears, frustrations, hopes, and dreams—and what drives them. That work prepares us to begin to live and lead consciously. Then and only then can we begin to ask others in our organizations to work and lead in a conscious way. When we are well connected with the person we are, beneath all the layers of insulation that protects and separates us from others, courage comes easily. Heart courage is rewarded with better results and a spirited workplace—a workplace in which people look forward to actively participating.

EXPLORING THE PATH OF COURAGE

(1a).   Begin watching for incidents in which you "generalize" by using categories or labels. The generalizations may be cultural or ethnic in nature, or they may be made by professional group (labels like "bean counters" or the "touchy feelies" in Human Resources). The generalizations may refer to political groups or to government regulation or intervention. They may be about your clients, customers, or employees or about situations rather than people. At the end of the day, take a few minutes to make notes after each generalization about the specifics you missed as you shielded yourself from your heart by using generalizations.

(1b).   After you have identified incidents in which you generalize, begin listing the assumptions you bring to interactions because of the generalizations. Challenge those assumptions by asking yourself, "What if the opposite were true?"

(1c).   Now select from one of your generalized categories one person with whom you will interact tomorrow. Challenge the assumptions that you bring to your generalizations about that individual by asking, "What if the opposite were true?" List for yourself the ways this relationship or interaction may be changed by removing your old assumptions and assuming instead that the opposite *is* true. List for yourself the possibilities for new positive outcomes for the organization when you go into each interaction with the person without the insulations of generalization to separate you. Before you encounter the person, replace old negative assumptions with new positive ones. When you catch yourself about to respond based on negative beliefs, ask a question to get clarification instead. At the end of the encounter, make some notes about how this meeting differed from other meetings you've had with that person.

(2).   If someone had come in to assess your organization every five years for the last fifteen to twenty years, what commonalties would they have found? What qualities are "contagious" to newcomers? When new ideas are sought, what are the limits or accepted views of reality that confine the input? What if the opposite were true?

Chapter 2

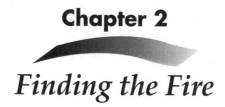

Finding the Fire

"Fires can't be made with dead embers, nor can enthusiasm be stirred by spiritless men. Enthusiasm in our daily work lightens efforts and turns even labor into pleasant tasks."

. . . JAMES MARK BALDWIN[1]

Why is it that the Joes of the world are able to consistently get their people to achieve the impossible and the Teds of the world can hardly get their employees to continue to accomplish the usual work of the day? Both are committed to helping their organizations achieve the potential they envision for them. Both are committed to doing exactly what the consultant encourages them to do. Yet try as they may, the Teds of the world just can't seem to pull their companies together, and some actually push their organizations apart.

This question has haunted me much of the thirty years I have spent working in different companies, and finding an answer has driven me in recent years. Although I seemed to know intuitively that the answer has to do with leadership, I focused on measurable, quantifiable, and behav-

---

1. James Mark Baldwin, in Glenn Van Ekeren, *Speaker's Sourcebook II: Quotes, Stories, and Anecdotes for Every Occasion* (Englewood Cliffs, NJ: Prentice Hall, 1994), p. 130.

ioral aspects of management—what people *did*. The more I looked, the more contradictions emerged. Often leaders appeared to *do* the same thing but got different results. Sometimes they *did* different things but got the same results. One thing was certain: The leaders who consistently achieved remarkable ends were able to tap a vitality that spirited the whole organization almost effortlessly toward their goals.

I began reading a lot of books that mentioned the importance of "respecting the spiritual nature of people" in companies that were happy, healthy, innovative, quality-focused, and productive. I also read about the lack of "respect for the spiritual nature of people" in co-dependent and addictive organizations. The authors mentioned "the spiritual nature of people," but they didn't elaborate on what that meant. When I began asking people I thought might know about this "spiritual nature," I got vague, puzzled looks. Some recommended other books. One organizational consultant said, "I work with spirituality in the workplace all the time. I *rarely* use the word." Hmmmm.

Just as I was beginning to play seriously with the idea that something as intangible as spirit may be the component I was seeking, I was invited to work in a company where spirit was everywhere. The leader embodied the characteristics of my leadership model in a way that other clients had not, but there was something more—the way people interacted with each other and with their customers and still maintained the bottom line. The company had experienced phenomenal growth by conducting a business that often carries negative overtones in a different, positive, and people-focused way.

What a dynamic organization it was! I eagerly looked forward to each day I was at the work site. What incredible enthusiasm! The word *enthusiasm* derives from the Latin meaning "to be inspired by a god," and this work group was inspired. What esprit de corps! They definitely had something special: They definitely had spirit. I wish I could say that I figured it out immediately. I was still trying to figure out what "respecting the spiritual nature of human beings" meant, but I seemed to be observing it firsthand. And it just felt good to be there!

At the end of the project, when I retreated to my office to reflect on all that I had seen and felt, the skeptic in me finally gave up. It was now clear to me that spirit is the key to the workplace dynamism I had sought—the source of creativity, health, quality, energy, meaning, and life. It is also clear that it occurs naturally in every relationship, whether between two people, two hundred, or two thousand. All we have to do is discover spirit buried under rules, procedures, practices, organizational culture, and personal barriers.

WHAT IS SPIRIT?

Spirit. The origin of the word reveals the life-giving nature that ancients recognized in it. Descending to English from the Latin *spirare*, "to breathe," spirit breathes life into each of us. The first dictionary definition of spirit is "the vital principle or animating force traditionally believed to be within living beings." These are words that are about truly being *alive*, and alive is what these companies are. Spirituality, distinct from religion, is a challenging topic because it can be such an important part of religion in its pure form. Respectfully discussing the spiritual nature of people in the workplace without invading the realm of personal religious freedom or being perceived as proselytizing a sectarian religion is even more challenging. It is essential to my spirit that I be as open and respecting of the spirits of others as I would hope them to be about mine.

If spirituality isn't necessarily religion, then what is it? Some have described a beautiful sunrise or sunset as having a spiritual nature. I have certainly experienced it when I've climbed up to a mountain precipice and marveled at the splendor of surrounding peaks and valleys below. Some people may feel a spiritual connection when they listen to a great piece of music, and others feel it at the birth of a child. Spontaneous spiritual moments shed light on the word's origins in *spirare*, "to breathe." Spiritual experiences cause us to gasp for breath or to give a heartfelt sigh when we feel connection to a greater order.

In the workplace, spirituality may emerge when a particularly competent co-worker offers to help us with an overwhelming project. Our sigh of relief expresses more than getting out from under work. It taps human connection, faith that the job will be done right, and a sense of community. Spirituality may be something as simple as feeling listened to attentively by a co-worker who sincerely wants to understand without judging. Spirit can be felt by people working together so well that it is like breathing together.

Describing spirituality is a bit like wrestling with a lovable octopus—the closer we get to the animal, the harder it is to embrace completely. Spirituality is more about meaning than about definitions. Definitions are the stuff of brains, but spirituality isn't brain stuff. It's heart and soul stuff. Thoughts just get in the way; words are only symbols.

Over time, I have acquired bits and pieces of understanding from other writers. Many hours in meditation have helped me get out of my brain, to shut down intangibles, and to access the wisdom of the ages, a part of me I had long neglected and ignored. Even now, the only thing I know for sure is that spirit and spirituality will be somewhat different for each person. Yet I am almost as sure that people share many elements in common. Because the concept of spirituality, outside of a religious context, may be new to many, I will make my best effort to share what it means to me, both personally and in the workplace.

Spirit is something I am. I experience it more like a place than a thing. I can share a lot about what it is like to me, how I got there, and what I feel like when I am there. Yet until I had been there, I couldn't really know it or experience it. The journey to spirituality is personal. Until we take it, our two-dimensional, knowledge-based brain has a hard time conjuring the multidimensionality of wisdom and spirit.

It's like trying to experience the vitality, sights, sounds, and smells of Hong Kong by watching a slide show. We may get an idea of what we think it may be like, but only when we've been there can we know how different it is to experience the real thing. Spirit is a place in me. When I am there, I know it. It is a place where I am loving, peaceful, caring, trusting, and connected. It is a place where I am open to other people and different ideas, where I accept others as they are, and where I am respectful of our differences. It is a place where I see an abundance of talent and ideas and resources that we can create.

Although I describe my place of spirit in qualities that describe my relationships with others, living from spirit is ultimately about my relationship with myself. It is a feeling of being full within myself. There is none of the neediness that prevails on the Path of Fear where we are looking for others to fill us with approval, love, trust, caring, and connection. When I am abundantly full of spirit, I have all that I need and plenty to give to others.

In my place of spirit, I am inspiring to others and aspiring for myself. It is a place where I am creative and accepting of my intuitions. When I am in this place I call spirit, I have *complete* belief in myself and in the rest of humanity. I see an abundant world full of win-win relationships rather than a competitive world of win-lose ones. I see a friendly world that wants me, and everyone else, to win.

Spirit is a place where I am totally present and focusing on who I am with and what I am doing in this moment, unwilling to lose even one instant to living in the past or the future. I am filled with wonder, expansiveness, enthusiasm, peace, and joy. I am playful. It is a place in which I know whatever I do is a gift for me and others, at the very least, a gift of learning. It is a place in which I *cannot* fail; I can only grow. It is a place where I face fear openly and consciously but am not afraid. I have courage. I am safe within myself, completely safe. Spirit is something I am, not something I do.

Deepak Chopra, a physician and popular writer about body–mind–spirit relationships, has called spirituality the domain of increased awareness.[2] When I am living from spirit, I am aware of who I am and who I am not. I am consciously aware of things and people around me, and I am aware of my own feelings, motivations, and reactions. I am also consciously aware of how we are all connected in an intricate web that puzzles my brain only when it tries to understand how such connectedness can be. From the increased awareness of connection with spirit, I come to know that all events in my life have been part of a divine plan to create the remarkable person who includes both what I like and what I don't like about myself.

When I *am* my spirit, the sense of connectedness to all things extends beyond people and events. I cannot observe a beautiful sunset, stand on a mountaintop, or experience the birth of a child without feeling that I am part of something greater. It may be Nature, the Universe, God, Goddess, or the Great Spirit. *How* I experience that spiritual connectedness is not important. *That* I experience it is.

When I *am* my spirit, I am also keenly aware that I have a unique purpose in life. In my soul, I know that there is a specific reason for my being on this earth. We need not compete among ourselves: each of us has a different purpose here on earth. Like a complex mosaic, we each add to the richness, and without any one of us, the missing contribution leaves a hole where our work was to be. When I am my spirit, I find meaning from achieving my special purpose and in helping others to achieve their own.

THE FIRE WITHIN

Work bridges a critical gap between the spiritual and the rational in each of us, a gap that is continuously seeking wholeness and completion. Spirit is a fire within each of us that ignites us with passion, purpose, love, energy, and courage. This fire dwells in each of us and sets us ablaze when we are near *our work*—not merely our job or career but a personal calling or purpose that is spiritually and emotionally sustaining. This work beckons our creativity and fills us with energy and enthusiasm as we embrace opportunities to become all we can be. When we work with spirit, we accomplish more with less time, energy, and resources. We leave work with more energy than we had when we came. When we work with spirit, we look forward to going to work as an important part of self-expression instead of dreading it as something we have to do until the pension comes in.

This work doesn't have to be in the creative arts; it can be in anything that we do with spirit and from spirit. Creativity, by its simplest definition,

---

2. Deepak Chopra, "The Seven Spiritual Laws of Success," public television special, 18 March 1996, UNC-TV.

is coming up with a new way to do something. It may be a new painting, piece of sculpture, or musical composition, but far more often creativity surfaces in incremental improvements that we make daily in our lives. When manufacturing employees figure out how to cut scrap and waste while reducing bottlenecks and improving the quality of products, creativity is at work. When a law firm figures out an innovative approach to a challenging case, creativity is at work. When medical office staff improves scheduling so that it minimizes both physician and patient waiting time, that is creativity. When the staff of one client brainstormed how to energize Monday morning staff meetings, the result was two or three minutes of stretching at the start of the meeting. That was truly creative! (It not only works, but they've stuck to it. Meetings work better and the staff feels better, too.)

As intense as the yearning for creativity and passion in our work is, there is another part of us that yearns equally to be rational and to develop our mental and physical capacities. This part yearns to be productive and to produce the "things" we need for physical survival. This is the part that most of us have overused in our workplaces to the exclusion of our other part.

Work offers us a unique setting in which to bridge the creative with the rational and productive and to bring a sense of wholeness to our lives. In simpler cultures, work, play, and art are not distinguished; people put their whole being into everything they do and bring creativity, passion, and artfulness to the simplest of tasks. In his book on rediscovering the art in our daily work, Dick Richards writes that when art became a job, "A wedge severed artfulness from work."[3] If we are to be alive in our work, it is time to put spirit back into our work.

Mary Baechler, CEO and co-founder of Racing Strollers, brings a similar concept, learned from Sufi practice, to her successful company today. "Any work is good work," she says, "and our first job is to do a good job at whatever we do." Many describe a spiritual approach to work as bringing consciousness and a spirit of joy and service in the doing of the work to any job. This idea is clearly reflected in the widely documented life of Mohandas K. Gandhi. He brought this spirit to everything he did, whether it was leading a protest, weaving his own cloth, or cleaning toilets.

In one client group, I posed this question: If you go to the office and do all the things you normally do, but instead of saying you are going to work, you said you are going to play, what difference would it make? The resulting dialogue produced several chart-pad sheets of outcomes that the

---

3. Dick Richards, *Artful Work: Awakening Joy, Meaning and Commitment in the Workplace* (San Francisco, CA: Berrett-Kohler, 1995).

participants thought would be positive changes to their organization. Among them were:

- We would be less conscious of time
- We would be more flexible
- We would do things that were "not in our job descriptions"
- We would have more variety in our work
- We would have greater passion for what we do
- We would be more tolerant of others' shortcomings or differences
- We would make fewer but better decisions; we would involve more people and be more focused
- We would be more creative
- We would have more face-to-face communication with more information exchange, deeper relationships, more opportunity to ask questions and to clarify misunderstandings
- We would have less stress and stress-related sickness and injuries

Most of these results could have come from a course on modern management, but they didn't. They came from a question that asked people to look at their work as play and to change the relationship to work.

I asked another work team I was facilitating what it would take for each of them to experience joy in their work. One team member responded incredulously, "I couldn't have joy *at work*. Joy is what I have at church or home."

It has been said that when we change the metaphor, we change the world. *Narings Lev*, a Swedish term for business that means "work as nourishment for life," is being explored by small groups in this country as a new spiritual metaphor for our work. How may the stress and discouragement of the above team member have changed had she chosen to make her work part of her spiritual practice by choosing joy and service in what she did? What if she'd chosen to be more playful? When we unleash our passion to work from spirit, it feeds us; it truly does nourish us. It gives us vitality and energy to take home.

LEADING A SPIRIT-RESPECTING ORGANIZATION

In a lot of ways, leading a spirit-respecting workplace is easier than managing a traditional organization; the former takes on a life of its own. At the same time, leading such a workplace is also harder, especially for those who are compelled to control the uncontrollable. Most of us have clear ideas about what should and should not happen in organizations and about our responsibilities as leaders of those organizations. These ideas became the rules by which we do our work. They simplify the workplace and the way we do our business by keeping everything on a superficial level.

When we choose to build a spirit-respecting and spirit-nurturing organization, we also choose to give up the illusion of simplicity. We choose to give up the rules by which we have lived and operated, and we develop a tolerance for ambiguity enabling us to reap the harvest that the complexity in our organizations can yield. We build an environment for courageous leadership to emerge at all levels and in everyone who works for us. We make it safe to take risks, to try new things, and to stretch our creativity.

Thomas Watson, former chairman of IBM, talked about such an environment when he said, "If you want to increase your success rate, double your failure rate." Companies on the Path of Fear spend incredible amounts of time and energy wringing their hands for fear something won't go right. This attitude does not create an environment in which leadership emerges from the ranks. When bosses are afraid of making mistakes, no one else is going to get too innovative in identifying either problems or their solutions.

Greg Steltenpohl, co-CEO of the hugely successful and innovative juice company, Odwalla, Inc., talks about building a "leader*ful*" company. Although much trendy thinking and writing refers to leader*less* organizations, Steltenpohl asserts that organizations need leadership. He indicates that at Odwalla, everyone must exercise leadership. "We want a company *full* of leaders."[4] The company dramatically multiplies its capacity by enabling every person to use a watchful eye, creativity, and a commitment to produce top-quality products in a way that respects both the environment and the people who work for Odwalla. This leaderful company accomplishes what no single manager or small group of managers could ever do.

MAKING IT HAPPEN

I strongly believe that there are no rules about what we should do in organizations but that we can get some guidance about leading in a way that provides an environment for leaders to emerge at all levels in our organizations. After sharing the results of his studies on how our way of being in the world influences our tendency to have a heart attack in *The Trusting Heart*,[5] Dr. Redford Williams reviews teachings from various religious tra-

---

4. Greg Steltenpohl, conversation with Kay Gilley, Hilton Head Island, SC, February 1995.

5. Redford Williams, M.D., *The Trusting Heart: Great News about Type A Behavior* (New York: Time Books, 1989), p. 145.

ditions. He finds that Jesus, Jewish scholars, Buddha, Confucius, and Lao-tzu all had similar messages and that all of them recommended living in ways similar to those that he had discovered would reduce the odds of having a heart attack!

Throughout these religious traditions we find a preferred way of being, described as one wherein we are advised to:

- Look for the good in others, rather than the bad
- Treat others well, just as we would like to be treated ourselves
- Cease to be so concerned with our own selves, but direct our attention and acts more toward other beings, even all creation . . .

Finally, we have seen in many traditions the idea that as humans we contain something within us . . . that somehow motivates and enables us to follow the preferred way.[6]

The work that leaders must do in order to be more courageous and spirit respecting is to find that "something within us" and to learn to live from that spot. That, I believe, is the *being* of a leader. When we learn to live and work from that spot, we are free of the ego-driven need to view everything from our own perspective, and we are able to focus "our attention and acts more toward other beings." For our organizations to become collections of healthy and creative human beings working together in community toward a common goal, leaders must free themselves of measuring everything in terms of ego-win or -loss. To live in this way seems essential both to living the "golden rule" common to these various spiritual teachings and to seeing each individual contribution as unique and important.

Despite the millions of dollars spent on effective communication, motivation, diversity, stress reduction, and other training programs, the most significant thing that can be done to accomplish all these ends has, so far, been neglected. Most organizations would be dramatically improved places to work if leaders only did the soul-searching necessary to bring this loving and respectful way of being to all their interactions, and to build an environment for others to do the same kind of soul-searching and bring that consciousness to the workplace.

However, we cannot be good leaders by just providing a workplace where people relate better to each other. When organizations falter because we aren't being effective when we relate to each other, we ultimately fail in our collective responsibility to provide a place to work together and to supply income needed to sustain our life needs. We can-

---

6. See note 5 above.

not let ourselves fall into either/or thinking. We cannot choose between having a spirit-respecting workplace or a productive, rational, and effective workplace. Neither of these options is sustainable. We must choose to create *both*!

As I work in organizations, I discover that a few simple truths about who we *be* in relationship to ourselves, the organization, and its members assist us as we create a whole and sustainable workplace. The few simple truths about being that seem to pervade heart leadership are:

- Leaders create an environment that invites and supports spirit
- Leaders are conscious and intentional
- Leaders recognize that everything is a choice
- Leaders see possibilities
- Leaders respect people and the process of involving people
- Leaders live integrity: they walk their talk
- Leaders are committed
- Leaders are connected to others
- Leaders ask questions, listen, and create space for answers to emerge

On the surface, these truths may seem easy to do, even intuitive to some people. The truths are not about doing: They are about being. When they are viewed as ways of being, the truths are much more challenging. We must move beyond saying trendy words and instead live those words deeply.

Experience shows me that, as simple as these truths sound, they generally are not the things that most of us as managers or even as human beings have been taught or have practiced. Two critical components seem to be implicit in being able to lead by these few truths. First, we must see the need to unlearn behaviors that may have served us well at one time but no longer seem to work. Second, the unlearning—and the new learning—is a lifelong process.

It has been said that we all behave rationally within our current frames of reference. As we choose to lead in a spirit-respecting way, our frame of reference or our metaphor changes. What seems perfectly rational when we think of people as flesh and blood robots who need to be driven, no longer seems rational or even mildly reasonable when our frame of reference becomes one that includes spirited human beings infused with untapped energy, vitality, and creativity, in search of life and meaning in their work.

The finite rules we develop in a fairly stable world no longer work in a world of constant change and chaos, fed daily by an escalating pace of technology development and new global markets. The learning of thirty, forty, or fifty years isn't unlearned overnight. Life and work always present new lessons for us, lessons that require us to explore, refine, and adapt our understanding of what we knew.

The second critical component in being able to lead by these simple truths is the realization that the unlearning and new learning never end and require constant practice—the commitment and practice required of a discipline. We didn't learn to walk the first time we tried, but crawling eventually outlived its usefulness to us. Although most of us can see how inefficient and foolish we would be to depend primarily upon crawling into our offices and boardrooms, we continue to run our companies according to a model that we began to learn not much later than the period we learned to walk. The model we use, even when it is infused with participatory activities, is one of parentalism, one in which managers are ultimately assumed to have the answers, and one in which those answers or even the right to have those answers is rarely, if ever, questioned.

EXPLORING THE PATH OF COURAGE

(1) What do spirit and spirituality mean to you? What are your experiences with spirit in the workplace? Is yours a spirit-respecting organization, or is it spiritually dead? Make a list of ten things that you can change to make your workplace more spirit respecting. Change them!

(2) If you chose to go to the office and do all the things you normally do, but instead of saying you were going to work, you said you were going to play, what difference would it make? Make a list. How would the impact of your playful behavior change others' experience of you at work? How would such behavior change your relationships at home and in the community? What if everyone at your workplace were more playful? What difference would a more playful attitude have made at a time when things were not going well at work?

(3) What would it take for you to experience joy at work? What would be the impact on your life of more joy in your work?

Chapter 3

Choosing the Courageous Path

"Courage is not the absence of fear; rather it is the ability to take action in the face of fear."

...NANCY ANDERSON, *Work with Passion*[1]

Leadership can and does occur at all levels in organizations; it emerges when people have the courage to incorporate the few simple truths of being into their whole lives. The more we live from our spirits, the more we recognize that we do not have work lives, home lives, community lives, lives as employees or employers, and lives as parents, spouses, or children. Each of us has one life, and it is seamless and continuous. When we view our lives as segmented, we begin to experience stress. When we experience our lives as a whole, with the same truths and values governing all parts, we experience peace.

A closer look at the few simple truths of courageous leadership demonstrates how those truths can and indeed must be lived in all parts of our lives by each of us. Although the examples focus on people in traditional management roles, I have witnessed some dynamic displays of these leadership qualities by people throughout organizations. In fact, in spirit-respecting organizations, the role of the boss, manager or leader is

---

1. Nancy Anderson in Glenn Van Ekeren, *Speaker's Sourcebook II: Quotes, Stories, and Anecdotes for Every Occasion* (Englewood Cliffs, NJ: Prentice Hall, 1994).

almost unnecessary; those roles are played by everyone at different times and in different projects. If we are to have spirited organizations, it is important that leadership qualities spread infectiously from individual to individual and that everyone have faith, commitment, and determination to create workplaces which will improve our organizational competitiveness and also increase our individual and collective satisfaction with our work and with our lives.

INVITING SPIRIT

Spirit was as natural as breathing to all of us at some point in our lives. Only when we learned that people could hurt us, retaliate against us, or use us to protect their ego position while damaging our own, did we become afraid to live from spirit. To the person who is charged with responsibility to produce results from a work unit, control seems safe. The unit may never achieve its potential, but control can usually ensure an outcome that is acceptable by traditional standards. (One manager, who has a dynamic industrial plant that he ostensibly manages, says of traditional workplaces, "We've figured out how to get 10 percent from our people, and we've figured out how to make the system work by only using the 10 percent.")

The courageous leader, however, does not accept mediocrity. "Good enough" serves neither the work unit nor the people in it over time. It doesn't produce results that will retain competitiveness in quantity, quality, cost effectiveness, or any other measure of organizational success over time, and it doesn't stimulate or energize the workers, either today or over time. With faith of spirit and commitment to guide them, courageous leaders make themselves available for what wants to happen. With general goals about service, quality, and purpose to guide them, the work unit can unleash its creativity and spirit to learn how to do its very best, and it can continue to learn how to be better and better, day in and day out, over time.

For most managers, what I call the control thing is born of a host of fears. We are afraid that the unit won't meet expectations, that we might lose our job, that the unit will go out of existence. We are afraid that if people do well without us, we will lose our jobs. We are afraid that we will be embarrassed before our peers for trying something new and for which we can't guarantee results. We are afraid that when we lose our jobs, we won't find others, that those who supposedly love us will go away. So we settle for "good enough." When we settle for good enough, it is because we have become so attached to what we believe things must be that we are unable to let go of the attachment in order to approach greatness. When we are willing to accept that control limits us and blocks our potential, we begin to approach the courageous leadership we need to survive in the ever-changing, fast-paced global marketplace. Joseph Campbell said, "We must be willing to get rid of the life we've planned, so as to have the life that is waiting for us."[2]

There is a much better organizational life waiting for all of us if only we are willing to let go of our attachment to the organizational life we had planned. As we let go organizationally, most of us discover that there is a much better personal life waiting for us than the one we had planned. There are no lines in our lives: how our lives are in one place is how they will be in all places. When we begin to live from spirit at work, we will begin to live from spirit in other dimensions of our lives as well. When we are courageous, we are able to face ego-driven fears and accept them as guardians to ensure that we carefully and diligently consider our risks, rather than as prison guards to prevent us from action.

In Taoism the concept *wu wei* means "without doing, causing, or making." In essence, it means that we don't force things that don't want to happen. We look for innovative, effortless ways to accomplish our outcomes. *Wu wei* has been compared to water flowing over rocks. It doesn't flow in a linear, mechanical way; instead, it more easily accomplishes its task by being sensitive to the laws of nature, tumbling over and around obstacles.

In his book *The Seven Spiritual Laws of Success*,[3] Deepak Chopra describes what he calls The Law of Least Effort. He encourages the reader to observe and learn from nature where even the most important functions happen easily. "Grass doesn't try to grow, it just grows. Fish don't try to swim, they just swim. . . . Birds don't try to fly, they fly."[4] In bringing this law to human application, Chopra says, "Least effort is expended when your actions are motivated by love, because nature is held together by the energy of love. When you seek power and control over other people, you waste energy. When you seek money or power for the sake of the ego, you spend energy chasing the illusion of happiness instead of enjoying happiness in the moment."[5]

As leaders, when we make ourselves available for what wants to happen and we act from love, we choose the easy and effortless route to

---

2. Diane K. Osbon, ed., *A Joseph Campbell Companion: Reflections on the Art of Living*, (New York: HarperCollins, 1991).

3. Deepak Chopra, *The Seven Spiritual Laws of Success: A Practical Guide to the Fulfillment of Your Dreams*, (San Rafael, CA: New World Library, 1994), p. 53.

4. See note 3 above.

5. See note 3 above, 55.

our objective rather than using a forceful, directive, and combative approach to the same challenge. In order to reap the benefits of either *wu wei* or the Law of Least Effort, we must create an environment in which those who work with and for us experience safety in making suggestions, in being creative, and in trying new things.

Neither a learning nor a loving environment can emerge from a directive, hierarchical workplace or from a controlled society such as ours without some nurturing. Part of the natural rhythms of *wu wei* acknowledge that seeds thrown upon hardened soil will rarely sprout. In an environment that has been manipulated until its ability to function naturally has been disabled, nature requires assistance in preparing the soil and planting and watering the seeds. This assistance is the work of the leader. Patience rewards the leader who is willing to commit to creating an environment for spirit to emerge and to support that spirit when it does.

LEADING FROM THE HEART

Most of us spend much of our lives on autopilot. Traditional managers autopilot their way through interactions and decisions; they operate from assumptions or certainties that haven't been challenged for a long time, if ever. When we depend on old assumptions, we automatically filter out a lot of important information. Early explorers graphically proved that they did things differently and got very different answers. When they changed their assumption that the world was flat to one that the world was round, they literally discovered a whole new world. Many leaders discover that when they begin to challenge some of their most basic assumptions, they too make very different decisions, and they too often discover a whole new world of possibilities. When we lead from the heart, we want as many people as possible challenging as many "realities" as possible, contributing as much pertinent information as possible, and collaboratively making the best decisions for the enterprise.

One of the projects I frequently do with groups of leaders helps them identify what things they need to do well as an organization in order to successfully achieve their organization's purpose. The process gives them tangible insights about what and how to do business, and at the same time it also helps them learn the important leadership quality of intentionality.

A group that I worked with recently determined that it had to be good at "communicating" in order to be successful. After discussing whom they needed to communicate with, what needed to be communicated, and how it needed to be communicated, I challenged the underlying assumption. "Why," I said, "would we *not* want to communicate?"

Blank stares and a long silence came my way. Finally, I clarified the question: "What if, instead of wanting to communicate, the organization determined that the opposite was true—that it didn't want to communicate. Why would we not want to communicate?" More silence followed. Finally, a meek voice or two started what ended up being some of the most useful input of the series of sessions. There were a number of reasons some people wouldn't want to communicate.

Fear of loss	Avoidance of uncomfortable topics
Fear of misinterpretation	Fear of failure
Loss of power base	Fear of change
Fear of conflict	Fear shortcomings would be revealed

This is important information for a group that wants to foster communication.

All the reasons that people don't want to communicate can be summarized as FEAR. The group determined that in order to encourage people to communicate, they would have to create an environment that was safe for communication to occur in. Without challenging the basic assumption that everyone wanted good communication, this company would have moved along rosily putting together good communication development strategies that focused on techniques and mechanisms; a few months down the line management would wonder why the changes weren't working.

Even more deeply held than our assumptions about our organizations and activities within them are the autopilot roles for our behavior. Usually these roles are so old that we aren't even aware of them or of the way they cripple our organizations and the ability to respond consciously. In the process of identifying autopilot roles, a management group identified one person as their idea man. Upon examination, they discovered that they enabled his role so well that others in the group had abdicated their individual responsibility for idea-generation. At the same time, they realized that since idea-generation was his role, they rarely seriously challenged his ideas and limited their input to refining the details.

When we lead from the heart, we recognize that everything we do in the workplace is based upon assumptions. When we are conscious and intentional, we consciously identify what our assumptions are and then challenge them. We bring to consciousness the underlying beliefs upon which our ideas are based and then we consciously challenge them, because we know that with only one perspective (our own) for input, we cannot possibly be accurate in assessing conditions. Until we have the courage and intention to challenge our every assumption, we find ourselves operating reactively, feeling as if we are always putting out fires, without having a clue about what caused them.

EVERYTHING IS A CHOICE

Leaders recognize that everything in business—and in life for that matter—is a choice. When we say we don't have time or money to do something that we think would be good for the company, we are actually saying that there are other things on which we choose to spend our time or money.

For instance, it is not uncommon when I go to a company to hear employees complain about the poor training they received to do their jobs when they started work. Management most often responds that they didn't have time for training because they needed the person to do the job. So instead of investing a few days at the beginning of the worker's employment, the individual was put right to work. The employee flounders and takes lots of co-worker time to obtain, in a hit-and-miss fashion, information that might have come to them in an organized presentation if they had been trained. Most of the learning they receive comes in the form of negative feedback when something is performed incorrectly.

An employee who had no effective training period needs extra time to reach full productivity, and accidents are more likely to occur. The employee's self-esteem usually dips from the high amount of negative feedback, and co-worker productivity falls because of the large number of interruptions. Co-worker attendance may even fall as people become frustrated with frequent interruptions they experience when working with the newcomer. The lack of investment in employee training at the beginning of employment is a choice to spend much more money over time, probably not a conscious choice, but a choice nonetheless.

A leader recognizes that we are always making choices. It is only when a choice is recognized that more information will be sought, more questions asked, and the situation assessed consciously and objectively. The leader who leads from the heart considers not only productivity issues (that in this case would support training), but also considers the impact of the lack of training on the spirits of the employees. Newcomers who come to think of themselves as inept because they are slow at learning will take a long time to recover self-esteem and self-respect, if they ever do. The co-workers, who become frustrated with the lack of commitment to the newcomer's learning and success, are neither inspired, trusting, nor very connected to the enterprise.

When I have worked in union environments, I have often discovered employers who feel that they are at the mercy of the union and that there isn't anything they can do about the situation. What they are really saying is that they have not been willing to choose to change the situation, either because they didn't want to admit that they didn't know how or because they were unwilling to make the changes in themselves that would be required to change the relationship. Trapped by their own adversarial attitudes, they are unwilling to choose to be partners with the union in creating a better workplace. Some have been so trapped by adversary mentality that they will actually negotiate conditions that work to the employer's detriment in order to resist what the union wants.

At a medical center where I worked earlier in my career, the CEO insisted that an outside negotiator rather than human resources staff be used for bargaining a new labor agreement with the nurses. Before the new negotiations, wage rates had been so low that the human resources staff was having difficulty competing for nurses, who were in short supply at the time. The CEO and the negotiator, without input from human resources management, developed the negotiating strategy.

They succeeded in reaching their targeted settlement, but very soon, the human resources staff was unable even to approach satisfying the hospital's need for nurses. Within months, highly paid temporaries were being flown from all over the country to fill the most crucial positions. Other work units had to stop operations temporarily because of lack of staff. Within six months, the hospital was forced to go back to the union and say, "We want to increase the wage scale we agreed upon with you because we can't fill the positions at the current rate." To this, the union politely said, "We could have told you, but you wouldn't listen."

The heart leader recognizes that everything is a choice; he or she makes the commitment to feed the process with information in order to discover the best choice possible. Sequestered planning toward a goal that creates an unsustainable position just to be able to say "We won!" wastes time and resources and damages trust and morale. Robbed of critical information from those doing the work, executives inevitably make bad choices that heart leaders wouldn't even consider.

SEEING THE POSSIBILITIES

Spirit-respecting leadership sees the positive possibilities in every situation and makes risk-taking much easier. An environment that encourages people to experiment with possibilities and to make mistakes is fertile ground for creativity and innovation.

We are programmed from early childhood to expect the worst. "Don't talk to strangers!" we are told, as if every human being we do not know will kidnap or molest us. We bring that attitude to the workplace. We write policies for the 5 percent of employees who are problems rather than the 95 percent who are not. We want written contracts for everything because we have no faith in the integrity of our fellow human beings. What we focus on truly does determine what we miss. For many of us, focusing on the negatives of life has completely erased our awareness of the much more predominant positive.

Until proven otherwise to me, I always believe that everyone is doing the best he or she can. Some people may not have had the same advantages in life, education, training, or exposure to new and stimulating ideas that I have had. When I believe in a person and behave as if he or she will succeed, the chances of success increase dramatically. This phenomenon has been called the Pygmalion effect, after the play[6] by George Bernard Shaw, in that the clever Henry Higgins trains a flower girl from the streets of London to be a fine lady of society. He is able to accomplish this feat because he strongly *believes* he can do it, and she is able to become what he wants her to be because he believes in her ability to do it.

Some years ago, a group of school children were accidentally mislabeled at the beginning of the school year. The group that had previously shown potential was labeled "dumb," and those who had experienced learning problems in the past were labeled "bright." The teachers, acting on these assessments, treated each group as it had been labeled. When the error was finally discovered, testing was done to discover the impact of the labeling upon the students. IQ scores of the students who had been labeled as "dumb" dropped significantly, even though these were the "brighter" students. At the same time, the other students, those who had experienced learning problems in the past and had been treated as bright, scored higher on their IQ tests.

People consistently live up to our expectations of them. A manager working for a former employer of mine had talked about a new product for at least two years. Focusing on potential problems, he sat on the project and prevented product development from proceeding. Employees who had originally been zealous about the project began to support his doubts. A new manager came in, seized the project, turned it over to two groups of employees, and in less than thirty days a successful product was on the market. The second manager saw the possibilities and believed in the employees' ability to make it happen. The employees succeeded.

A few years ago I went to a company that had been marginally profitable for many years. The workers in this company had been treated as

---

6. Shaw named his play after a mythological king of Cyprus who carved a statue of a woman and then fell in love with it. At his request, Aphrodite brought the statue to life.

mindless robots who could perform only what they were programmed to do, and those doing the programming hadn't been doing a very enlightened job. Not unlike the school children already discussed, the workers had been labeled unproductive, wasteful, uncreative, and unsafe, and so they assumed those characteristics.

The employees were trying to buy the company, which was burdened by significant debt, and I had been brought in to conduct an assessment of the potential for turning the company around. My assessment was that the workers had incredible ideas and motivation, and given the opportunity, I thought the company could demonstrate dramatically improved productivity, materials usage, quality, and safety (relieving a significant insurance burden).

The company, however, was allowed to close because the financial wizards didn't think such gains were realistic. They looked at things—I looked at people and at their spirits. The financiers preferred to see the company fail and to lose their investment rather than take a chance that their negative worldview was wrong!

A real leader has the courage to challenge assumptions and thereby to discover which assumptions are self-limiting beliefs. Questioning everything becomes the leader's most important job. Questions like "What is the evidence?" "What does that mean?" "Are there other possibilities?" and "What if the opposite were true?" help us to discover what keeps our organizations from greatness. They bring into view a positive world of possibilities that may have been concealed by limiting assumptions we brought to the decision-making process in the past. A significant portion of what we use in our everyday lives was labeled "unrealistic" by the doomsayers of the past. "When early microcomputer developers tried to sell their ideas to the larger established companies in the 1970s, they were laughed at, and inventor Chester Carlson pounded the streets for years before he could find backers for his 'Xerox' photocopying process."[7] Is this realism?

Negative thinking is pervasive in our society, and people are often lauded for their ability to find the negative aspects of a project. The mark of a leader, at whatever level, is maintaining the belief that something positive *can and will* happen and then supporting others in helping to make it happen. A significant level of spiritual connectedness is demanded to enable a healthy dose of optimism to balance the knee-jerk negativism that abounds. The dogged pessimist always seeks exception. I consistently hear "You don't really understand *my* company," or "You don't under-

---

7. Roger Von Oech, *A Kick in the Seat of the Pants: Using Your Explorer, Artist, Judge, and Warrior to Be More Creative* (New York: Harper & Row, 1986).

stand the people that work here. They are from dysfunctional back-grounds." (That's a favorite!) And there is always the "what if?" What if the project fails? What if we lose money? What if we lose a lot of money?

Personal motivation guru Anthony Robbins tells about the after-math of his discovery that an employee had stolen a significant amount of money from his company. Initially, he says, he was angry and felt victim-ized by the man. Over time, he came to realize that the theft occurred because of the way he ran his business. Later he came to believe that he could actually share what he had learned in seminars with others. Once he was able to adjust his thinking and accept that the theft had been a gift of learning for him, the event spun him into a new, extremely lucrative area of business.[8]

The leader knows that as long as people do anything, they are going to make mistakes. (Even a .350 batter is "failing" two out of three times at bat!) The leader sees the positive possibilities and encourages people to grow and try new things although he or she knows people make mistakes. In "continuous improvement," the leader focuses on possibilities that have been created by what she or he has learned rather than focusing on what went "wrong."

The leader who truly believes in the people who work for him or her cannot help but openly display that belief. Providing the support for employee-generated projects becomes natural. Leaders who believe in their people are rarely disappointed. When belief is merely a veneer, this fact is communicated nonverbally. Belief cannot be segmented. The leader inte-grates the "wide-eyed optimist" view either into all parts of life or into none.

LEADERS RESPECT PEOPLE

Respect is a word that has taken on new meaning as I've come to under-stand more and more about leadership. To understand the kind of respect that a leader guards tenaciously, one has to turn to the root meaning of the word. The word *respect* means to "look again." When we respect people, we give them the benefit of the doubt; we are willing to look at other con-siderations or to look again at the old ones and to say there must be some-thing here that we initially missed. We challenge initial assumptions. We see positive possibilities. With a second look, we usually see perspectives that we have missed at first glance.

---

8. Anthony Robbins, *Personal Power: How to Get What You Really Want: The Power of Focus*, learning series by Robbins Research International, produced by Guthy-Renker Corp., Irwindale, CA, 1989, audiotape.

Leaders respect people. They respect their employees. They respect their customers. They respect their suppliers. They respect their competitors. They respect their neighbors and the community in which they operate. They respect themselves. Their intention is to look twice at relationships, impacts, and needs from the perspective of each group with whom they are involved. Respect begins with recognizing that every person who works with and for us has a spirit.

Each individual has a specific purpose in life that is their source of purpose and meaning: What brings life to them and them to life. As leaders, we have a responsibility to help each person in our workplaces to achieve his or her purpose when it is known, to uncover it when unknown, and to discover how the purpose can be uniquely experienced in this particular job in this workplace. One employer has said that it is "immoral" to do anything less.

A British manager I know explained what happened when he started looking for the uniqueness in each of his employees. Jobs were carved up and reshaped so that people were doing those tasks that naturally interested them. Workers who had been marginal performers began to excel. His whole department developed new energy. They have spirit! Martin Buber, a philosopher and a theologian said, "To understand the heart of another human being is the ultimate spiritual achievement."[9] As leaders in workplaces, knowing the hearts and spirits of each of the people that work with us, and sharing our hearts and spirits with them, gets to the crux of this new view of respect and the spirituality from that it rises.

When leaders take a second, closer look, they see that the lines between groups of people blur. The leaders begin to see that although their employees serve them, they must also serve the employees. They must ensure the basics: a healthy work environment, the necessary tools in good repair, the training that is needed to do a good job, the removal of impediments to accomplishing the company's vision and the employees' personal purposes. The leaders serve employees and themselves best by providing an environment for creativity and an involvement in making a difference in the organization.

Many managers respond to events of the moment. If a person isn't doing his or her job, managers may not exercise the respect that would allow them to ask, "Is there something that the company is doing or failing to do that is causing this to occur?" It is well accepted among proponents of quality programs that 95 percent of employee performance problems are caused by the system, yet it is rare that I see managers looking to themselves and the system when an employee has a problem.

---

9. National Public Radio, *Weekend Edition/Sunday*, Robert Ferrante, executive producer, Robert Malesky, show producer, 5 December 1993.

An example of the system's failing an employee occurred many years ago and forever stands out in my mind. I had just become the first personnel manager of a long-established company. Managers, who had been accustomed to running their own fiefdoms, were a bit disgruntled at suddenly having procedures to follow. Late one Friday afternoon, a department director stormed into my office, saying, "I want to fire Mary, and I want to do it now. She's simply not working out." Because neither job descriptions nor training programs were yet in place, the manager, after some discussion, agreed that the three of us should have a talk.

The employee, who was in her first real job after graduating from high school, was just as frustrated as the manager. She had been floundering about, trying to figure out exactly what she was to do and how it was supposed to be done. The only instructions she received came in the form of negative feedback when she had done something wrong. The director and I clarified what Mary was to be doing, and we arranged for training and feedback to occur. We also encouraged her to ask questions and suggested appropriate people for her to ask for different types of information. The employee was very appreciative; she had feared that there was something wrong with her because she wasn't "getting it."

Within a month, the same manager was back in my office, but this time he was singing Mary's praises. By the time her annual review came around, she rated highly in every category. That was at least fifteen years ago, and when I last heard, Mary was still working in the same department and still doing a great job. What I had encouraged the director to do is what leaders routinely do: to respect, to take a deeper look at what might be going on.

The respect that leaders have for people goes beyond respect for individual people. Leaders know that the people who do a job know more about the work than anyone else. They want workers involved in decision making, not because it is the trendy thing to do or because it makes people feel good, but because it is the best way to get all perspectives and to make the best decisions. Leaders respect the process of involving people. When they are tempted to make a quick decision because others want to move forward, leaders resist and take time. If a decision is worth making, it is worth making right. This is not to say, in situational leadership language, that when there is a fire we need to call a meeting to decide whether to call the fire department. It is to say that when we provide the right environment and a fire occurs, employees automatically organize around all aspects of responding to the emergency; they call the fire department and respond to many other aspects of employee and property protection.

A health care organization that I have worked with spent a good deal of time discussing the purchase of new scales to weigh their patients. The scales they had been using didn't seem to last long. To many this may seem like a decision that the administrator should have made. "If the scales we use are breaking, buy better scales," people may say, but this organization was committed to involvement. When I observed the scale-buying meeting, I must confess I initially thought that the group decision making was being carried to the extreme. Twenty minutes later, however, at least six different reasons, in addition to the quality of the scales, had emerged as possible causes for the breakage. Before making a decision, the group developed a strategy to test the different hypotheses.

The temptation to barrel ahead and subvert the process "just this once" is an inviting one. Another management group I know of was switching to a new production system. Once the equipment was in place, there was peer pressure to make the transition. The group didn't invest the time to explore and learn about the dozens of activities related to the new equipment which also had to be changed. The group not surprisingly stormed on with the transition, which was a disaster. What followed was a complete shutdown of the facility for days. After the ill-fated transition, several people shared their concern about various aspects of the transition, but under pressure from their peers, they hadn't respected the need for process, information generation, and inclusion before the change.

Leaders respect the idea that people make a positive difference. A manager with whom I have talked at length about leadership shared with me an interesting story about the importance of respect. He was formerly active in a national labor union, which, at the time, was widely acknowledged to be involved in disreputable activities. Yet, despite that reputation, many workers continued to cling to the union. The reason, he was convinced, was that it was the only place in that each member was respected for the job he did. Members were treated as if the work they did truly made a difference. It brought meaning to their lives. The union fulfilled a need that would have been satisfied in a spirit-respecting organization.

As groups of executives explore respect in their work together, they inevitably discover that before they can really respect others, they must first respect themselves. The relationship that managers have with others is simply a reflection of the one they have with themselves. The manager who jumps to judgment without asking questions or looking for positive outcomes probably does the same with him- or herself. The manager who won't listen to others probably hasn't spent much time listening to what his or her inner wisdom has to say. The courageous leader respects people and knows that respect begins with self-respect.

LIVING INTEGRITY

Living integrity is one of the few truths of heart leadership. One manager I interviewed in my research called it "walking our talk," but it is more than acting in accordance with what we say. Integrity is a wholeness that encompasses the belief system on such a deep level that it is impossible to sever what we believe from how we act. Integrity is believing, thinking, speaking, and acting in complete accordance with personal values.

I have spent a lot of time exploring my personal integrity, how I work, and for whom I work. Some clients who had proven difficult to work with approached employee participation and involvement from a "make them *feel* they're important" perspective rather than from a perspective of "I believe they *are* important." It seems to me that when workers are truly involved they believe that they truly are valued and important. It can't be an act; people see right through that. There are even clients who, I believe, intellectually accept the participatory process but on a deeper level, driven by fear and a need for control, still act as if most of the wisdom emanated from the executive suites.

Roughly 90 percent of what we communicate is non-verbal, and almost 50 percent isn't even related to body language or other non-verbal signals. That 50 percent is a sense people have about whether another person is being completely straight. When the leadership-ownership-management is not in complete integrity internally, people seem to know. When what leaders are saying and doing isn't completely congruent with their deeply held beliefs, people intuitively know. Research continues to show that aware people can tell when another is lying. They can't tell you how they know, but they do. And they're nearly always right.

When two leaders say the same words in front of groups of employees and one builds commitment whereas the other just provides a distraction from the work of the day, it is integrity that makes the difference. One leader speaks from the heart with complete commitment and integrity. The other goes through the proper motions but knows that changes will never happen. And the employees get the message almost instantly.

Many times when people act in a way that is not congruent with their deep beliefs and values, they do so not with intent but because they lack clarity about what they believe at heart or because conflicting beliefs create mixed messages within them and send mixed messages to others. Some people act out of sync with their integrity when they feel themselves being pulled in different directions; they are torn between doing what they know is right and what they believe is expected of them. Finally, integrity becomes an issue when individuals haven't chosen to examine the messages that their actions send to others. In these circumstances, it is essential to our integrity to seek a deeper understanding of our values that brings expression to our souls and to become conscious and intentional about ensuring that our every action is compatible with our values. It is absolutely vital to our integrity to know what we truly believe.

These mixed messages often emerge in the area of conflict. Most of us give lip service to the importance of getting different perspectives in decisions, but we often fear that we won't be able to handle the conflict that may erupt. Defense mechanisms and other such behaviors that follow can stifle the expression and exploration of different opinions.

When I work with leaders in guiding them to discover, explore, and understand their own integrity, I question them repeatedly on one value to help them gain more and more clarity about their own beliefs. When a person tells me teamwork is important to them, I ask what teamwork means, what teamwork looks like when it happens, and what it looks like when it does not. I ask how the person exhibits teamwork. I ask the person to assume that teamwork is not important, and I follow with questions about the areas of personal life in which she or he fails to demonstrate teamwork.

People often discover that although they intellectually espouse teamwork, other beliefs about control, perfectionism, self-reliance, and responsibility create mixed messages within them. The result is a high-level of personal stress within themselves and the communication of mixed messages to others, which can lead to a perceived lack of integrity. If we are to lead, people must connect with us. If people don't know what we stand for, what we believe in, or even who we are as people, the ability of others to entrust us with leadership and by extension commit to "followership" is going to be crippled.

LEADERS ARE COMMITTED

The word *commitment* is tossed around a lot these days, yet I observe very little *real* commitment. When I ask people what commitment is, the answers I get don't sound to me like commitment. Sometimes they sound like obligations or like mild interest. At other times, people make a commitment as long as it isn't uncomfortable, doesn't upset the routine, or guarantees a known outcome. I wonder whether we have completely forgotten what a commitment is. Several years ago, a sign on the bulletin board at a client's office caught my eye. It spoke of commitment so simply and so eloquently that I have often used it in my work and in my own personal development:

> There is a difference between interest and commitment. When you are interested in something, you do it only when it is con-

venient. When you are committed to something, you accept no excuses and produce only results.

The New Year's resolution that is attacked with zeal for three or four days is not commitment. Commitment is deciding how we are going to be on this earth, making it happen, accepting no excuses, and producing only results. Many of us say that we are committed to values, a vision, a course of action, or other group decision when in fact we are not. Often we haven't explored what we pledge to support thoroughly enough to understand what commitment means. We should not commit to anything until we know that the commitment is in alignment with our core values and purpose and until we know we will be able to do whatever it takes to ensure that we keep the commitment, accept no excuses, and produce results.

Lagging commitment sometimes emerges because people get into a project and discover that keeping the commitment is more demanding than they had anticipated. Commitment may require skills or abilities that need honing or may call for confronting unanticipated resistance. I believe that we rarely commit to a challenging course of action without discovering fear-producing obstacles for which we could not have prepared. Does this mean that we stop? If we are truly committed, absolutely not. It does mean that when we experience fear, we tap our core beliefs for support and keep our commitment *in spite of the fear*, that we know our value as human beings lies not in producing perfection but in fulfilling our commitment with flexibility and a spirit of learning.

Commitment *does* require discipline to consider and act consciously, to assess our outcomes and to learn how to get closer to being what we hope to be next time around. We must carefully examine our commitment, consider what may be going on *within us* to undermine our resolve, and consider how events of the past may impede our ability to fulfill our commitment today. Critical to the concept of commitment are the realization and acceptance that there is no half-commitment. It is impossible to *try* to keep a commitment. We either keep it, or we don't.

> "Try? There is no try. There is only do or not do" (Yoda, in *The Empire Strikes Back*).[10]

Commitment is *doing*, not *trying*. The very essence of living from spirit is keeping all our commitments, starting with those we make to ourselves.

---

10. George Lucas (story), Leigh Brackett and Lawrence Kasdan (screenplay), *The Empire Strikes Back*, 20th Century-Fox Productions, 1984.

The origin of lagging commitment often lies in lack of intentionality or strategic will to make the commitment happen. We often make a commitment without asking ourselves the questions that define it or outlining what we need to do to make it happen:

- What does the commitment require?
- What must I do to make sure the commitment is carried out?
- What must I refuse to do to make sure that it is carried out?
- How do I measure my progress?
- What support systems or mechanisms do I or others need to make sure that the commitment is carried out?
- Why wouldn't I want to be committed to this?
- What situations test our commitment?
- How do we respond in those situations to ensure that we keep our commitment?

Companies spend significant amounts of money developing visions, values, missions, and guiding principles without going the next step and developing strategic will. It is easy to talk the talk, but walking the talk requires that we search our individual and organizational selves for what gets in the way of keeping our commitments.

Stonyfield CEO Gary Hirschberg is an eloquent spokesperson for the social responsibility movement, and he is clear about a company's responsibility to make a profit while being socially responsible. That achievement requires organizational will. "Watch companies that have leveled off or are on the down swing to see if they just sort of throw the mission out with the bath water. . . . When business is flat, it is interesting to see the impulses there to carve into the mission."

In talking about his own company and their commitment to both the family farm and to wholesome, environmentally safe products, he says, "If we're doing something with ingredients, doing something with our farmers or doing something with our crops that waivers us away from our mission, alarms go off because I just know it isn't going to pay for us. . . . People respect you and will come back to you if they believe you are sincere in supporting your mission."[11]

I repeatedly see managers saying that they want more involvement to happen. They never ask the critical questions, "What will happen that will undermine my own resolve and what do I need to do to ensure that I

---

11. Gary Hirschberg, "Is Corporate Responsibility Good for the Bottom Line?" Keynote address at the Transforming the Soul of Business conference, sponsored by the National Institute for New Corporate Vision, Hilton Head Island, SC, 8 February 1995.

don't slip in a pinch?" A manager that I know once told me that he wanted to be doing leading-edge work in his company, yet he persisted in perpetuating traditional management programs and practices. It was as if he thought saying the words without doing anything different would make it happen.

Another person I know said repeatedly that she wanted to improve her relationship with her former spouse but continued talking about him in derogatory terms and blaming him for their problems. She continually reverted to her standard ways of doing things when dealing with their joint custody of their children and cast everything into a win-lose framework. Although she said she wanted to improve the relationship, she didn't ask those critical questions that would have helped her develop the intentionality to make the relationship change. A commitment is meaningless without consciously developing the intentionality—the will—to make it happen.

CONNECTING WITH OTHERS

Leaders in spirit-respecting workplaces are deeply connected with everyone. Leaders love, value, and respect both themselves and others. Trust is assumed, and faith is a given. Trust and faith are unconditional. They cannot be earned; they can only be lost. When we are warm, caring, and sympathetic—truly putting ourselves in each other's shoes—we bring people together in a new dimension.

When we lead from the heart, we focus on what we have in common, what connects us rather than what separates us. If we are to be leaders who respect the spirits of our workers, it is imminently important for us to realize that every person is part of something greater than the spot he or she holds on the organizational chart. Each is a living, breathing human being with hopes and dreams, creativity waiting to take form, and purpose to be realized. Each is deeply connected to family and friends. Each is deeply connected to the community. We are all integrally connected in the human race and in the cycle of generations that continues to unfold minute by minute. We are all woven into an intricate web of life, a symbiotic relationship out of which we either retain the integrity of the whole and all emerge as winners or, by extraction or damage of even a single thread, all dissolve as losers.

When we seek connection, we give up win and lose games. Win and lose is not a game that is possible when we live from our spirits. Instead of falling into a competitive mode of reaction, we seek perspectives on situations that allow all of us to win. When we become angry because an employee has filed a grievance against us, and we decide to get even, we may win a personal game of vengeance, but we all lose in the long run. We probably missed the learning from the grievance, or we wouldn't be angry in the first place. The employee may lose a job that is needed. The company loses an employee in whom it has invested and who may hold the creativity needed for a significant competitive breakthrough.

A leader who leads from the spirit wants to discover what action or perception motivated the grievance, so that both employee and manager can learn from the situation. In this way, we all win. We are better leaders because we have learned. The employee is probably a better team member because he or she feels important, listened to, cared for; more important, the employee understands how we can work together better and is likely to be much more committed to the employer because he or she feels safe addressing concerns and making mistakes. That very security may be what allows the employee to feel safe enough to try that winning innovation. Every situation has the potential to be win-win when we will let it be! Every situation has the potential to build connection, if we let it.

As we seek connection rather than separation, differences are honored as part of our uniqueness that is the spirit of each of us. We create connection when we let go of attachment to a particular way of doing things and focus instead on achieving our purpose. There may be many ways to achieve the same purpose. Each of us needs an outlet for creative expression, to learn and grow, and to use our abilities in a way that is uniquely suited to our own talents. When the desired end is achieved and everyone is respected throughout the process, there are not right or wrong ways of doing things, only different ways.

One client of mine received almost universal kudos from employees for a checklist that had been compiled early in the company's short history. The list contained what had to be accomplished during the shift, and employees were free to determine how and in what order things were completed as long as the customers' needs were met. One after another employees told me how wonderful it was to complete their work in the way that worked best for them individually. They frequently learned better ways of doing things from each other and from brainstorming sessions and could unleash their creativity to rise to new levels. The respect for individual expression created connection throughout the organization. Leaders focus on what connects us rather than on what separates us, and they honor each person's uniqueness for the dimension it brings to the organization's learning, growth, and continuous improvement.

ASK, LISTEN, CREATE SPACE

The power of the question may be the most underrated and overlooked leverage we have in our organizations. It is a powerful decision-making device and a powerful learning tool. Discussions during meetings often degenerate to A's promoting one perspective and B's promoting another perspective and a subsequent compromise or a win-lose decision. Little group learning occurs, and because the focus has been on A's and B's perspectives, many other possibilities are overlooked. Questions can help us discover new possibilities and understand all alternatives.

Most of us aren't accustomed to thinking in terms of questions; we have to practice developing information- and idea-generating questions and then learning to sequence them to help us bring understanding to the issue on the table. One of the hardest things for people I have worked with to do is to learn to ask an open-ended question that generates information, especially when they think they know the answer. They tend to ask either questions with built-in answers or yes-no questions that don't produce new thinking. "Wouldn't you say that collections are the accounting department's responsibility?" is the kind of question they often ask. Such questions really leave themselves open only to agreement or disagreement, a yes or a no. Thought-provoking questions may be "What are all the points in our process at which we could increase our collection percentage?" or "If everyone in our organization took responsibility for collections, where would leverage points occur?"

It has also been my experience that "Why" questions generate little that is useful and often lead to blame-casting, glory-grabbing, defensiveness, and win-lose thinking. "What" questions tend to be the most useful early on, and "How" questions make a useful contribution only when "What" has been well defined.

I often ask groups, "What would be different about your decision-making if you started every process by asking, 'What do you want?' " They discover they currently spend much of their decision-making time focusing on what they don't want rather than on what they do, and changing their decision-making process forces them to define both their desired task and their process outcomes. Others say, "We would have to know what we want!" because their dialogue reveals they take off in hot pursuit of something often without knowing what they are pursuing. They also discover that more participation is required when they start by asking what they want. It is also easier to participate when you start with a defining question rather than responding to someone's specific idea of "how" to do something. Other outcomes from such questions include happier participants, more productive use of time, more narrowly focused scope, greater buy-in of the resulting decision, and better opportunity to avert disaster.

Groups rarely ask the defining questions that determine what they are going to do; they jump in and try to figure out how to do it. Along with "What do we want, individually and collectively?" some other "What" questions that are instrumental in early stages of problem assessment and decision making are:

- What does that mean to you?
- What would it look like if that were happening?
- What would it look like if that weren't happening?
- What are the reasons that we would want that?
- What are the reasons that we wouldn't want that?
- What are the assumptions upon which that is based?
- What if the opposite were true?

I often ask groups to focus completely on developing questions that they should be asking in looking at a particular problem; much to their amazement, they sometimes figure out what the problem is without even answering the questions. The process of simply identifying the questions brings clarity to the issue. By thinking about an issue as something we know little about, we can bring our curiosity to it and playfully ask questions to help us collectively learn things that we can never learn when we start by applying our ideas about "how to handle" the problem.

In addition to providing an effective vehicle for decision making, question-asking is the most valuable learning device that I know of. Managers who get into an answer mode often benignly develop dependency relationships that leave them feeling "pecked to death by goslings."[12] They aren't able to see that which is quite apparent to the outsider. People come to the manager for an answer, and the manager gives one to each of them. The people go away, they have another question the next day, and the manager gives them another answer. A leader, on the other hand, gives people something better than an answer. He or she gives people a question that leads to a learning process. The questioners learn how to think about a problem or a situation and can obtain a tool that they can use over and over again.

For example, an employee may ask, "Is this something we need to keep?" The manager can give a quick "yes" or "no," but the next time the employee needs to know whether to keep something, the process must

---

12. Erma Bombeck.

repeat itself. No learning has taken place. The manager who takes time to talk people through a thought process gives them a foundation on which to build future decisions. A set of questions may go like this: "What are the reasons that we would want to save it? What are the reasons that we wouldn't want to? Are there similar things you've encountered that would tell you what to do? What do you think we should do? What would the consequences be if we did that? Are those consequences that we can live with?" The manager helps the employee find an answer. Although this technique would not be used with a new employee, it is extremely effective with trained employees, and managers often discover new thinking on an issue by listening to the employee's thought process.

When organizations are built on a culture of having answers, the organization fails to access massive amounts of data and countless new perspectives and at the same time builds dependency relationships that leave managers overworked and stressed from frequent interruptions. People know a lot. Yet in a society that rewards having the right answer, workers and even managers are reticent to offer their wisdom for fear they will say the wrong thing. They watch carefully for signals about what the boss is looking for before saying anything. If the average I.Q. of people in a group is 120, then more often than not the collective intelligence of the group is 60. People are afraid to build on their individual knowing, they are afraid to expose their ideas because they fear being wrong or because they can't "prove" something they know intuitively. This is why it is so important for the leader to recognize his or her role in helping people discover they have the answers and then providing them space for discovering the answers.

One highly educated management group I have worked with had fallen into the dependency role to such an extent that, with one exception, each member told me in personal interviews that they were not able to make decisions as a group. They hadn't had any training, and the executives of the company had not created space or provided an environment for decision making. Every time they began to process a topic, executives would grow impatient with process and would step in and make the decision for the managers. It had happened so consistently over so many years that the managers no longer believed they were able to make decisions.

Silence is uncomfortable to most of us in our Western culture. When there is a gap in a meeting during which no talking occurs, most managers feel they need to rescue the group either by giving them an answer or by changing the subject. This attitude creates a co-dependent relationship. Providing space means just that: The leader can accept a few minutes of silence. I have yet to encounter a normal group in which, after two or three minutes of silence, someone doesn't jump in to rescue the group from the space for thought and reflection. When I throw out challenging questions to a group, I am patient in letting time lapse. When comments come, they are usually something like, "Do you know the answer?" or "It's so complicated and confusing," or even "I don't know." With dogged persistence, I tell the group, "I don't know the answer, but I am sure that it is in the room." Without fail, it is. One person finally comes up with a piece, another almost always has something to add, then another and another add pieces.

The same thing happens in one-on-one meetings. The "don't know" or "confused" response is a common defense mechanism. Once adequate training has been given and the employee has developed a level of familiarity with both the individual job and how it fits into the larger organization, then when the leader assures the employee that he or she has great faith that the person has the answer, it frequently comes. In responding to questions with questions instead of answers, the leader often probes to assist accessing the answer. This process must not consist of defined questions such as "Have you thought of doing XYZ?" Such questions are just answers with a question mark at the end. Open-ended questions, such as "What are the possibilities?" "Are there other possibilities?" "Have you ever dealt with a similar situation?" "What things do you think might be important to consider?" stimulate the employee's thought processes.

One executive that I have been working with on his question-asking techniques proudly reported to me that he'd used it with the manager of a satellite operation. He reported that she had not only included all the things he would have suggested, but she had added a few things he hadn't thought about. He was equally pleased with the effect of the exchange on the manager, who seemed pleased to have figured the problem out herself. Most important, he recognized that the next time a similar situation came up, she wouldn't need to call him.

Most of us know a lot more than we know we know. An effective leader is able to help people discover both that they have the answers they didn't know they had and that they can make meaningful change. It may even take an extended period of space. If the leader is comfortable saying, "Why don't you think about it for an hour or so? Then we'll get back together," the space that is created often allows ideas to germinate. (It is critical that the leader keep his or her commitment to follow up; otherwise the employee may feel abandoned and discouraged if an answer hasn't come.)

Building healthy interdependent relationships rather than co-dependent ones seems desirable. Not unlike my management group who realized that fear often impedes communication, you will find that fear is usually the basis for co-dependent workplace relationships. Knowledge and information are power bases for many managers. If they parcel out information piece by piece, as it is needed, managers ensure that people are dependent on them, that they are needed. They become the co-dependent, the person who enables the dependent party to remain dependent. At the same time, employees who live in a society that punishes mistakes and insists there is one right answer for every situation are actually glad to continue to be dependent, a situation that entails few risks.

Not long ago I had occasion to witness a man I'll call Bill, a high-level executive in a large corporation, panic almost to the extent of becoming irrational at the prospect of losing his co-dependent relationship. Bill had engineered that managers reporting to him at several sites around the country knew just enough to do their jobs, but not enough to work autonomously. Earlier, Bill had talked about how busy he was and had boasted that these managers called him two or three times every day to get help with crises at their plants. In the past Bill had always been able to designate those named to manager positions and thus had ensured continuation of the dependency relationship. When the company decided to build a new site, a new decentralized selection procedure was used. Sue, a competent and knowledgeable prospective manager, became a finalist for the job. Bill quickly realized that Sue wouldn't need him as the other managers had. Classic organizational politics ensued. Bill was able to survive one more time.

Real leaders are able to see through the Bills. They are able to see that if companies are to achieve their potential, everyone in them must use all the knowledge they have. When leaders ask questions, they mine the knowledge that others have while broadening their own understanding of situations, and they increase the collective intelligence of the organization.

A NEW TOOL

If we, as leaders, are to provide space for spirit to emerge, we need a new tool that seeks to challenge our assumptions, our creativity, and our spontaneity rather than to restrict and to control in order to ensure outcomes with which we are familiar and comfortable. We need tools that help groups of people learn to think together so that as a group they can discover things that would have been impossible to learn outside the group setting.

As a communication process, *dialogue* has gained great respect in recent years. *Dialogue* literally means "to think through." Dialogue significantly differs from discussion, which is based on individual thinking, advocacy, defense, conversion, and movement to consensus, decision, or both. Groups using dialogue seek to develop a deep understanding of an issue's sides and depths; they flood themselves with information and try to understand relationships and to discover the meaning of each alternative for their various frames of reference, until a solution emerges. When in dialogue, groups focus on learning to resolve problems together. They agree to put aside certainties or assumptions in the belief that flawed decisions are often based on false assumptions. In a spirit of discovery, participants agree to be open to many possibilities, any one of which may be workable. Instead of presenting defended positions that are narrowed to achieve agreement, people try to expand the inquiry by asking more and deeper questions. It has been my experience that people literally come to be of one mind as the concerns and perspectives of each person are explored.

For example, a dialogue about installation of new technology may begin with questions about what the equipment should do when it is operational. Thus far dialogue differs little from discussion. But as the dialogue continues, items like "provide better customer service," "cut costs," or "increase competitiveness" are explored in depth. What does it mean to provide better customer service? What happens when that aim is achieved? What does better customer service look and sound like? What gets in the way? Even questions like "Why wouldn't we want to give better customer service?" are explored.

Once the group has "learned" its desired outcomes, the dialogue shifts to learn how the outcomes can be accomplished: What must be done well in order to achieve them? When the group identifies one concern, such as "understanding the new technology," then it delves deeper into what it means to understand the new technology, what skills are needed, who is involved, and how an understanding of the technology is measured. Groups who believe they can quickly understand even the simplest of issues discover that each person may understand only one dimension moderately well. Dialogue enables the group to take understanding for the whole team to a deeper level than anyone imagines.

The dialogue process may be compared to peeling an onion. When we look at the onion with its skin on, we have an idea of what it looks like. As we peel off the skin, we find something different. As each successive layer is peeled away, we discover more and more, including some undesirable side effects, such as a strong odor and a tendency to evoke tears. When we get to the core, the onion looks smaller and smoother than we may have thought when we started. At the same time, we discover that, as a result of the peeling process, we are different (teary eyes and cleared sinuses) for having gone through the experience. Participants in the dialogue process inevitably discover two things. First, through the group process, each participant gains a much clearer picture of whatever topic is being explored. Second, as a result of the exploration, we find the talents and abilities which each person brings to the decision and implementation changes.

The more clearly we understand all dimensions, or the range of possible solutions, of a problem, the better our decision is. Decisions in companies often focus on a symptom perceived to be a problem. Through the dialogue process, participants come to understand that the problem may be quite different from the symptom that precipitated the dialogue. For instance, absenteeism is often identified as a problem, but dialogue almost always discloses that poor attendance is instead a symptom. Dialogue may reveal that there is a negative reward system at work: when an employee misses work, others do distasteful work for them. Dialogue may reveal one of a number of other possibilities: supervisors don't do performance evaluations, poor performance evaluations don't lead to any negative consequences (termination or loss of pay increase), people with poor attendance continue to be employed resulting in mixed messages about attendance. Each of these individual problems would be addressed differently. Yet it has been my experience that when absenteeism occurs, it is most often addressed with a bonus or reward program that responds to the symptom, rather than discovering the real problem and tackling it directly.

Dialogue helps leaders discover how one action supports or impedes other actions. Executives often decide they want to achieve a particular outcome in a company, but they don't take the time to explore the breadth of the changes that must be made to produce that outcome. For example, it is currently trendy to say we want top-level customer service. We want employees to exercise a high degree of initiative in delivering quality customer service, but we punish them when they break rules in the process; the business thus never motivates the employee to the degree of personal entrepreneurship needed for top-level service to occur. Dialogue enables leaders to ascertain the many practices and policies that must be changed at the same time that it also reveals the new training and new practices that must be implemented to support new behavior. Dialogue gets people intensely involved in developing solutions and creates a great commitment to implementation. It engages the spirit, intelligence, experience, and wisdom of all involved and allows them to make their unique contributions to the spirit of the enterprise.

In Part 2 of this book I discuss at length helping leaders unlearn some of the things that get in the way of living these few simple truths. For most of us, learning to live these truths of being becomes a lifelong discipline to be practiced over and over again as we learn more and more about what they mean. Just when we think we've "got it," we slip, and, as the old song goes, "pick yourself up, dust yourself off, and start all over again!" Fortunately, slipping does not carry the negative charge for the heart leader that it does for the traditional manager, who had to have all the answers and had to be perfect. In a spirit-respecting workplace, everyone is learning, including the boss.

EXPLORING THE PATH OF COURAGE

(1) List your own personal values and closely held beliefs. Then, make a list of four or five times in the last month when your actions didn't reflect those beliefs and values. (Excuses don't count. Either you reflected your values or you didn't.) Ask yourself how you could have acted differently so that your actions would reflect your commitment to your values. Take each of your values and, using the questions about commitment in Chapter 3, page 47, develop personal intentionality guides to ensure that your actions reflect your values in the future.

(2) Think of a recent situation in which your actions reflected that either you had no choice or the choices were so limited that you felt as if you had no choice. Ask yourself, "What were the other possibilities that I didn't consider?" "If there were more, what would they be?" Any time you catch your internal voices exercising judgment about the new choice you have identified, ask yourself, "What if the opposite were true?" (Hint: Don't forget that consciously choosing to take no action, to delay action, or to solicit more ideas from others are choices.)

(3) Focus on asking open-ended questions for a day. Open-ended questions merely express curiosity and lack built-in answers. What new perspectives do you discover? Did you help others gain new insights as well?

Chapter 4

Unleashing the Spirit Cycle at Work

A few years ago, if someone had asked me to write about spirit in the workplace, I probably would have responded "What? Religion hasn't got any place in our organizations. In fact, mixing the two could lead to legal problems." In the early '90s, in fact, a participant in a staff session organized to write a statement of a company's vision and values accused me of trying to establish a corporate religion. The owners of the business and I were incredulous. I hadn't said anything about religion but was simply trying to help the organization identify the driving forces in their work. In addition, my own personal beliefs were sacred to me, and I held in the highest respect the right of others to have personal religious beliefs. As my work with creativity, leadership, and quality continued to evolve, I began to be aware that this employee knew something about spirituality that I was just discovering. Although she, not unlike many others, confused spirituality and religion, she did understand that the driving forces in our work and the values at the core of our organizations and at the core of our selves are spiritual.

GENERATING THE SPIRIT CYCLE

Early in my research about leaders who promoted creativity and quality, I had the opportunity to visit a small factory run by one of these instinctive leaders whom I call Bert. Bert was a fortyish entrepreneur who had started and run his small manufacturing job-shop operation for about ten years, first alone, and after he married, with his wife. As we toured the facility, Bert told one story after another of innovations that his factory workers had made in the way they did their work. Some changes improved safety. Others resulted in gains in productivity. Still others refined packaging and assembly. There were even computer programs designed to revamp the way products were engineered. As Bert walked around and talked about these innovations, he became demonstrably excited and enthused talking about what his workers had accomplished.

This man seemed to have the key I'd been seeking. What, I asked him, did he *do* to encourage people to make all these improvements? (At that point, I still thought it was something he *did*.) At first, he didn't understand the question, and after several attempts at clarification, he could only say that he didn't do anything. The workers had done it all. In frustration, I was forced to satisfy myself with the knowledge that whatever he was doing occurred without any thought or effort on his part.

What was setting these people on fire was happening on a deeper level, and it was generating what I call the Spirit Cycle. I use the term *Spirit Cycle* to describe the way people relate to one another in a spirit-respecting workplace that produces a self-perpetuating energy. These relationships escalate into a virtuous cycle whereby openness, trust, and respect improve work relationships. Better work relationships lead to more communication and to a better understanding of how our work relates to that of others. As we come to understand how our jobs relate to each other, we discover better ways to work. This result leads to more trust, openness and respect, and to improved bottom-line returns. Each behavior reinforces the other and culminates in a cycle that produces more and more of the same.

THE SPIRITLESS, VICIOUS CYCLE

When these spirit-generated behaviors aren't present, a different, vicious cycle is generated; this cycle slowly but surely sucks the life from an organization. In one instance I remember particularly well, management ego was costing a company thousands of dollars. The company manufactured large, high-quality wooden furnishings for commercial buildings, in a factory that was housed in an old manufacturing site, with several large cracks in the concrete floor. The raw materials used were very large sheets of expensive, flawless wood. When I visited the factory, I saw large sheets of cherry plywood, costing several hundred dollars a sheet, being worked on. Dollies moved both sheets of wood and finished furniture around the work site. The dolly frequently became unbalanced when moved over a crack in the floor, and the wood or the large pieces of furniture toppled over. To prevent damage when the furniture inevitably fell off the dolly, often into machinery, employees used their bodies to block the fall. The workers had so much pride in craftsmanship that they risked physical harm to save the finished pieces. The result was almost always both an on-the-job injury *and* damaged goods. Not surprisingly, the company was burdened with astronomical workers' compensation premiums, significant volumes of scrapped materials, and low morale from craftsmen who witnessed the destruction of weeks and months of work before the pieces ever left the shop floor.

As we tried to identify ways to cut costs and improve safety, almost 75 percent of the workers identified this one situation, yet most had been afraid to mention it to managers, who let workers know they "weren't paid to think." The few who had been courageous enough to mention it were told it would cost too much to fix the floor. Imagine the incredulity of being told that a repair that would have cost a few hundred dollars was too expensive when it would have saved thousands of dollars in materials, finished goods, and insurance premiums! How much ego does it take to bring a company to the verge of bankruptcy rather than bringing more spirit to the workplace?

This company was located just about a mile from Bert's company where workers' innovations were received with open arms and words of encouragement such as "Go ahead and do it!" or "Develop a proposal, and let's do it!" The furniture company, driven by egoism, resisted allowing natural forces to improve it from within and closed its doors forever just a few months later. Bert's company that nurtures the spirits of its workers to be leaders at every level is alive, expanding, and doing well. If an organization is to be healthy financially, the choice cannot be *either* profit *or* spirit. There is no choice. Both must happen, and they must happen continuously. Real leaders have the wisdom to see the relationships of the Spirit Cycle and bring to the workplace the trust and well-being that allow the cycle to begin.

POSITIVE ENERGY IN THE AIR

A closer look at Bert's facility shows us more about the Spirit Cycle. The moment I walk into Bert's office, I sense something different. There is a lightness that is welcoming beyond the nice smile and friendly patter of the receptionist. The office is relaxed. People interact in a friendly, supportive way with each other, customers, and even the boss, as he comes to meet us. Bert greets us and enthusiastically begins to tell us about his small company with the pride usually reserved for a first child or grandchild. Using standard quality jargon, he talks about the connection he and his employees have with their customers and the pride they take in delivering a first-rate product that they are always trying to improve. He talks about how they are able to work in the present by debriefing every situation, learning from it, and moving forward to current projects.

At least a half-dozen times during our less-than-one-hour tour, individuals come up and make suggestions about how to do something differently. Always his response is similar. He asks a few questions about how the idea will work and whether they've involved others who would be affected, then asks the employee if he or she thinks the idea will work, and finally encourages the person to go ahead with a trial, after he makes sure the employee has determined how to measure the performance of the innovation.

Bert's way of communicating with his employees is respectful of them and their ideas; he makes sure the employees retain ownership of their ideas. He honors their ideas almost as if each is a work of art, which in a way it is. A workplace innovation taking form is the expression of individual creativity. Bert inspires people as they aspire to a better product, to a safer workplace, and to a conserving of the small company's resources. Several times Bert stops and shows us an innovation that someone had made in a piece of equipment or in an operation. He always tells us the name of the person who generated the idea. Even though we don't know Mary Dokes or Howard Samson, he wants to make sure that he respects and honors their contribution.

Risk-taking in the form of new ideas or even communicating with the boss about things that need to be improved is apparent everywhere. This group puts workplace fear to rest. Bert has faith in the people that work with him (*with*, not for); he trusts them to give their ideas thought and research, and they have faith and trust him to receive these ideas respectfully. The more he respects their input, it seems, the more they give it. Thousands of dollars were saved in process improvements and improved safety standards; even new product lines had been conceived of and facilitated by workers. The company virtually explodes with creativity.

In addition to encouraging people to develop their creativity at work, Bert also encourages people to expand their personal horizons by taking classes of personal interest to them. He introduces us to a young woman who had just completed her bachelor's degree after several years of working on it part time while holding a clerical job in the company. He beams as he tells her story. He also tells us about others who have taken seemingly unrelated classes only to discover that they learned something that was useful to them on the job while pursuing their own personal passions.

In recent years, it has been trendy to talk about the "whole" person, to remember that people have a life beyond work. Bert lives that attitude: He not only respects people's lives outside of work but encourages a blurring of the lines wherever possible. A playpen in one office attests to his commitment to helping a young woman bond with her toddler. Bert cares about the people that work with him. He shares their hopes and dreams and encourages them in any way he can to experience a full life. His commitment to them is obvious in the returned commitment they give to the company and to its growth and prosperity.

RELATIONSHIPS ARE DIFFERENT HERE

As we watch people interact at Bert's facility, it is clear that there is an unusual quality of relationship here. When people talk, they are really present with each other. Even though there are many activities, including a group of strangers touring the plant, around them, their focus is on the person with whom they are talking—completely. They listen carefully. They ask questions of each other to understand what the other is talking about. The pace is slower and more studied than I am accustomed to witnessing in the workplace. The level of respect with which each speaks to the other truly honors both people. People are also attentive to relationships often neglected in our workplaces, such as the relationship between work and its effect on other people and their jobs. People take care to explain how and if an idea impacts others and how the input of those others has influenced the evolution of the idea.

Even more important, I continuously observe a strong presence of the relationship between what Bert and his co-workers want to create in their every action. The ideas that are often part of a vision statement or of organizational values that hang on the wall come to life here. Some of the things that I observe in almost every conversation I overhear are:

- How does this action affect this customer?
- How does it affect our ability to serve other customers?
- Does this action reflect the way we want to do business?
- How does this action tie in with our operational goals?
- Have you talked with everyone involved?
- Does this action affect other operations beyond your own? If so, have you talked to the people involved?
- Is this action something you feel good about doing?

The intentions of the company have been clearly articulated and integrated into every action by everyone.

As I reflect on my observations, I am nearly certain that the quality of relationships are a reflection of Bert and the quality of his relationship with himself, and his attitude seems to be contagious. He is courageous and gives power away, over and over again. He isn't caught up in defensive postures to make himself look good; he knows that he is only one part and that every single person has an important contribution to make. He trusts and respects and encourages others. He knows that life is a learning process, and he easily learns lessons from unexpected outcomes. He communicates all this from his very being.

THE PROOF IS IN THE PUDDING

Although my interaction with Bert's company was brief, I do know that at the time I visited the facility, the economy was weak in his area of the country, yet his company had managed to prosper and grow. It had introduced new products and expanded into new markets, including international ones. A new source of income was generated when employees developed a computer program for one of their processes that was then marketed to similar industries. When last I heard, the company was introducing a new product line that integrated their advanced technologies into a more traditional product.

In manufacturing facilities, the physical condition of the plant is often a reflection of many aspects of the business. Bert's site was spotless. Regular preventive maintenance, a process "owned" by each operator, allowed the company to avoid delays caused by downed equipment. Bert bragged about the company's safety record, which allowed the company to save significantly on workers' compensation insurance in an industry with traditionally high experience ratings.

Although I don't know about Bert's facility, in other spirit-generating companies where I have worked, attendance is high, in no small part because of the low-stress level of the atmosphere and avoidance of stress-generated illnesses. It is also a reflection of the company's willingness to work with people and with the demands their personal and family lives necessarily make on them. Because there is a high level of trust and respect for the whole person, people can honestly talk about their desire to attend a child's school performance and can take off an hour to support the child instead of having to fake an illness and take off a whole day to slip off to attend the performance on the side. People can be honest with each other and feel good about it. The commitment to the company grows each time they do.

THE SACRED TRUST

I remind the reader that talking about spirit in the workplace and the personal spirituality of leaders is fairly new to me, and it is something that I have mustered great courage to do. Even the skeptic in me has been convinced of the vital need for respect of our spirits and all that this subject implies if we are to survive as people, as organizations, as an economy, and even as a society. The price we have been paying in quantity, quality, price, availability, innovation, and stress-related illness for keeping spirit down has been too high, and it is a real, dollars-and-cents cost to the bottom line. Financial prudence and attention to productivity are also parts of the sacred trust that leaders hold. A leader who doesn't keep people focused on the organization's financial as well as spiritual goals is usurping trust. To do less jeopardizes the relationship of the leader to the workers. Safety in the relationship is required for workers to be creative and take risks. The leader who isn't financially prudent so that jobs may be jeopardized has missed an important part of the Spirit Cycle. If we are to have learning, continuous improvement, and quality over the long run, we must create an environment of personal safety, openness, trust, and respect.

The real bottom line is to have a financially healthy, competitive organization in which we needn't choose between *either* financial security and productivity *or* helping people discover creativity and meaning in their work. The real bottom line is that both are critical. Financial security cannot happen over the long run without meaningful work. Ruthless financial measures that produce short-term gains and demoralize people actually undermine the company's long-term ability to be competitive. When people see the heads of others rolling right and left, they are unlikely to stick their necks out and to suggest that management's way of running things is costing the company money. As we have already seen, this reluctance to participate is just one of many ways in which failing to respect the spirits of people in the workplace can hurt the bottom line.

TAPPING THE SPIRIT

This notion of bringing spirit into everyday life and especially into our work challenges me to translate the esoteric ideas of messiahs, Buddha, saints, and gurus into their meanings for me in my everyday work life and for millions of others who try to create a better way of working together. There appear to be two keys for understanding the Spirit Cycle. The first

The Spirit Cycle

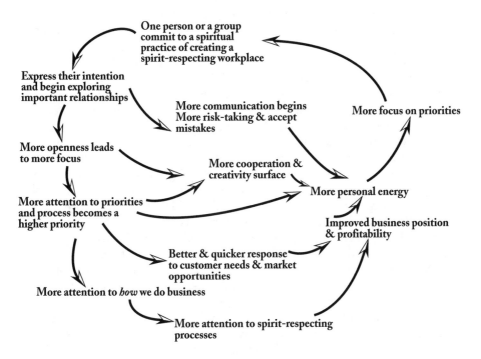

Figure 4-1. The Spirit Cycle.

is seeing our work as a spiritual practice, like practicing on an instrument or at a sport to get better and better at being what we hope to be. I believe there are three components to a workplace spiritual practice. The first is to know what we want to be—what kind of workplace we want to create. The second is to make a commitment to bring consciousness to every act and become a nonjudgmental observer who knows when the act I do, as I am doing it, is being done in a way that supports what I want to create. The third component is to make a commitment to learn from each act how to move closer and closer to what we want to create. In spiritual practice at work, I may choose to respect others more by making sure I really hear what they are saying. I must adopt a stance of naïve inquirer and listen without judgment to truly understand what others are saying. I must ask questions to understand others' ideas and let go of my ego-driven assumption that after a sentence or two, I know exactly what the other is saying.

Once I know what I want to create, I start observing myself in action. Initially, I notice that when I plan for communication, I can really observe myself and learn a lot I have been missing. I also notice that when someone comes up to me when I am stressed or in a hurry, I slip into old ways of *re*acting instead of *inter*acting. As time moves on and I practice more, I even get to the point where I begin to notice that I relate to others in a more respectful way. Over time, my focus shifts from noticing when I act the way I want to, because that is the exception, to noticing when I slip in my commitment to higher-quality communication, because I have evolved to the point that slips are now the exception.

I have been told that the word *sin*, which has come to have a strong religious context relating more to crime and punishment than to learning, evolved from a medieval archery term meaning "missing the mark." In work-a-day spirituality, our *sins* occur when we miss the mark. In the case I have just described, sin occurs when I don't relate to others in the way I have chosen. In the context of spiritual practice, however, this sin should not be the source of punishment but of measurement. By learning from *how* I have missed the mark, I can come closer to my goal the next time. As anyone who has mastered a sport or learned to play a musical instrument knows, when we study the pattern of our misses, we get insights into how we can move closer and closer to the mark.

The second key for understanding the Spirit Cycle is developing spiritual practice to consciously create compassionate relationships in our work. Stephen Nachmanovitch describes compassion as "the ability to relate to and identify with what we see, hear and touch: seeing what we see not as an *it*, but as part of ourselves."[1] From a spiritual perspective, we are all part of a larger whole. There is no person and no act that is not part of ourselves, and we cannot continue to injure ourselves and expect either a healthy work atmosphere or a healthy bottom line for very long. Understanding the fundamental relationships in our work and in our lives as part of a spiritual practice moving toward creating more compassion—seeing those with whom we have those relationships as part of ourselves—is critical to unleashing the Spirit Cycle.

I believe that there are four key relationships that define what our workplaces are; awareness of these relationships can lead to a conscious move to a spiritual practice that can change them. The *first* of these relationships is the most important. It is the relationship that each of us has with ourselves. It is the most important because the relationships that I have with others, with my work, and with life in general is a reflection of

---

1. Stephen Nachmanovitch, *Free Play: The Power of Improvisation in Life and the Arts* (New York: G. P. Putnam's Sons, 1990), p. 169.

the one that I have with myself. Compassion is definitely needed in the relationship I have with myself. In one group that was examining their relationship with self, a woman said, "If I talked to my friends the way I talk to myself, they wouldn't be friends very long." And that is what most of us are reflecting into the world. Only when I can accept myself and my relationship with myself can I begin to observe how my being affects others and how it affects my work. Only when I become aware of who I am and what my relationship with myself is can I begin to think about changing it. To use the spiritual practice model described earlier in this section (Tapping the Spirit), I can't come to know that I want to communicate with others in a more respecting way until I come to know that I am not already doing that. I have no motivation to do so until and unless I come to know that the impact of my current mode of communication is stealing the energy—the very life—from my workplace environment. And, as I come to be more aware of my relationship with myself, I probably discover that it is stealing the energy and life from me as well.

The *second* relationship that is important for me to understand in generating the Spirit Cycle is my relationship with my work. When I define my work as producing results, I approach it very differently from the way I would when I define my work as being a partner in a team that produces results. A mind shift occurs with the latter definition: I drop my ego-driven perspective that when I don't make something happen it won't happen, and I allow a creative collaboration toward a common goal to occur. I begin to observe the ways my efforts to force and control have actually impeded what I want to occur. A group can change before my eyes when, for instance, the "idea man" begins to see his relationship to his work as "the teacher of idea-generation." An overworked research librarian can change her relationship to her work by redefining her job from "research" to "helping others understand how to use research resources."

In each of these cases, not only does the person achieve a new level of freedom and energy toward a "new job" but others in the group discover within themselves new capacities that they had once abdicated. There is probably little that I do that produces more visible and moving results than helping people redefine their relationships with their work. This change impacts leadership at all levels of the organization; the stories we have created for ourselves, about what we have to be and how we have to be that, cripple us individually and collectively.

Philip Berrigan, writing about his time in prison in the early '70s, describes his work with prisoners and his experiences of that work: "I can imagine no greater joy or satisfaction than witnessing people slowly gaining control of themselves, breaking the slaveries that afflict them. It's like being a spectator at creation."[2] When people redefine their relationship with their work, it is truly like "breaking the slaveries that afflict them," and I, like Berrigan, have felt the gift of "being a spectator at creation." Although there is a freedom that impacts a whole organization when those at the "top" redefine their relationships with work, it is one of the most touching of human experiences to see people who have always experienced themselves as "just doing what I'm told to do" stand up and own the ability to change their workplace in a strong and powerful way.

The *third* relationship that impacts the Spirit Cycle is the relationships people have with their co-workers at all levels. Those relationships come to be very spiritual. Each person is accepted, valued, and respected as a unique and precious human being, apart from the job. Leslie, a clerk, doesn't "do a job." Leslie, the human being, is an important part of our team, and her principal work is clerical in nature.

People aspire to fulfill themselves. They inspire others. They have faith in and trust one another. They learn from one another and support each other. They look for better ways to perform their own jobs so that others' work becomes easier or better. Understanding people's relationships with their co-workers simultaneously opens another set of relationships that are the linkages between various jobs, functions, and processes, which we may have never realized are related until we began coming to know the people in those jobs and talking about how we can work together better.

The *fourth* relationship is that with the larger environment: people in other divisions of the business; our customers, suppliers, contractors, and even competitors; government regulators, our legislators, other government officials and the laws they write and enforce; accountants, lawyers, or consultants; the physical environment and whether the way we do business respects Earth and other species and the resources we leave for our grandchildren and their grandchildren. In a spiritual context, we come to know that all things are connected. When we examine what our relationships are with each component in our larger environment, we become aware of how much of our dissatisfaction may have been of our own making; then we can consciously create a different relationship. Every group I have led through an examination of their "larger environment" has discovered that they had the power to change the relationship with even their "most dreaded" outside group simply by choosing to do so.

---

2. Philip Berrigan, *Widen the Prison Gates* (New York: Simon & Schuster, 1973), p. 62.

THE COURAGE FACTOR

As many in Eastern Europe have discovered, when long-suppressed and undeveloped spirit is released, an often frightening transition begins. To bring spirit to an organization requires that the leader commit to having the courage to be calm amid chaos, to actually sustain the tension until adequate learning can occur, to maintain personal spirit, and to have faith and trust in both people and process. Giving orders doesn't require personal courage. That's only one reason that so many managers who give lip service to employee involvement revert to old modes of operating when the going gets tough. They lack the personal courage to endure over time.

Courage doesn't come in a bottle to be taken as needed when symptoms of weakness occur. To live the kind of courage required to bring spirit to the workplace requires the leader to take time to experience the relationship with ourselves and to discover what spiritual leadership is about. It also requires acceptance of emotions—ours and those of others; emotions drive most actions whether we acknowledge them or not. When emotions are accepted, we can acknowledge fear or anger or resentment, and explore the sources of those very real emotions. With a shared understanding of where people are personally, the organization can move ahead. When emotions are denied, they unconsciously drive our actions and reactions. We do or say things that aren't in keeping with our expressed values system. We do and say things that undermine the goals of the organization.

As Carl Jung said, "That which we do not bring to consciousness appears in our lives as Fate." Without self-knowledge, our reactions are driven by events in the past, often events totally unrelated to the current situation. Without self-knowledge, we do not recognize the disconnectedness of our own reaction. Events we create are blamed upon Fate, the market, our employees, our competitors, or other handy scapegoats. When we have made the commitment to the spiritual practice of relationship exploration, we are able to deal with matters on a conscious rather than a reactive level. We are *completely* present, in the present, at all times.

The managers in the company who wouldn't repair the floor were driven by emotions—fear, anger, resentment, jealousy, and other emotions that frame the situation as a win-lose decision. By being unwilling to accept and explore those emotions so that decision making occurs on a conscious level for the good of the company, the managers let unconscious emotions drive destructive decisions. When the emotions and experiences that insulate us from others are pulled into consciousness, we take the ego out of our decision making and create connection.

We are then able to take win-lose out of decision making and transform it into win-win. When we view the world as a whole in which we are all connected, we know win-lose is a game no one wins. It is not possible in our organizations for one person or one group to lose in the long run without the organization also losing in the long run. We may refuse to take an employee's suggestion to fix the floor and "win" that round, but when the cracked floor leads the company into bankruptcy, we all lose. The owners lose their investment. The employees lose their jobs. The managers lose their positions of ego power. The customers lose a source of goods upon which they may have been dependent. An organization with incredible potential is lost.

Leadership is different from management. Leadership is a state of being; management is a way of doing. A leader's being launches the Spirit Cycle. The leader *gives* service to those who work *with* him or her. Managers *receive* service from those who work *for* them. Leaders do not act for ego gratification or personal rewards. Leaders give of themselves to others. Leaders are real people involved in real working relationships with other real people on a conscious level. Spirits are unleashed when an environment allows and encourages each and every person to achieve his or her workplace potential. A leader is able to achieve personal potential *because* others are achieving theirs. The organization wins because the people win, and the people win because the organization wins. Under everything is that core deep within each of us, the heart and soul that binds us across time and space.

SPIRIT: THE VITALITY THAT'S BEEN MISSING

Without our spirits, we are never fully alive, individually or organizationally. Spirit is not our whole life, but it is an essential part of the whole of our lives. Spirit brings vitality and energy to us, individually and organizationally. It brings balance to life. It provides an anchor in times of adversity and transition. For too long, people have been asked to place their spirits on a shelf. They have been socialized to believe that it is not appropriate to bring their hearts, emotions, and spirits to work, to school, to community groups, to government agencies. Spirituality has either been relegated to a few minutes of meditation each day or to church on Sunday; more likely, spirituality has been quietly tucked away and forgotten. Most of us have chosen to put it away because it has been too painful to know the joy and exhilaration of spirit and not bring it into the rest of life.

Without spirit, an organization does not thrive. When we have severed people from their spirits, what is left are last gasps for a shallow existence. The strength is gone. The fullness is gone. The ability to flexibly weather the storms of change are gone. The balance, beauty, and compassion are gone. Burnout runs amok. And these things are gone from all of life—work life, family life, social life, and community life. Without spiritual nourishment, we move through life anesthetized from joy, love, and emotion, pulled down by progressive resignation and fatigue.

When we acknowledge the spiritual dimension, we choose to accept that organizations are living systems, made up of living human beings. When people are treated like machines, they act like machines. When they are treated as the human beings that they are, they bring more to work. They are more involved; they are present in their jobs; they are creative and committed. With spiritual nourishment, they thrive! They have the spirit that we have longed for in our workers. They have the spirit we have longed for in ourselves. When we see that all things are connected, we know that we cannot foster relationships that use people up without knowing at the very same time that we are planting the seeds of our own destruction. When we see that all things are connected and connect to us personally, we know that even one act of disrespect can create a ripple through every relationship in the organization.

When we collectively commit to a practice of creating more compassion in significant relationships—with self, with work, with others, and with the larger environment—we have found the start of the virtuous cycle that becomes the Spirit Cycle. We live openness, trust, respect, and faith, which produce more openness, trust, respect, and faith. When we open more to each other, we open to working together better and producing more effective results. And we feel good too. A man I know described the feeling he experienced as his heart began opening. "My chest feels as big and full as it might be if I weighed fifty pounds more than I do." I have had a similar feeling when I am aware of being part of all things; a wave of overwhelming emotion sweeps over me and leaves the area around my physical heart with a warm vibration that slowly takes over my whole body. When we can bring that feeling of oneness—of true compassion—to all of our work relationships, we are ready to unleash the Spirit Cycle.

EXPLORING THE PATH OF COURAGE

(1) Look at your relationship with yourself. What do you find? Do you respect yourself? Do you accept yourself? Are you able to acknowledge feelings different from those that society or business culture may tell you to have? How do you talk to yourself? If you talk to your friends the way you talk to yourself, are they friends for very long? If you commit to a spiritual practice (as defined earlier in this chapter,

in the section Tapping the Spirit) of transforming one quality, what impact can you alone make in your workplace?

(2) Look at your relationship to your work. How may you redefine that relationship in a way that creates new possibilities for you and your co-workers?

(3) What kind of relationship do you have with the "larger environment"?

(4) Think of three or four important decisions, incidents, or crises you have dealt with lately. This time instead of thinking about tangible components, try to identify the emotions experienced by you and by other parties to the incident. How did those emotions drive the various inputs to the decision? If those emotions had been acknowledged and addressed before the discussion, think of at least two or three components of the discussion that may have changed.

Chapter 5

Learning Is the Heart of It

The illiterate of the future will not be the person who cannot read.
It will be the person who does not know how to learn.

. . . ALVIN TOFFLER

Imagine a bull's-eye target with several arrows tightly clustered approximately four inches low and to the right of the center. Then imagine the frustration of such consistent "missing the mark." Many managers who try to lead organizational change have similar experiences: They get close but somehow they always miss the mark. The frustration mounts as their consistency at missing the mark increases. "Why?" they ask. Finally, many give up and say, "I just don't believe any of it can work. I've tried so many things, and none of them works." What they are really saying is, "I haven't been able to allow them to work because I've been unwilling to own my part."

A spiritual practice ceases to be a practice without the learning that draws us closer and closer to our target. Without learning, spiritual practice is simply a study in failure; without learning, we never draw closer to the target. Over the years, it has been increasingly clear to me that whatever we want—our target—is generally unattainable in a sustained way until we look at why we *don't* want what we think we want and make peace with the "not wanting" part of our goal as well as the "wanting" part. If we are to lead from courage, we must understand the sources of our fears. We must understand what disguises them from us so that we believe we are angry, frustrated, irritated, or confused. We must be conscious and aware of what is driving us. We must also understand our own spirits and the nature of spirit if we are to know how to respect the spirits of others. Getting to this point requires considerable experiential learning and personal development over a period of time. You might call it learning of the heart.

Part Two of the book is devoted to sharing some of the more important lessons that I learned as I discovered how to be increasingly in touch with my own spirit. These lessons will not necessarily be the same for everyone, but it is my hope that, by sharing them, readers will begin to challenge their assumptions about what they have believed. When we are open to looking at new perspectives, our own spirits will present us with just the right lesson for us.

I'm not sure whether my personal or my professional quest came first. For a long time, I thought they were separate. Over time, as I continued to learn and grow, I began to see the paths growing closer and closer until they merged. Finally, as I began to live from my spirit more and more, I came to understand that there are no lines in our lives. We do not have personal lives and business lives. We have one life. But it took me years to discover that.

As the idea of employee involvement began to surface in a popular way in the early '80s, it made incredible sense to me. I began working at sixteen, and in every job I had experienced lines between management and employees which were counterproductive to both. Employees had great ideas they rarely shared with management. When ideas were shared, they were often received in a patronizing way and were never acted on. Occasionally an idea would be adapted or adopted, and a manager often took credit and responsibility for implementation. As I heard and read more about it, the idea of more active employee participation became exciting to me. After many years of work in personnel, human resources, and general management in traditional workplaces, I had the opportunity at the age of forty to go to graduate business school and pursue my interest in participatory work systems.

I had thought for some time that I was getting distracted from this interest, first by an interest in developing creativity in individuals, then by workplace creativity. After that the link between quality and participation, which is now well accepted, distracted me. Then it was leadership and how leaders and managers differed. That distraction evolved into the concept of leadership at all levels, until healthy companies and co-dependent and addictive organizations—seemingly opposite sides of the same issue—emerged as interests. After a while I began to realize that I wasn't going off in six or seven directions: There were common themes across the topics. In fact, there were many similar characteristics in workplaces with high levels of personal and organizational creativity, in quality-focused organizations, in healthy ones, and in those in which leadership was encouraged and respected at all levels.

- People feel connected to the whole organization. A common vision of purpose, greatness, and values is shared by people throughout the organization. People follow the high road; work hard together; collaborate; discourage internal competitiveness because they're all on the same team.
- There is a deeply held understanding that the organization is a system. Change anywhere creates change everywhere.
- Individuals are respected. Employees are valued for their uniqueness, their humor, and for the whole person they bring to the work, which is enriched by a variety of experiences outside the workplace.
- There is openness and flexibility.
- Leadership occurs at all levels. Ideas and risk-taking are encouraged. People who generate ideas are given leadership or high involvement in implementation.
- Mistakes are accepted, even celebrated, and used for learning. The continuous improvement ethic prevails from the factory floor to office to warehouse to the break room and executive suite.
- The organization is seen not as an isolated entity but as part of something much larger: a series of linkages from supplier to manufacturer to distributor to customers and between employees, co-workers, teams, and companies. People have faith and trust in the system.
- People enjoy coming to work.
- There is respect for the spiritual nature of human beings.

My exploration was guided by the very things that I was coming to know were essential to spirit-respecting workplaces, and they were things that I had rarely experienced in the workplace. First, there was a spirit of openness and continuous learning. I happily admitted I didn't have the answer and soon learned that I probably wouldn't find it in one place. The search for and the refinement and reworking of ideas led me. I was committed to learning what the mysterious answer was—truly committed. There was no "trying" to find out. I was quite intentional and would not be dissuaded. When I'd found two or three pieces, I could easily have given up or decided I'd learned enough. But *discipline*, which means to teach or to be a disciple, prevailed; I continued to learn more and more over time. I was practicing a discipline. I was moving closer and closer to the mark. (I still am. That is one reason this book is in its sixth rewrite. I continue to uncover more pieces.)

MIDLIFE OPENS NEW POSSIBILITIES

Some time ago, I was at a meeting during which lengthy discussion was given to whether a crisis, trauma, or other "wake-up call" was a requirement for creating openness to new ideas. A decision was never reached, yet there was a deeply shared sense that a willingness to accept different approaches to thinking was certainly accelerated by a sudden awareness that old ways of operating were no longer working. There were countless anecdotes about businesses who were willing only to look at new ways of working when bankruptcy or a new competitor was at their doorstep. There were even more stories about business owners and executives who became willing to look inside themselves and their way of relating to family, friends, and employees only after they had lost a valued spouse to divorce or a child to drugs.

Although I cannot speak for anyone except myself, I know that in my case a midlife transition propelled by a traumatic divorce, deaths of several significant family members, and a serious injury to myself encouraged me to be more receptive to exploring possibilities than I believe I would ever have been otherwise.

It seems important here to talk just a bit about the well-known terms *midlife crisis* and *midlife transition* and the differences between them. I have come to understand that some change at midlife is a normal part of our growth and development process. Midlife is a time of taking a psychological inventory of what is working in our lives and what is not. It is a time of seeking more meaning in, and purpose to, our lives, a time of beginning to think about leaving a legacy or about whether the world is different because we were here. It is a time when we begin to acknowledge our mortality and to know that if we are going to do things differently in our lives, we had better get started. It is a time of personal housekeeping, sorting out what we want to keep and what we want to eliminate from our lives. The things that get changed may range from losing those twenty extra pounds to getting a new hairdo to leaving a spouse or a career of twenty years.

This transition can be worked through either consciously or unconsciously; the more conscious the process is, the less likely it is to become a midlife crisis. Addressing the midlife transition consciously may include some of the kinds of searching that I am describing in this book. It may involve counseling, support groups, taking classes—particularly classes about career or life exploration—reading self-help books or journals, reading any books that are different from what we normally read, taking a sabbatical, taking a vacation alone, particularly to an isolated location where there is plenty of time for reflection. The conscious searching process allows us to discover what isn't working, to decide how we would like to be, and to go about creating the change we want. We may undergo personal or marriage counseling or engage in frank discussions about what needs to be different to change a job from one that discourages us into one that taps our spirit.

Whatever people finally choose to change, when the process is a conscious one, first, we are able to identify and solve the real problem, and second, we are able to involve others around us in the transition so they can make appropriate changes in their own lives. The dynamic that is playing out to your dissatisfaction in your marriage may be equally unsatisfactory to your spouse. The two of you may decide to create a new relationship that works better for you than the stereotype that you have been living for years.

Whatever the outcome, people who engage the midlife transition actively and use it for growth, development, and improvement often find themselves happier, feeling physically better, and even looking younger than they have in years.

I am not an authority on the subject, but I think that there are at least two means by which this normal midlife transition escalates into a midlife crisis. The most obvious way is exemplified by the culturally stereotypical forty- or fifty-year-old man who has an affair with a woman younger than his daughter, leaves his wife of twenty-five years, buys a red sports car, and elopes to Aruba with the younger woman. This man is usually unhappy with his life, but rather than consciously exploring what is troubling him or what isn't satisfying him, he looks for a quick escape. Thereby he creates such turmoil in his life that years may pass before he begins to be pressured by the same qualities about himself that he failed to deal with when they first haunted him. Unless engaged in a conscious process of change, the person caught up in such a situation is likely to find his or her life (for women are as well as men may behave in this way) reiterating itself again and again.

The second way in which the midlife transition can become a midlife crisis is exemplified by what is known as the "wake-up call," which is actually almost the reverse of the first crisis possibility. The wake-up call is an experience we are faced with in life's school when we receive a lesson that we hadn't planned to learn. A wake-up call may occur when our spouse walks out, our teenager gets into serious trouble, a job is lost or a personal business fails, serious illness strikes, or a close friend or family member dies. Suddenly what we assume to be a predictable world is no longer what we thought it was. People upon whom we had counted aren't there, explicit or implied promises are broken, people close to us begin to engage in "acting-out" behavior. This is the hard way to cope with the midlife transition. Usually hitting us unexpectedly, this way forces us, contrary to our wishes, to make dramatic changes in life "cold turkey." The upside of the wake-up call is that it often propels its victims into counseling or other conscious searching processes and allows them to create a truly happy life. Although I don't know of anyone who has really enjoyed a wake-up call, those who accept it as a gift of learning often reflect upon the period as "the best thing that ever happened to me."

Others, however, choose not to use the wake-up call as a gift. These people are angry and bitter, and they engage in blame-casting at every opportunity. Sadly, instead of renewed vigor and spirit for the second half of life, this group seems to get physically ill or depressed, to become less and less pleasant company, and to adopt an attitude of resignation that tends to persist for the rest of their lives. Their anger and bitterness seem to create a self-fulfilling prophecy of more anger and bitterness. Much of what I was learning in my personal exploration complemented the professional research I was doing. Each presented new ways of looking at life. When I discovered new things about myself, I was also able to understand for perhaps the first time how these same qualities impacted our workplaces.

To Learn, We Must Be Open to the Possibility of Learning

Finding the time to write a book while running a busy consulting practice was a challenge. Not long before the time I had blocked off on my calendar for writing, a time when I would refrain from taking any new clients, a local businessman came to me. His was an organization that had experienced phenomenal growth and success, and unlike so many growth companies I had worked with, this company had continued to enjoy a positive reputation with both employees and customers. Although the company was a little different from most of my clients, I was intrigued; before I knew it, I found myself rearranging my writing schedule and fitting the organization into my work schedule. Later I was chagrined because I thought my actions violated my intention and commitment and belittled the value I placed on writing this book. I thought I had let greed distract me from my purpose and my integrity.

Two hours later, talking on the phone with a consultant friend, I was castigating myself for giving in. This wise friend always seems to have just the right question. She asked, "What do you have to learn from them?" That was an interesting question (a question we might all do well to ask ourselves about perceived diversions). Well, I thought, perhaps the leader embodies the characteristics of my leadership model in a way that other clients did not. I was partially right, but there was something more I had to learn from the company: my first conscious lesson in *wu wei*, or making myself available for what wanted to happen. I had availed myself of the opportunity to examine a spirit-respecting organization from the inside. This surrender was new to my hard-charging, goal-driven life. It felt good but not very comfortable for a while.

More often than not life's school seems to know just the lesson we need at just the right time. When we are open and flexible and make ourselves available for what wants to happen, we accept the lesson we have to learn. Countless times in my own life and in the lives of those around me, "chance" provides personal and professional lessons that make what we had planned much more meaningful. Other times, we gain a new skill that makes us more effective at our original task. Still other times, we meet a new acquaintance who makes us aware of additional resources that make the project easier, more successful, or both. Despite my discomfort with surrendering early on, I have actually come to embrace the opportunity to be in the unknown. Those bent on forcing things to happen exactly how and when they plan them miss these opportunities.

THE GLUE

The glue that I had been looking for in the successful organizations was a spirit that manifests itself as a positive belief in people, and a belief that the organization can handle whatever comes its way. There is a consciousness, intentionality, and commitment to living from that belief system. The organizations that didn't have that spiritual quality about them were only giving their people a longer leash but a leash nonetheless. The leash is a negative, nonspiritual belief system. Virtually all the ingredients that allow creativity, quality, participation, leadership, and health to flourish in an organization are qualities of the spiritual nature of human beings which I'd been seeking to learn more about. It became clear to me that if we are going to unleash the Spirit Cycle in organizations, the negative, nonspiritual belief system has to go.

My new client organization had a spiritual quality, which was a source of enthusiasm, of esprit de corps. I looked up my evolving definition of spirit, and there it was: love, peace, kindness. There was caring on a level I had not encountered in an organization, real connection. There was respect for each other and for the work of each and every person. There were trust, faith, abundance, openness that continues to astonish me. There was acceptance of people as they are, with their foibles. There was joy, creativity, a high level of acknowledged intuition, aspiration for individuals and the company, and flexibility. The acceptance of mistakes was at a level that I'd only heard about. There was personal accountability. There was complete belief in the people both inside and outside of the company. My friend had been right. They did have something to teach me.

When I looked, it became more apparent to me that the organizational "glue" I had been seeking wasn't really glue in the traditional sense at all. That kind of glue locks things into a rigid, inflexible form that is unable to respond to changes in the operational environment. Spirit glue is more like a complex series of interconnections throughout the organization which hold it together and allow it to respond to new challenges in a unified way, yet able to flex and change to meet new conditions. Thus open sharing of information is practiced, and everyone cares that everyone succeeds. Incredibly creative and ever-changing configurations allow the flexibility to meet each challenge in an optimal way. Shared joy at how good we feel about what we do together and confidence that we will prevail if we live our vision and values are part of the connectedness. This glue holds the organization together and allows the freedom to flex and change to meet conditions on the daily basis that today's changing environment requires.

By this point, my paths of discovery were coming together. Once I had figured out the organization piece, the personal piece fell into place almost instantly. The underlying glue I had been seeking in my personal life was an anchoring to my spiritual core. This core had periodically emerged—I would get headaches and stomach aches when I found myself working in a way or on a project that didn't respect my own spirit. Whenever I experienced stress, it was almost always when I'd been working on a project that didn't respect either my own spirit or the spirits of others.

The purpose of this description of my personal journey to spirituality is to underline that spirituality isn't a box that we suddenly open one day. Discovering spirit is a journey, not a destination, and it is a journey each person has to make, believe, and live before asking others to do it. Any number of people in an organization may seek spirituality simultaneously with each other's support. This work is to be encouraged, yet it is the work of individuals working together because they choose to do it. The CEO cannot simply say one day, "We are going to respect the spiritual nature of our employees and customers!" and expect everything to change. When the CEO *becomes* his or her spirit, then it can happen—and not until then.

We cannot ask others to do their spiritual work until we have done our own. It is only when we have done our own work that we discover the patience to know that this growth doesn't happen overnight whenever we develop a "just do it!" attitude. It doesn't happen to everyone the same way; what is easy for one may be extremely difficult for another. Sometimes we have to keep encountering "life's lessons" on a particular issue, over and over, until one day with the gentleness of a feather drifting to the ground, we suddenly find ourselves shaking our heads and saying, "Now I get it!" Other issues may require a more direct approach. The intense lessons of the wake-up call usually shorten the learning curve for those who are so blessed.

Spiritual voyages are about learning and continuously moving closer to the mark. Learning is largely a process of doing something, finding out what works, analyzing mistakes and learning from them, and trying again. Learning absolutely requires us to be willing to make and accept what we may perceive to be mistakes or failure and to experience every attempt as one step on the road toward what I am seeking. When we can begin to see an outcome as just one part of an unfolding of events which produces a gift of learning that we need for the step, every outcome becomes a success. What we learn may not be what I choose to learn, but if I choose it, it is a gift nonetheless. When I am able to accept what Susan Jeffers calls "no-lose decision making,"[1] I am ready to accept the outcome and go in the direction the process takes me. There are no failures, only feedback. For learning to occur, I become part of the process. I cannot control the process; I surrender to it and follow where it may lead.

For me to stay in this place of continuously surrendering to what is unfolding has been one of my biggest shifts from my goal-driven, make-it-happen mode. I have a quotation from an article written by a colleague of mine, reprinted and strategically placed around my office and home as a constant reminder to accept that what happens is what is supposed to happen, and, whatever it is, it happens exactly when it is supposed to.

"Spirit works in strange ways; it is largely unimpressed with my controlling efforts to schedule or influence it."[2]

The learning that occurs when I let go of my attachment to how things should be, how things are going to be, when things should happen,

---

1. Susan Jeffers, *Feel the Fear and Do It Anyway* (New York: Fawcett-Columbine, 1987).

2. Michael Scott Rankin, "Spiritual Entrepreneuring," in *The New Bottom Line: Bringing Heart and Soul to Business*, eds. John Renesch and Bill DeFoore (San Francisco, CA: New Leaders Press, 1996).

or where we are going to be when this is all over is learning to let go of my attachment to what my limited brain can conceive and to open to new and greater possibilities. The learning requires that I let go of judgment that this event, outcome, or person is good or bad. Events, outcomes, or people are not good or bad: they just are. When we learn to accept each event, outcome, or person as exactly what is supposed to be in this moment for us to get to where we want to be, we are able to be in a place of continuous learning of the heart—to be in our spiritual practice as a way of living and being.

At many points along my journey, if I had been determined to rationally control the process, I would have been taken on a lengthy detour. It was essential that I make myself available to the learning that presented itself when I was ready for just that lesson. For instance, if I had insisted upon writing this book on the original schedule, I would not have worked in the spirited organization that allowed me to connect leadership and spirit. I would have written another "how to do it" book, and I might never have made the connections that I have come to believe are essential to identify the magic so integral to dynamic organizations. When we make ourselves available for what wants to happen, we respond to our intuitive senses and open ourselves to creativity and new learning that might otherwise have been missed. We cannot fail. We can only learn from these experiences, and it is learning of the heart.

Until we have gone through this growth process ourselves, we never have the understanding that is so essential to lead an organization full of unique spirits, each on their own journeys. This voyage is also shared because of the many interconnections and weaving of different elements of my personal journey with my professional one. In our culture, it is most common for people to treat different parts of their lives as discrete: work life, personal life, relationships, and so on. As we come to understand our own spiritual natures and those of people around us, we come to know that our lives are not neatly packaged into separate boxes. We have a life—one life. Our work is part of it. Our personal needs and relationships are part of it. There must be congruity across all parts, or the incongruities slowly destroy us.

Finally, my experience is shared because it was very different from a typical formal, cognitive learning experience. Much of the learning we do formally is comprised of theory and examples, learning pieces and parts, putting them together, either step-by-step or by cause-and-effect. It is a linear, left-brain, rational process. Once our left brain has learned whatever is being learned, then the learning can be given over to the right brain, as a whole, where it becomes part of our "autopilot" system. (Have you ever headed home from work with the idea of stopping for bread at the store and suddenly found yourself in the driveway at home? The right brain takes over the process of getting us home each day on "autopilot.")

There is much that we have learned over the course of our lives that has become so integrated into our thinking that it is virtually impossible to pull the pieces and parts out and explain them. Someone with an advanced degree in engineering may have trouble trying to explain to a third grader why a paper airplane won't fly. It is my belief that most spiritual learning is a right-brain process, a learning process that comes from looking at the whole picture and trying to integrate pieces into a whole as a whole. This learning might be described as playing with pieces of a puzzle until our subconscious mind can put together the right picture. When we make ourselves available to nonlinear learning processes we access parts of our brains that are usually missed. It takes courage, faith, and trust, and the self-confidence of a leader. It takes knowing that there are no failures; there is only learning.

This journey has spotlighted for me the importance of patience in the continuous improvement process. Peter Senge has described creative tension as being the gap between what we desire (the vision) and what currently exists (current reality). He says the tension can be resolved in two ways: "By raising current reality toward the vision, or by lowering the vision toward current reality."[3]

When I know what I want (the vision—in my case peace of mind, and understanding of what sparks companies), when I am willing to persevere and continue raising my current reality toward the vision, I come closer and closer to my vision. When I lower my vision toward current reality, I never reach the original vision. That is what would have happened had I chosen not to follow the process 100 percent, had I taken one of the easier detours, or had I "got stuck in my head" and demanded a quantifiable solution. I could have lowered my vision by stopping somewhere short of what I perceived as full spiritual connectedness. There were several points along the way where that would have been possible (and far less tortuous). I may have got *an* answer but not the one that would ultimately give me the level of understanding and peace of mind that I sought.

All that said, I would be misleading to imply that any of us ever "gets there." Like a mirage luring us farther and farther along, full and sustained peace, joy, and love are elusive. Just when we think we're almost there, life presents one more lesson. At one time, I believed in an

---

3. Peter Senge, "The Leader's New Work: Building Learning Organizations," in *New Traditions in Business: Spirit and Leadership in the 21st Century*, ed. John Renesch (San Francisco, CA: Berrett-Kohler, 1992), p. 81.

end point of constant bliss and acceptance. As my journey progresses, I have come to believe that *there* is an attitude or state of mind that whatever occurs is deeply beneficial. With my deeper connection to spirit has come an "attitude of gratitude" about the events of life and how we experience them. Events that at one time may have generated anger, guilt, embarrassment, or shame as I judged them *wrong* or *bad* are now just accepted as part of life. A set of questions almost instantly pop into my mind. What do you suppose I have to learn from this? What is the lesson? What is the gift? The discipline of learning becomes automatic. As I get closer to that final state of mind, I find myself observing my behavior almost as if watching myself on stage. A friend was in the process of making a major decision in a way that I found myself reacting to quite negatively—to the point of irrationality. I felt as if I were watching myself shouting, crying, and raging. As I watched for a while, I became angry at myself: I thought I'd left that kind of behavior behind. Finally the wisdom began to unfold.

I had lessons to learn. First, I discovered I had become pretty self-righteous about my growth, and it was humbling to see how much work I still had to do. Second, I needed to learn on a new level that decisions aren't good or bad; they just are. It is what we do with what happens after we make our choice that is important. Third, everyone has choice, and no matter how well meaning, we cannot enact others' lives for them—a lesson that is a continuing challenge for many parents! I learned many other lessons, not the least of which was the importance of having the courage of my own convictions, and staying the course.

The Learning Process Never Ends

A business friend of mine once said, "Any discussion of spirituality needs to consider *learning* as integral to being on a spiritual journey." Spiritual growth is not a task with defined parameters and a decisive ending. The learning and the process continue; the journey is without an end. The true destination is the process of the journey itself, the process or practice of drawing closer and closer to the mark, learning to be ever more conscious of how we *be* in our relationships to ourselves, others, and the experiences of life. Just because I am writing a book about my learning certainly does not mean my journey has ended. Like everyone else, I am still learning. I continue to seek even more understanding, to learn each day about myself and the companies in which I work. Life continues to present all of us with lessons that require us to seek ever deeper levels of understanding—about our spirits, our manufacturing processes, or how we relate to our customers.

I have come to understand the need to be comfortable with chaos and confusion. What I've learned about confusion is this: It is only when I believe that I have the answer that I am truly confused. This world is complex, and businesses are complex systems. The need to have *the* answer may cause us to simplify complex situations to an extent that actual conditions are no longer accurately reflected in our reality. Our need to simplify comes from our fear of not being able to handle the complexities of a situation as they arise. When we can trust ourselves to respond to the situation's needs moment by moment by moment, we can be comfortable not knowing *the* answer. At that point we muster the courage to look at the whole complex situation, accept the confusion, and begin learning.

When we lead on the Path of Courage, complex situations, confusion and apparent chaos do not deter us from our learning. From our spirits, we know there is deep order in what is occurring. If we have the openness, the patience, and the courage to ask questions and generate more and more information, we put ourselves and our companies in the position to begin to see order in the chaos. We begin to see how events and conditions relate to other events and conditions. As we get more and more clarity about what is, then leadership on the Path of Courage enables us to deepen and broaden the understanding. Rather than racing to a quick decision, we ask even more questions and generate still more information. When asked about what outcomes we want to create, we react not in a survival mode that suggests an attitude of "How do we pull this one out?" or "How do we keep X from happening?" but in a mode of leading from our spirits. We have faith we can create desired outcomes that are consistent with our purpose, vision, and values.

The journey is life, and life is about learning. When I believed I had the framework in place, I learned that the concept of a framework is an illusion, too structured for the amorphous nature of either the workplace or personal spirituality. If I have anything, I have what I believe to be some basic truths about spirit in our companies. New learning adds color and dimension to my understanding but does not change the basic truths. The journey is continuous fine tuning of the picture I have of those truths.

STEPS IN A PROCESS

Spirituality is an "inside job." We each begin by discovering and living our own spirituality. Discovering our spirits is work which we do in ourselves by ourselves. Others may support and encourage us, yet each person's journey is unique and personal. We can support others in their personal journeys, but we must respect the uniqueness of each journey.

Each person must find a personal path. There are no road maps, only an endless network of paths that lead us to a higher level of consciousness or a way of being that is mindful of how everything we do is part of a much larger whole. The path that has called me is of integrating spirit and work. Others may find health and nutrition to be their path, and their practice may be to be conscious of everything they put in their body and to be committed to an intentional way of eating. Others may find their being in exploration of nature or the environment, and their practice may be to have a heightened awareness of how each act is either a contribution to the health and sustainability of the environment or a destruction of it. Acceptance and respect of another's chosen path that differs from ours is part of our own spiritual development.

I have read and observed a lot, and I believe that much of my learning is similar to that of others who lead and live from their spirits, whatever path they have chosen. What I share is what worked for me. It may work for you; it may not. Something else may work better for you. Although it is my belief that no one can tell you how to go about becoming whole with your own spirit, there seems to be some commonality among paths many have taken. A client of mine who read the fourth rewrite of this manuscript was incredulous after reading a few chapters. He said, "If I had not seen the copyright date on this, I would have sworn most of it was written about me and my company." Most of the book had been written long before I started working with him, but the commonalities between journeys are significant.

Either consciously or subconsciously, the journey usually begins when we come to the realization that our personal or organizational lives are not what we know they have the potential to be. We see other people and companies doing things we wish we were doing, but we don't seem able to do these things. Aspects of life that used to be easy become a struggle. Aims that we worked toward seem empty when we finally get them. Things that were simple begin to be more complicated. Work isn't joyful or fun, and we always seem to be playing catch-up. Increasingly, we may experience depression, physical pain, illness, or loss of energy. We lack a sense of purpose or direction. On some level, we know this isn't how we want to live, and we ask, "Is that all there is?"

We begin to play around with replacing statements with more and more questions. Instead of saying, "That's the way we do it," we begin to ask, "What if we did it a different way?" "What if" questions begin to liberate us. Eventually, the questions begin evolving to, "What is the worst that could happen if we did it a different way?" Later, the question changes more: "Could it be any worse than what we are currently experiencing?" This is the stage my friend Kris King calls, "Making the unacceptable acceptable!"[4] Finally, once we accept that the status quo no longer works and new ways of being appear to be acceptable, the final step in the process is taking the step. The journey begins with a single step, and it is a step each of us must take alone.

The learning process may be faster for some than for others. It was my experience that making the decision and mustering courage to take the step, although related, were separate stages in mental process and in time. Taking the plunge is not unlike deciding to jump into a cool swimming pool on a hundred-degree day. We tell ourselves it will feel good once we make the jump. We may even dip a toe in the water to confirm that the water feels cool and pleasant. We see others enjoying the refreshing coolness. Yet we know that the difference between the temperature of the air and that of the water is going to be shocking when we hit the water. We also know the only way to enjoy the cool, refreshing pool is to accept the shock. Finally we jump. The shock hits us, and then what exhilaration and refreshment we experience. Why did it take us so long? Some of us spend only a fleeting moment deciding the water is where we want to be. Others take much longer—and need lots of coaxing. Some may even decide they prefer to swelter in the heat and never jump.

LEARNING OF THE HEART

This learning is learning of the heart, not of the head. Reading about it does not bring it to the heart. We often spend years helping our heads to discover what our hearts must have known long ago. Our unconscious has the knowledge, but it is usually inconvenient to acknowledge that fact. This knowledge doesn't "fit" with popular personal or management trends or with most of our personal or business lives. So we stuff it into the anteroom of our hearts for a more convenient time, then discover there are no convenient times. There are just times.

The longer we resist accepting that our hearts and spirits hold wisdom that our brains can't comprehend, the more out of sync our lives become. As a friend reminds me, "The longest journey in the world is the eighteen inches from the head to the heart." Without my spirit, I had no passion, no spark. I was driven and didn't know what was driving me or what I was being driven toward. I just seemed driven to go faster and

---

4. Kris King, Transforming Fear (workshop led by K. King at Wings Enterprises, Inc., Eugene, OR, April 1993).

faster, to try harder and harder. In *We*, Robert A. Johnson describes what I now see was my constant state of being before I discovered my spirit:

"When one side of human nature grows out of balance with the other, it becomes a tyranny in the soul. . . . The greatest force in the psychic universe is the demand for completion, for wholeness, for balance."[5]

"The demand for completion, for wholeness, for balance," gnawed at me from the inside. At first it gently nudged me; later it forcefully poked at me. My need for completion persisted and did whatever it would take to get my attention. Even after the need had my attention, I tried for a long time to attend to it as a brain job, tried to learn from books and other people. But satisfying demands of the spirit isn't a brain job that can be learned from others. It's a heart job and a soul job.

After I finished writing this book and was far into the editing, I was researching what I thought was a different personal question. I picked up a book I had read long ago and as I skimmed through it, I was surprised to note several themes similar to those about which I had just finished writing. Reading the book earlier had not brought understanding to me. Understanding was accomplished only after significant inside work. In fact, similar themes could probably be found in many other books that I've read over the years. But the ideas just didn't "take" until I was ready, until I let my heart do the work and bypassed consulting my brain.

Seminars, counseling, and books may help. An organizational change project that focuses on developing organizational learning may help. A personal tragedy or wake-up call may jump-start the process, but we have to do the work ourselves. We must be willing to jump in. Sticking your toe in the water won't give the same results. The real work and the real understanding do not begin until people jump into the water.

As you read Part Two of this book, I hope you discover some tools for spiritual leadership; but the tools are different from those to which you may be accustomed. These tools help you *do* things. These new tools are tools of *being*. I hope that my learning will help you discover the courage to begin your own journey on the Path of Courage. Perhaps the readings in my references will provide additional insights to you as they have to me. This book is not a prescription for the journey is one of self-discovery. No other person can tell you where your journey takes you; otherwise the journey isn't yours and doesn't respect your spirit. The journey to our spirits is an inside job. Each of us must do it alone.

---

5. Robert A. Johnson, *We* (San Francisco, CA: HarperCollins, 1983).

EXPLORING THE PATH OF COURAGE

(1) Think of a time that you fought to force an outcome but failed to produce what you had hoped to achieve, a time that you didn't make
yourself available for what wanted to happen. Try to recall as many
significant decision points as possible, and write them down.
Perform an exercise in "what iffing." At each of the decision points,
list as many alternative courses as you can think of. Pay particular
attention to alternatives you resisted. Ask yourself "What if I had
made myself available for that alternative?" Have fun with this. Be
as imaginative as possible, because some of the "off the wall" alternatives often suggest approaches that challenge our assumptions
about what is possible.

(2) If you experience resistance to the nonlinear, nonrational approach
to self-development, explore the reasons why you are unwilling to
make yourself available for what wants to happen. Ask yourself,
"What does that mean to me?" Ask yourself, "What if the opposite
were true?" and "What are other possibilities?" What are you able to
discover about the source of your resistance? Try to remember a time
when you tried to force something that really didn't want to happen? What was the outcome? What really wanted to happen? How
may your life, your work, and your relationships have been different
if you had surrendered to *wu wei*?

(3) There are two normal midlife transitions. If you are nearing or past
midlife, reflect on your own transition. Was yours a conscious one?
Did you get the "blessing" of a wake-up call? Did you get the call
and still not wake up? Are there still areas of your life that require
conscious searching to create for yourself the life you want?

Part 2

Exploring the Path to Leading from the Heart

Chapter 6

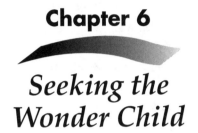

Seeking the
Wonder Child

For most of us, our search for spiritual knowing is rewarded over the years in bits at a time. Yet spiritual knowing is with each of us all the time, but until we have done some organized self-discovery, most of us don't know we have it. The things that touch our hearts have always touched our hearts, but we may not have been aware that we were being touched. This experience is a little like turning the radio to 89.9 for a message you need to hear which is on 94.5. We get a message, but the message isn't really connected to the heart until we tune the dial a bit.

An important part of discovering spiritual knowing is learning to be aware of ourselves. Most of us have been socialized to ignore or stifle the gifts our bodies send us to help us be aware of our spiritual knowing—the tear in the eye, the lump in the throat, irritability, or nervous energy. It may be a big step to become conscious of the fact that we are having a spiritual reaction and to accept that reaction as a gift that says, "There's something here you should examine more closely." When we learn to recognize that our spirit is trying to communicate with us, we have come a long way toward achieving spiritual knowing.

When we were infants, our spiritual natures were unlocked. A newborn knows nothing but faith and trust, freedom in expressing emotion, safety in forming attachments, and openness to new ideas and experiences. Carl Jung first wrote about the spiritual infant I am talking about. He used the phrase *Wonder Child*. John Bradshaw writes and speaks at length about the Wonder Child.[1] He has even made *WON-DERFUL* an acronym for the spiritual qualities each of us possesses early in life.

W — I am full of a natural sense of *Wonder,* exploration, and risk taking.

O — I am *Optimistic.* I have childlike faith, openness, and trust.

N — *Naïveté;* I create new and empowering experiences for myself.

D — Healthy *Dependence* allows me to form attachments and make commitments.

E — I laugh and cry and am comfortable expressing my true *Emotions.*

R — I have natural *Resilience* and flexibility.

F — I enjoy *Free* play, Freedom and spontaneity—transcending habit.

U — I have a *Unified* wholeness that makes me special, Unique, and wonderful.

L — I *Love* and am *Loved* for who I *am* not what I *do.*

Bradshaw's description of the Wonder Child helps me understand clearly and succinctly the spiritual being in each of us. At the same time, it helps me understand why it is so hard to rediscover the qualities each of us brought with us when we came into this life. Parents carry the incredible responsibilities of nurturing and protecting a newborn so that the child reaches adulthood in reasonable physical, mental, emotional, and spiritual health, and of providing enough socialization to function in day-to-day life. Parenthood is an awesome undertaking. Some parents are loving and do their very best, and some parents have dysfunctional parenting skills. All parents are challenged to balance the child's need for physical protection and socialization with the child's need to retain the Wonder Child's characteristics. Until the last two decades, precious little was available to guide parents. What has become available is often conjecture; even now parenting is largely instinctual. Most often instinct has led, frequently and appropriately, to protecting the child's physical being first.

If a two-year-old walks toward a bonfire, the parent's natural instinct is to keep her or him from walking into the fire and getting

---

1. John Bradshaw, *Homecoming: Reclaiming and Championing Your Inner Child* (New York: Bantam Books, 1990), pp. 30–31.

burned. The parent feels terror, and the child becomes frightened. As the parent sweeps the child out of harm's way, the act may dampen the toddler's natural sense of wonder, exploration, and risk taking for decades, if not for life, a result that is of course the farthest thing from the parent's mind. The child may wear scars for life, not physical scars from the fire which was avoided, but scars to the sense of wonder, exploration, and risk taking.

Parents grapple with balancing the fostering of a three-year-old's faith, openness, and trust and the need to communicate that some strangers may injure the child. Children are told for their own protection not to speak to strangers. They probably do avoid injury from strangers but may lose their Wonder Child characteristics and develop a view of the world as a dangerous place.

When part of a four-year-old's special uniqueness is the tendency to urinate whenever and wherever he or she feels the need, the parents must teach the child that this part of uniqueness is not all right. They do it not because they want to squelch the uniqueness but because they know that when the child goes to school using the restroom will be expected.

How does a parent provide a child with the skills needed to survive to adulthood without destroying his/her wonderful spiritual characteristics? The answer is that try as they may, most parents don't. By the age of five, most children have developed their picture of reality that will take them to adulthood. Most of us carry that picture with us much longer. Depending on the overall quality of our parenting, we may carry the childhood view of reality into midlife and beyond.

Our socialization process involves many other people who continue to chip away at our Wonder Child. Schools teach us there is one right answer to everything and establish norms for acceptable behavior which are far less useful when we carry them into other arenas and areas of our lives. Our peers, especially in our teen years, teach us that there are some things which are natural to us that may be unacceptable to their group.

When we study business in a traditional institution of higher education, we are more than likely taught that there is a right way to do things and a right way to be. Some chipping away happens because of gender. Males are socialized not to show emotion, and females are often socialized not to be assertive about what they believe. The corporate culture(s) in which we work may carve away other pieces. A job that otherwise would have been quite satisfying for me created a lot of stress in my life because the culture didn't respect a person's need for balance, time with family and friends, and time for rest and renewal. Every socialization process can move us farther from who we truly are and limit our sense of creative possibilities.

LETTING GO OF OLD REALITIES

Ken Moses, a psychotherapist and lecturer, compares a five-year-old's reality to being in the middle of a large, empty eggshell where we can't know anything about what's outside. One day a crack appears; try as we may to repair or ignore it, the crack continues to widen and eventually sucks us out. We then discover a whole new reality with new options and possibilities . . . in another, bigger eggshell. One day it too will crack.[2]

The process of leaving each broken eggshell carries with it the incredible fear of the unknown. We feel safe in our protected environment where we know how things are, and we know the rules. We know how things work. We may feel cramped, uneasy, unhappy, even extremely limited. A child who is pulled back from a fire at the age of two may never explore anything interesting. Even as an adult, he or she may do only safe activities, such as talking guardedly. A child told not to speak to strangers may distrust people in general and not be open to relationships. Children who are told it is unacceptable to be unique at the age of four may never use their creative talents and may never do what they truly want until they are absolutely certain that such acts are acceptable to other people—and maybe not even then.

The socialization we have during adulthood can create another confining eggshell. In a company that focuses on this quarter's results, we may never run our project or department as well as we know we can. We may fail to invest in training because it increases our expenses. We may fail to empower our employees by increasing their involvement because we are unwilling to exchange lower short-term productivity during the training period for substantial gains later. We may fail to develop a new idea or product because it takes two to three years to see a return. We may fail to take the time to build business relationships that may pay off in the future because that time will take away from closing a smaller sale today.

We may not ever achieve our potential as leaders or individuals, but we know what the rules are in the limited reality of our eggshell. We know our place. We know our limitations and have learned to live within them. We don't know the rules outside the eggshell. We don't know that outside the eggshell there is a way to build relationships for the future and close today's sale without working excessive hours. We don't know where and how we fit in the workplace or the world outside our eggshell. It may be better . . . and it may be worse. Rather than using our natural naïveté,

---

2. Kenneth Moses, "Shattered Dreams and Growth: A Workshop on Helping and Being Helped," (presented by Resource Networks, Inc., Evanston, IL), at Portland, OR, April 1993.

creativity, and sense of wonder to explore a more expansive reality and create empowering new experiences for ourselves, we choose to stay in the limiting reality we know.

Discovering our spiritual self requires that we step outside the eggshell. Not only must we step out of the eggshell, but the nature of eggshells is that we can't explore the new one until we leave the old one. We may get a glance from a distance now and then, but we can't really explore the new reality until we let go of the old. Once we let go and explore the new reality, we can never, ever return to the old one. Most of us actively resist letting go of our eggshells for as long as possible because it takes incredible courage to let go of our old reality without having any idea about the new one.

The word *courage*, remember, derives from the Latin word for "heart." When we have the true heart courage to let go of the eggshell, we begin to gain access to heart and soul. For those of us who have long denied our feelings and our spirit, accepting that our heart and soul are important parts of ourselves is frightening, maybe even embarrassing, especially when we have been vocal about denying those parts of ourselves or when we are in a family or organizational culture that denies those parts.

As long as we deny our feelings and spirit, we can pretend we aren't afraid. We don't have to act upon the positive spiritual belief system. Once we discover a new way, we are at a point of no return. Once we know our spirits, and are congruent with them, we can no longer deny that they exist. Once we know we have a spirit, whenever we don't live in a way that is congruent with that spirit, we are out of personal integrity, and both our bodies and our minds have a way of haunting us with stress and pain until we become realigned with our spirits.

Facing the challenge of escaping from our negative realities takes something pretty dramatic like a wake-up call. Even at that, accepting a new reality takes lots of time. The first step in learning and growing is recognizing an unacceptable old reality (paralleling feeling uncomfortable in hundred-degree heat when a cool swimming pool is at hand). We become tired of expecting the worst of people, of the constant stress and fatigue from continually fighting to keep our spirits (and theirs) down. We find ourselves saying and doing things we don't want to say or do. We are tired of looking at other people doing things we want to do and wishing we were doing them. Even when our personal and professional lives are going well, we may sense an incredible longing or have a sense that something is missing. We keep acquiring more and more things, but still feel empty. Something has to change.

The next step, remember, is psychologically preparing to accept the worst our new reality can present (parallel to sticking our toes in the swimming pool). We examine the worst possible outcome and make it acceptable. People may take advantage of us; they may be taking advantage of us now. What is the worst that can happen? I may attempt to write my first book and fail. I will have learned one way not to write a book. People may think it is foolish for me to be singing a karaoke solo when I obviously cannot sing. I think it is foolish to miss all the fun. Besides, why does making a fool of myself matter? If people don't respect my singing, they may respect my courage. If I just sit here waiting to have fun, there is surely not much to respect. When I explore the positive possibilities of the worst-case scenario, change doesn't seem so bad after all.

Last comes the hardest part (jumping in the swimming pool). We come to know that each of us is empowered to make the difference. Despite the challenge and the fear, we *choose* to grow. No one else can make us choose; we must take the step alone. Even if it is a baby step, we must do it alone. Each of us personally chooses how to see the world, how to experience events. Each of us chooses the meaning an event has in our lives. By choosing in accordance with our spirits, even outcomes we may once have considered the "worst," take on new and positive meaning.

MUSTERING COURAGE AND DISCOVERING FAITH

There was a time when I cringed at the prospect of any living being saying or thinking anything that was less than 100 percent positive about me. I lived my life according to what I thought were the rules. Following the rules was how I made sure people thought about me in a positive way. When I didn't know what the rules were, I didn't try. I didn't want to get something wrong and have people think ill of me! Our spirits do not judge ourselves or others. Such judgments are chains with which we bind ourselves. Our spirits are free and comfortable, flexible and resilient, about taking risks. When we live from spirit and don't get the outcome we thought we wanted, we accept and explore the outcome we got and look for meaning in that. The unplanned outcome can become an unexpected gift when we make ourselves available to that possibility. For spirit, an outcome isn't right or wrong, good or bad. It is just an outcome presented to us for learning. The undesired outcome can provide a much richer path of growth than the one we planned.

Leaving my judgmental, controlled, and controlling self and living in accordance with my spirit was a complete turnaround. Although I didn't know what it was going to be like, faith helped me to discover my spirit. I believe that it is essential to our spirits to develop comfort with paradox and ambiguity, and one of the most perplexing and frightening paradoxes most of us face and eventually accept presents itself early in our search for our spirits. We can't really discover our spirits until we find the faith to believe that each of us has a spirit that is a vital aspect of who we are, yet faith is an important part of spirit that we need to discover! We can't discover our spirits until we have faith, and we can't have faith until we discover our spirits. To the linear thinker, this observation creates a chicken-and-egg phenomenon from which all but the most courageous retreat.

Spirituality isn't linear. To develop comfort with any of spirituality's paradoxes, including the faith-spirit paradox, we must let go of our linear thinking. We must accept that our linear brains don't and can't know how it will work. At the time I was working on the spirit-faith paradox, my niece gave me a card that I keep on my desk as a constant reminder. It says:

> "Faith is knowing that if you must step off a cliff, either a step will appear or you will be taught how to fly."[3]

We need to remember that we are well programmed with a lifetime of instruction, socialization, and linear, analytical, quantitative thinking. One of the biggest challenges we face in learning to lead from our spirits is to become aware when our automatic responses activate. Once we begin to identify the situations that pull us out of our spirits, or begin to recognize our own symptoms, we can begin to know what we need to do to "keep the faith."

Faith is essential to spirit—faith in ourselves and faith in others. Faith is knowing that we can't know what will be put before us to learn, but knowing that when we "step off a cliff, either a step will appear or [we] will be taught to fly." The prospect of taking the step alone was incredibly frightening to me as it is to most people I have known. Yet taking the step to discover and be in accordance with our own spirits is a step that must be taken alone. Others may point the way, but each of us must take the step ourselves.

As frightening as it was to me to take the step alone, that fear paled in comparison to the even stronger fear I had about the judgment my friends, family, and business associates might have had about my newly discovered spirituality. (Before I connected with my spirit, I was very concerned about what others might think. That was part of my automatic response.) Did I have the courage to face the criticism I expected? Still more challenging was trying to figure out how I would work. Much of the work I have

---

3. Steve Blenk and Susan Blenk, *Blenk Cards* (Sequim, WA, 1992).

done was based on a negative belief system about people in workplaces. My business was just getting to the point where it would provide me with a comfortable living. Of course I hated about 80 percent of what I was doing, which was based on what I'd been taught rather than what I knew in my soul. Still I'd spent a lot of time, energy, and money building the business. What would other business leaders think? What would those in my Rotary Club think? Did I have the heart courage to risk throwing it all away? Yet even as I asked myself these questions, I knew that to do anything else was quickly becoming unacceptable. The very act of asking the questions is one of the ways we develop the courage to make the leap.

When I began acting in accordance with spirit, I began turning away clients and projects that didn't feel right to me. What occurred was surprising and very affirming. Each time I turned a project away, one I did want would replace it. The days flew by when I was working on projects with which I was spiritually aligned. The days that I worked on negatively-based projects seemed endless. Things I'd been willing to do just weeks before began becoming unacceptable.

I wanted to bring people together. I wanted to help leaders accept their own spirits and those of their employees. I wanted to help both people and organizations embrace learning as a way of life instead of as the latest episode in Management-of-the-Month. I wanted people to experience joy and satisfaction in their work. I wanted to help people and organizations achieve their potential. That was my purpose—what brought meaning to my life, set me on fire, and energized me.

The chronic pain from the injury I mentioned earlier began to trouble me whenever my thoughts and actions were not 100 percent congruent with spirit. What an incredible gift! Whenever the pain started, I knew it was time to go inside and check on what wasn't quite right. As soon as I made the adjustment in what I was doing, thinking, or writing, the pain subsided. My pain became like the lines on the sides of the highway: It kept me on track.

Change occurred quietly, mostly in my little office. When I was out in "the world," I found myself behaving in the old way. This old behavior was habit or maybe unspoken fear, not a conscious decision. I told myself and others that I was concerned about the impact my changes might have on my husband and his work. I now know I was actually more afraid for myself.

What I didn't and couldn't understand then is that when we choose to live from spirit, spirit becomes our ultimate authority. We must forever and always let go of our concern for what other people will think. We cannot live our lives in any way that doesn't nurture our souls. We cannot live in any way that is not in congruence with our own deeply held values, our integrity, and our being. As long as we choose to let the opinions, words, and judgments of other mortals distract us from our spiritual path, we are still on the Path of Fear. On the Path of Fear, we are always driven by real or imagined fear of what others will say or think and the fear of pain at our perception of their judgments. On the Path of Fear, we always sacrifice the peace and joy of our current experience while we strive for the future. But when I was still on the Path of Fear, I couldn't yet know that in my new reality on the Path of Courage what others happened to think would become irrelevant.

MOVING FORWARD

I had reached a point of no return. I had glimpsed what it was like to live from spirit in short, quiet times. I made my leap of faith when I made a conscious decision to transcend habit and to operate from Spirit all the time. I chose to sever some personal relationships that didn't support my spirit. Discontinuing a friendship with a fun-loving acquaintance whose values differed dramatically from my own was painful, but even while I was with that pain an incredible sense of peace came to me. I chose to sever a client relationship with an organization I'd often enjoyed but whose leadership I found to be firmly entrenched in negative beliefs about their people.

Why is it so hard to change? Why does it take so long? First, I had to accept that the belief system I'd lived with for over forty years was based on illusions:

- The illusion of finite rules
- The illusion that the world is a simple place
- The illusion that we can segment our lives and be positive human beings while working in a negative belief system
- The illusion that I can run my business and my life in a linear, analytical way and consider only the definable and quantifiable things I'd been taught to consider
- The illusion that all I needed to know about running a business I had learned in the graduate school of management or from workplace mentors and experience
- The illusion that if I can't touch it, see it, hear it, or measure it, it doesn't exist.

Accepting that my whole life had been based on mistaken illusions was not easy. My very survival had been assured by these illusions, and on some level I didn't know how I would survive without them. Not only did I have to accept that I had lived my life based on mistaken illusions, but I had to accept that the illusions and the rules that went with them had been robbing my life of joy, peace, love, creativity, energy, and humor. They were limiting my options and keeping me in chains. Next I had to accept that whatever living from my spirit may hold for me, it couldn't be worse than the increasing bind I was experiencing from my old perception of "life's rules."

- I was tired of being insecure about my ability.
- I was tired of attending seminars only to discover that I could have taught them.
- I was tired of waiting to get enough training, education, experience, or acknowledgment to prove that someone else thought I could do what I knew I could do.
- I was tired of watching others do what I wanted to do and could do but was afraid to try.
- I was tired of ignoring talents that were screaming to be exercised.
- I was tired of being halfway through my life and still waiting.
- I was tired of fighting my spirit.
- And I was tired—just plain tired.

Now I realize that I was waiting for courage, waiting to have the courage to trust myself and to have faith that I could handle whatever life handed me. Finally, I had to take that step alone with full knowledge that it would change my life, my work, and my relationships forever. As I took a few tentative steps, my knees began to knock. What would the great unknown hold for me?

After I took the step from old to new, it changed my life. I now do only work with which I am in complete integrity. I proclaim a worldview unpopular in many circles. I know that I have limited the places in which I can work because of the work I do. My concerns that I wouldn't be able to make a living were well founded. Some people won't hire me, and I wouldn't be happy working with them anyway. Other people now seek me out because they know I am able to help them build a happier, healthier, and more exhilarating workplace. I have faith the work will come, and it has.

I couldn't lead others from the heart until I knew my heart. I couldn't build spirit-respecting workplaces until I worked from spirit. When I did, I discovered wonderful things. I have entered the most exhilarating, invigorating, and creative time in my life. Each day is joyful and peaceful in a way I could not have conceived of a few years ago. My important relationships are much deeper and cleaner. There are new, affirmative relationships to replace the negative, draining ones. I hear the word *courage* a lot from my friends, but I could do nothing less. To change was a matter of life—my life. The courage has given me new life.

TOOLS FOR BEING ON THE PATH OF COURAGE

- The qualities of the Wonder Child are natural and are present in all of us. We only need discover them.
- The only way to move forward is to let go of limiting perceptions of reality, including perceptions about the importance of what other people will think.
- Comfort with paradox and ambiguity is essential.
- Courage and faith are gifts of spirit.

EXPLORING THE PATH OF COURAGE

(1a) Read through the list of Wonder Child qualities at the beginning of this chapter (page 94). As you read over each, ask yourself, "Is this the way I feel about myself?" If the answer is "yes," congratulations! You are on your way to living from your spirit. If you respond "no" to any of the questions, ask yourself, "What old realities must I let go of for this to be true for me?"

(1b) As you go through the realities which you must let go of in order to discover your Wonder Child, ask yourself, "What are the rewards for my old thinking?" Then explore the rewards for letting go of that reality. Become aware of times you choose old realities instead of new, empowering ones. When you catch yourself, make a conscious decision to let go of the old reality and to choose a new possibility instead.

(2) Review the illusions upon which my old belief system was based (in the section Moving Forward, page 102). What is your belief system based on? Make your own list, then go back and ask yourself, "If this belief is an illusion, what difference will it make to the way I live my life?" Choose one change that can have the most consequences in your life and work. Take a leap of faith: Simply choose to change the way you view one part of your life. Make a list of all the things you must do differently in your new belief system, and be conscious and conscientious about doing them.

Chapter 7

Reflecting: The Inner Door

Only that day dawns to which we are awake.

. . . Henry David Thoreau

People often ask me, "How do I get in touch with spirit?" The answer, I believe, lies in being—just being, in self-knowledge and self-awareness. It lies in listening to our inner wisdom and in trusting that we have the answers. It lies in trusting that we can know what we do not know. It lies in giving up the past and choosing to live in the present. It lies in letting negative thoughts and judgment give way to loving and trusting thoughts. It lies in understanding what motivates our relationships and what our relationships really are. Most of all, it is in being—just being.

We do not learn about spirit with our brains. We were born with spirit, and now we want to find it, again. How can we learn if not with our brains? We learn by listening and by being very still. We learn by breathing deeply and letting go of all the negative thoughts that clutter our minds with fear. We learn by letting go of all thoughts of this day, yesterday, last week, tomorrow, next week, or next year. When we are very still and listen, we can discover our own inner wisdom. The process is like prayer except that instead of talking, we listen.

Some may call the process reflection; others call it meditation. I prefer to call it listening. Whatever we call it, I believe, reflective practice is the inner door to our spirits. The notion of meditation may evoke thoughts of Eastern religions or mysticism, but in reality reflective practice is a part of all religions. It is clearly part of the Judeo-Christian heritage. The Bible has many examples of God or angels speaking to human beings. From Adam and Eve to Moses and Mary, the early heroes and heroines of Western religious tradition listened in order to hear God speak to them.

We don't have to go to India to learn listening. We don't even have to be associated with a particular group or religion. All we have to do to open the doors to our inner wisdom is to be quiet and listen. The inner door to our unconscious leads us to the place where the Wonder Child lies imprisoned. When we are still and listen, the door we have barred shut with fear and doing slowly and heavily creaks open—a wee bit at first. Gradually the door opens wider until oceans of spiritual wisdom flow forth. The wisdom is always with us and has always been with us. We simply have to listen. This wisdom is the source of our creativity, our intuition, our curiosity, our courage, and our safety. It is the source of our integrity, keeping us in touch with our values. All of these and more slip out the doors when we take time to listen.

LISTENING STARTS WITH RECEPTIVITY

Whether or not we engage in regular reflective practice, our wisdom tries to speak to us. When I become fidgety, agitated, grouchy, or experience physical aches or pains, it is usually an inner message trying to get my attention. Spirit speaks to us in pictures and experiences rather than in words. Unlike our negative voices, these messages don't come to us in complete sentences and words we easily understand. We don't hear, "Sit down and listen to me. There is something you need to look at in your life. You need to be more positive. You need to trust more and have faith." Instead the message comes to us as an ache between the shoulder blades or behind the left temple, or it comes to us as an agitated mood. Some may recognize it as a pressing need for a drink at the end of the day, a practice they have adopted to quiet the messages they don't choose to hear. Others may feel it as an escalating drive to *do*—a "to do" list that grows longer and longer and seems never to satisfy us. When we sit down and listen, the positive wisdom comes to us in words. We must first cooperate by lending attention.

Some may think it mysterious or even insane to talk of getting messages from within, yet virtually everyone has internal messages they listen to. They may be messages like, "Don't forget to stop at the store for bread on the way home," or they may take the form of a negative judgmental voice, saying "It is crazy to talk about listening to voices and inner wisdom." In our organizations, we frequently hear inner messages such as, "We better not trust them with this information. You know what would happen if it got out" or "That's pretty risky. Better play it safe. If you tried that, and it went sideways, it could cost you your job."

Jon Kabat-Zinn at the University of Massachusetts Medical Center, directs a program that teaches patients to find relief from chronic pain and stress-related disorders by using meditation. In an interview with Bill Moyers published in *Psychology Today*,[1] Kabat-Zinn said, "One reason that people take our program is that it's completely demystified. It's not anything exotic. Meditation just has to do with paying attention in a particular way. That's something we're all capable of doing." Kabat-Zinn clarifies meditative practice for the newcomer. "Non-doing does not mean doing nothing."[2] Instead he explains that the non-doing of meditation really cultivates stillness. This stillness opens us to our inner wisdom. As we develop a respect for the clarity that comes from stillness, our awareness begins to be heightened and receives dozens of subtle messages that we get every day, even when we are not meditating.

WORKING IT OUT WHILE WORKING OUT

When I started my journey, sitting for thirty to forty-five minutes and listening to my inner wisdom was beyond my comprehension. Yet as I look back, a different meditation was quite familiar to me. Although I didn't know what was happening at the time, for years I had accessed my inner wisdom when I ran. During the runner's high, I was in a peaceful state. I did my best problem solving then, when I was "out of my brain" and into my heart, my spirit, and my unconscious. I remember joking that when the president of our company heard the words, "I got the best idea when I was running last night," he knew he was in for some creative problem solving. I remember feeling a great sense of loss when a former partner took up running, and we began running together. At the time, I didn't understand why it bothered me. I really enjoyed spending the time with him. Now I know why: Running was the only time I spent in quiet reflection. When a running injury prevented running and walking, I discovered that I could experience the same reflective space when doing lap swimming.

---

1. Jon Kabat-Zinn and Bill Moyers, "Meditate! . . . for Stress Reduction, Inner Peace . . . ," *Psychology Today*, July–August 1993, p. 37.

2. Jon Kabat-Zinn, *Wherever You Go There You Are: Mindfulness Meditation in Everyday Life* (Los Angeles, CA: Renaissance, 1994), audiotape, side one.

I don't believe that it happens during the learning phase of any activity, but as soon as any uninterrupted, repetitive aerobic activity becomes automatic, I believe it is possible to use that time for meditation. For me it is important not to actively engage my brain in distracting activities—no television, no radio, no music. When my brain is engaged in listening to these stimuli, I am not able to hear my internal messages. When I am walking or running and talking with someone, my left brain is engaged, and I am not able to listen to inner messages. Others may find that different conditions work for them. What is critical is that the conditions don't actively engage the left brain.

WRITING FROM THE HEART

As I moved forward along my journey to spirituality, I also discovered that I could accomplish the same thing by writing. If I just sat down and started writing about what I was *feeling* and how I was experiencing people and events, I found that the door to my inner self slowly opened. Eventually, it began opening more quickly. This process is different from keeping a diary in which we write about what we do. Writing to reach the inner self goes on in our innermost core, in our very *BE*ing. And again it has been my experience that outside stimuli like music engage my brain and keep me out of my heart and spirit. Writing from the inner self has been particularly helpful to some of my clients who use it. "It's incredible. It's all there. I am able to see patterns I never noticed before," is typical of comments I hear.

DREAMS: ANOTHER DOOR TO INNER WISDOM

Dreams are also a good way to receive messages, sometimes very important messages from the unconscious. The Bible, Native American lore, and Greek, Roman, and other mythology are rich in examples of dreams that provide significant guidance to people who listen to, and seek to understand, their dreams. Dreams are our most effective source of the information that we are taking into our unconscious minds at almost forty-three thousand times the rate that our conscious minds process data. The unconscious mind plays continually with this information and tries to make sense of it. Finally, a picture materializes, and the wisdom is offered to us in the form of a dream.

When I started doing creativity research some years ago, I began consciously developing my capacity to use dreams. Before then I had been unable to remember more than one or two exceptional dreams a year and even then did not expend any energy on trying to figure out the symbolism. Although many people experience conversations and other verbal cues, most often my dreams were simply pictures. There were frequently a few, but not many, key words, as far as I recall. To take meaning from them, I had to develop an understanding of the symbolism. Volumes have been written on dream interpretation; often studies on creativity explore dream imagery. Anyone having difficulty accessing the inner self by the other methods I describe may want to do additional reading on dreams.

When I want insight on solving a problem or finding creative stimulus in a dream, I simply think about the problem as I am going to sleep. I say to myself that I want to have a dream that will give me insight into the problem, remember the dream, and wake up long enough to make some notes. I keep a scratch pad on my nightstand. When I am awakened by a dream, I jot down a few key words in the dark to remind myself of the dream in the morning. Upon awakening in the morning, I lie quietly for a few minutes, think about my reminder words, and reconstruct the dream in my mind. Then I jot down a few more notes. Two or three days may pass and additional dreams may occur before I figure out the significance of a dream. When I do, the dream or dream sequence often provides new perspectives or forgotten pieces which effortlessly resolve my situation.

In recent years I have adopted a practice that has yielded a bounty of unconscious dream material. Immediately upon waking each day, I write in my "dream log." When I remember a dream, I write down as many of its details as I can. Then I write, "What does this mean?" More times than not, a very clear message pours forth through my writing. Other days I may remember only a snapshot or two of the dream, but I still get a message from it. Sometimes I initially remember only a snapshot or two, but the more I write the more I remember. Regardless of what I remember about the dream, I almost always get an important message about what it means or a "message for the day" that keeps me in touch with spirit.

My experience with the dream log parallels other reflective activities. At early stages of the practice I often got little information about dreams, but when I came back faithfully, day after day, more and more unfolded for me. After a few months, it was not uncommon for me to log five to ten pages of dream material and messages. When a serious illness or the drugs associated with it caused my dreams to "stop," however, I found that I had to start almost from the beginning again with a snapshot or two and patiently build to my former levels of dream cultivation. It is now common for me to seek dream guidance in moving a group that has been "stuck." Often the approach suggested in my postdream consciousness is not the one my linear brain would have taken. I have a great deal of faith in this process, however, and the dream guidance has never failed me, although it often "pushes the envelope" of my work.

Some time ago I had the opportunity to visit a management class that a Native American woman was teaching; she used her tradition to look creatively at management practices. I had been personally moved and professionally intrigued by a ritual using the Medicine Circle which she introduced for stimulating reflection. A few months later I was facilitating a visioning process, and my dream guidance was to use the Medicine Circle. Using this kind of nontraditional ritual was pretty uncomfortable for me at the time, but I trusted my guidance. The result still amazes me. The group quickly and easily coalesced around a simple but powerful statement about what they wanted for their company. I have never seen such unanimity in a group that was creating a corporate vision, and the vision became a strong directive force for people in their daily organizational work lives.

As groups work together to heighten their consciousness about their work, oftentimes a "group dream" occurs, when one person's dreams reflect the process the group is experiencing. When a person is willing to share the dreams, their telling often causes their group to make a major move forward in their process work.

Many people experience discomfort in talking about their dreams, perhaps because dreams often speak in unfamiliar metaphors. My own experience, as well as that of colleagues who have developed "dream practices," is that dream telling is a rich resource resulting in an eager sharing of wisdom that our conscious brains aren't capable of assimilating.

THERE IS NO *RIGHT* WAY TO REFLECT

There are countless other ways for people to access their spirits. There are no right or wrong ways, only different ways. Whatever works is right. What works this week may not be what works next week or next month. With practice, we may discover new ways of quickly recharging or shifting gears when something negative pulls us down.

Most reflective practices relate to breathing which shouldn't be surprising since the word *spirit* comes from the Latin *spirare*, "to breathe." Deep breathing, which uses our diaphragms, seems to connect us with our spirits. Most traditional meditation and yoga practices involve slow, deep breathing. Some forms of meditation make it a discipline to focus on breathing and on letting go of thoughts that may drift in and out to distract that focus. Aerobic exercise also deepens breathing. When we are in a dream state, we usually have slower, deeper breathing. When I begin to feel agitated, nervous, anxious, confused, angry, or frightened, I can calm myself and connect with my spirit by taking a few deep breaths. I have also observed that clients who get angry or frightened take short, shallow breaths; when I encourage them to take deep, diaphragmatic breaths, they calm down significantly. Even this simple practice can dramatically assist a leader to stay connected to spirit.

THE SILENT RETREAT

For several years, I have taken three or four days once a year for what I call my silent retreat. For that period of time, I commit to maintaining silence and meditative activities and to performing only the most essential tasks of daily living. I prepare easy food in advance and often sustain myself on fresh fruit, vegetables, and raw nuts. I rarely go anywhere but usually choose a time when my husband is on a business trip or I house-sit for an out-of-town friend.

If I were to point to any one practice that has put my growth into "overdrive," it has been the silent retreat. The discipline of completely withdrawing from the activities of daily life produces learning that is deeper and faster than any seminar, counseling, or other growth activity in which I have engaged on my journey. As soon as I know I am not supposed to speak, I think of countless people with whom I need to communicate. I have forgotten to tell them something, or I need to arrange a trip or meeting, or there's something I've intended to share—a recipe, a compliment, a book, a joke, or just gratitude. For me the testing is so intense and the temptation to speak so great on the first day that I always wonder at both my resourcefulness at thinking of things to say and at my ability to let these thoughts drift away.

My commitment to engage only in meditational activities is similarly tested. It is an incredible challenge for me to walk by the same piece of mud on the kitchen floor for several days and not clean it up. While I am being, I notice dust that I don't regularly pay attention to, and I notice that my brain is trying to pull me back into doing. A claim check from the dry cleaners or shoe repair shop or the thought of my mother-in-law's birthday next week is a temptation to "do." I notice how intensely I am programmed to do, and I turn inward to being, again and again. It is the process that Kabat-Zinn calls cultivating stillness.[3]

---

3. See note 2 above.

It always takes at least a day, sometimes two, to still myself, but then I reap the generous rewards for commitment. Self-discovery and awareness move to new levels. Behaviors I had never related to events become apparent. I am able to see how I create or have created situations and relationships that are not what I want. I recall events and details of events from my childhood, events that explain the way I behave in metaphorically similar circumstances I encounter today. I always emerge from my retreat with a feeling of deep integration and complete peace, joy, harmony, and love, an amazing feeling, so different from the fidgeting and distraction of the first day. Although not as deep or complete, my daily meditation dips me into this space. But each retreat seems to take me to a new plateau where daily meditation goes deeper and faster and where I have a much higher level of awareness about my power to create the life I choose to live. My daily meditation and even my deep-breathing check-in help me to be conscious of how I function in the world. These routines help me to see options I didn't recognize before the time of reflection and assist me in leaving my old autopilot mode and living more consciously. These routines remind me that when I choose them, peace and tranquillity are amazingly close at hand.

SUSTAINING SPIRITUAL CONNECTION IN A NONSPIRITUAL WORLD

Much of the world is not very spiritual or positive. It is filled with negativity and bombards us on conscious and subliminal levels during most of our days. As the pace of doing quickens, we become more and more distant from our being and from our values and slip more and more into reactive doing. Rather than consciously accessing our unconscious for inner wisdom, we slip into letting our unconscious run our lives as Fate. We get further and further from spirit. When we spend time in reflection, we are being. We are our spirits. The Old Testament name for God is sometimes translated as "to be." Judaism has a higher life (I am) and a lower life (distant from I am). The lowest layer of hell in Buddhism is assigned to animals who spend all their time seeking food—doing—and no time in conscious contemplation of their being.[4] Being spiritual means spending time in reflection. Time spent being keeps us on track and keeps us in the present.

When I was finishing the first draft of this book, I talked with a friend about how the book would change my life. I remarked that I knew

---

4. Jacob Needleman, *Money and the Meaning of Life* (New York: Currency/Doubleday, 1991).

I had to change how I worked, but it was unclear to me what my new way of working would look like. I told her that I wouldn't need that information for a couple of weeks; I was sure that by the time I needed to know, my inner wisdom would make my new course clear to me. She responded to me, somewhat in disbelief, "It's nice you know that *you* have that." We all have that wisdom. Many deny it or don't create a receptivity or a space for listening. I haven't always wanted to be conscious about seeking it and am sometimes steered by the fearful parts of my unconscious. When I access what I am and when I trust it, I get clear, spiritual messages that keep me on track with my spirit and my deeply held values.

When we commit to developing our spiritual side, we need to cooperate by giving some time each day to becoming aware of positive beliefs about humankind. This much commitment is the least we can do. When we have committed to developing our spiritual side, we choose to check in with this inner wisdom before we make decisions. Our spirituality keeps us on track with our values. It keeps us in integrity. Our spirits guide us, if we listen and reflect and just be. Spirituality is the source of our courage—heart courage. In this state, we are one with our spirits.

TOOLS FOR BEING ON THE PATH OF COURAGE

- A regular practice or a discipline of reflection, meditation, or any activity that provides conscious listening to our unconscious mind, and inner wisdom helps keep us on balance, operating from our spirits, and on the Path of Courage.
- There are many ways to access this guidance. None are wrong. What works for you is right for you, but what works for you may change from time to time. In addition to traditional meditation, some ways that people have used are aerobic exercise without distraction, stream-of-consciousness writing, and dream logging.
- Whatever form of practice you choose to develop will probably take the commitment of a time, probably at least thirty days. Like any exercise you must get in shape before the practice happens easily.

EXPLORING THE PATH OF COURAGE

(1) Spend at least ten minutes at the beginning or the ending of each day writing about what you are *feeling* personally or what you are *feeling* about events and encounters with other individuals in the past day. Practice doing this writing for at least thirty days.

(2) Try keeping a dream log (like the one described in this chapter under the section "Dreams: Another Door . . .") every day for thirty days. Daily practice dramatically increases the number of insights.

(3) When you engage in a solo aerobic exercise, begin being conscious of your "runner's high." As soon as you finish exercising, write for a few minutes about what you feel.

Chapter 8

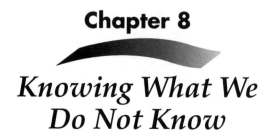

Knowing What We Do Not Know

If I don't know I don't know, I think I know. If I don't know I know, I think I don't know.

R. D. LAING, *Knots*[1]

We only know what we know—what we have been taught by books, by others, and by our experiences. That is all we know. Or is it? Is it possible that we do not know what we believe we know? That we know what we do not know we know? Once I was sure I knew how to get ahead: Get a good education, find a good company, work hard, do what I'm told, and be loyal. Promotions will come. I will move up the ladder and make more money as I go. I will retire with a gold watch, a good retirement, and a few years to live. This is what I knew a few years ago.

In less than a generation, most of what I and others thought we knew began crumbling. The good education isn't the right education for today. Once "good" companies are shrinking in size and number and are even disappearing. When the giants tumble, they leave behind broken people to reconstruct their lives. Other companies downsize, rightsize, flatten, reengineer, and decentralize. They leave millions of people scrambling, often

---

1. R. D. Laing, *Knots* (New York: Pantheon, 1970).

bloodied and bruised. Wages are frozen; benefits are reduced; pensions are underfunded; benefits are stripped from retirees. There is no ladder, no loyalty, no gold watch. There is only survival. So much for what I knew.

Making a leap of faith to change your belief system is simply a matter of choosing to do it. Your linear brain knows I've lost it, right? Yet what if I am right? I say finding the faith to live from your spirit is simply a choice. Your linear brain knows there must be more to it than that. I am saying to you that if you live your life from a place I call spirit, and if you have complete belief in yourself and the rest of humanity, you can provide the glue to hold your organization together and allow it the flexibility and resilience to respond to daily changes in the operating environment. What you're saying is that I'm wacko, right? Everything that is rational, cognitive, testable, believable, everything that you know to be true, says that spirituality has nothing to do with your organization, right? That's something we do on Sunday before the ball game, isn't it?

Enter a global marketplace, new technologies, and permanent white water; enter confusion and chaos. Just what is it that we know that is rational, cognitive, testable, believable that will be true five minutes from now? Try as we may to ignore or deny the evidence, our historic perceptions of reality are being distorted or erased daily. If we are truly rational, we know that there isn't much we really know for certain any more. What is knowing? Is it more than an illusion of one person's perception of the past? Can it be that what I thought was reality isn't what it appears to be at all because I'm looking through a strangely tinted lens? Can it be that I'm not the only one? Can it be that millions look through the same lens and think they see something that's not there? I have even suggested that something as rational as hard science is an illusion? It not only could be but is.

When the founders of quantum theory began to challenge Newtonian physics, their world became very confusing and unsettling. In *The Turning Point*, Fritjof Capra tells the story of Niels Bohr and Werner Heisenberg, two of the physicists who worked on early versions of quantum theory.

> In the twentieth century, physicists faced, for the first time, a serious challenge to their ability to understand the universe. Every time they asked nature a question in an atomic experiment, nature answered with a paradox; the more they tried to clarify the situation, the sharper the paradoxes became. In their struggle to grasp this new reality, scientists became painfully aware that their basic concepts, their language, and their whole way of thinking were inadequate to describe atomic phenomena. Their problem was not only intellectual but involved an intense emotional and existential experience, as vividly described by Werner Heisenberg:

> I remember discussions with Bohr which went through many hours till very late at night and ended almost in despair; and when at the end of the discussion I went alone for a walk in the neighboring park I repeated to myself again and again the question: Can nature possibly be so absurd as it seemed to us in these atomic experiments?
>
> It took these physicists a long time to accept the fact that the paradoxes they encountered are an essential aspect of atomic physics ... Once this was perceived, the physicists began to learn to ask the right questions and to avoid contradictions ... and finally they found the precise and consistent mathematical formulation of [quantum] theory.[2]

Quantum physics demanded a new lens, a different way of looking at things, and a different set of assumptions from those of classical physics.

Biologists who study single cells have encountered a similar unwinding of long-held beliefs in recent years. Scientists have long believed that the human mind and the brain were one and the same,[3] and they were separate from the body. They have been studied separately. There have been studies of how the brain influences the body and vice versa, but as separate entities. Diseases and malfunctions have been studied separately. Recent discoveries show that the chemicals responsible for memory, previously believed to be only in the brain, are located in every cell of the human body.[4] Like physics, biology also illustrates that what we knew is not what we know but only what we thought we knew.

WHAT IS IT TO *KNOW*?

> If you say to me, "The sky is blue," I ask, "How do you know?"
>
> To that question you may respond, "I can see it."
>
> "So you can see it," I say. "How do you know it is blue?"
>
> "I can see that it is blue," you respond, probably with a bit of irritation in your voice by now.
>
> "How do you know that the sky is blue? How do you know what you see is blue?"

---

2. Fritjof Capra, *The Turning Point: Science, Society, and the Rising Culture* (New York: Bantam Books, 1983), pp. 76–77.

3. Bill Moyers, "Healing and the Mind" (PBS Series), Spring 1994.

4. See note 3 above.

"I just know," you say.

And I continue to probe. "How do you know?"

"I don't know how I know. I just know it is blue because I can see that it is blue."

At some point in your fairly young life, you didn't know that the sky or anything else was blue. You had to be taught. You were taught that the color you saw in the sky was called *blue* by someone else who had been taught that the color of the sky was named *blue*, and before that, someone taught that person the same name, *blue*, for the color of the sky. And if you have children, you will likely teach them that name for the sky's color. We know that the sky is blue, and the grass is green, and so on. We just know it. We don't have to think about it. We don't have to explain it. In fact, most of us would be hard pressed to explain a lot of things we know to be true, as is evidenced by the preceding frustrating conversation.

These givens in life are the assumptions that we bring to everyday living. They are the things that we think we know. Because we assume that these things are true, we don't usually challenge them. We make other assumptions and sometimes decisions based on faulty information, because some of what we think we know isn't true. We used to know that what was good for General Motors was good for the country! Now we believe that what was good for General Motors was not even good for GM!

"How do you know there is spirit? How do you know that it has anything to do with work?" you may ask.

"How do you know there isn't?" I respond.

"I can't see it or touch it or hear it or measure it."

"So are you saying that to know that something is real, you must be able to see it, touch it, hear it, or measure it?" I query.

"That certainly makes it a lot easier to believe!" you say.

"Do you believe in gravity?" I ask.

"Well, of course!" you respond.

"Can you see it, touch it, hear it, or measure it?" I ask.

"Well, no, but I can see its effects!" you indignantly retort.

As I look around the room, I say, "I see nothing."

You pick up a spoon and drop it, "See! The effects of gravity!"

"I can see gravity's effects when I look for them, when you point them out, and I can see the effects of spirit in the workplace when I look. I can even point them out to you in a spirit-respecting workplace!"

When we begin to challenge what we know and don't know, we often discover that what we think we know is not true at all. Like Laing, we discover, "If I don't know I don't know, I think I know."[5] We think we know only because we don't know that we don't know. We are born with spiritual knowing. It is what we knew before we knew anything else. We trusted people to take care of us when we needed help. Why else would newborns cry out for help? As we grow older, we are taught things that contradict this deep knowing, and we begin to feel that we don't know the things that our hearts and spirits know. Again, like Laing, we discover, "If I don't know I know, I think I don't know."[6] For too long, we have depended only on what others have taught. We didn't trust our own inner knowing. Our companies, and indeed our civilization, are crying out for this knowing. We know. We just don't know that we know, so we think we don't know.

UNLEARNING

How does this discussion relate to the questions posed at the start of this chapter? If it is possible that we do not know what we believe we know, then by extension is it possible that we know what we do not know? If we hear the phrase, "once upon a time," our imaginations click on. In our mind's eye, we can conjure strange and mystical people, places and events with significant definition: a bean stalk large enough for a boy to climb into the sky, a shoe big enough for a large family to live in, or a wolf who can blow a house down with a deep breath. Not only can we do it now, we could do it when we were quite young. We were able to imagine then. The ability to imagine is something we had to *un*learn. Although we actually change our beliefs in an instant, most of us, especially in the beginning, spend days, weeks, or even years unlearning to prepare for that leap of faith.

In order to make space to learn something new, we must unlearn whatever is in its place, whatever contradicts the new learning. The old information must be destroyed before the new information can become a

---

5. See note 1 above.

6. See note 1 above.

functioning part of our knowledge banks. As we grow up, we unlearn that bean stalks can grow up to the sky before we can know that the giant one we had imagined was not possible.

For the sake of exploration, suppose that it is possible for bean stalks to grow to the sky. Imagine that our parents were the ones who were misinformed when they told us it was just a story, that bean stalks couldn't grow that tall and couldn't be strong enough for us to climb. We've lived all these years with a distorted view of bean stalks! We begin to behave differently. When we go to the feed store, we look for giant bean seeds, not the ones we traditionally plant in the garden. We don't mess with the poles when we plant these seeds, because these strong plants won't need support. We eagerly watch the plants as they grow upward, and we begin to plan an exciting adventure! Because we have unlearned our old belief system about pole beans, our expectations about the possibilities have been completely changed. We begin to have totally different assumptions.

I have suggested to you that the catalysts that can make your organization dynamic are spirit and respecting the spiritual nature of the human beings who work in it. I have asked you to know that you may have been viewing your world through a distorted lens. I have asked you to know that you and others are loving, lovable, peaceful, trusting, open, accepting, connected, creative, intuitive, and all the things that being in touch with our spirits represents. I have asked you to know these things, and you have said, "How can I know these things? They are not my experience."

Experience is the past. The past is part of an illusion. It was what you chose to experience, given what you had been taught. Quantum physics was not the everyday experience of Bohr and Heisenberg. That the mind can be located throughout the body had not been the experience of the traditional medical or psychological community. Each group of scientists had to learn to imagine things that were not, initially, within their imagining.

I am now suggesting that you can do this, *if you choose* to do it. Just imagine. You could do it when you were three. Your Wonder Child can choose what your experience will be right now. You can choose spiritual knowing over your perception of rational knowing. Everyone can. It is a choice.

Twentieth-century enterprise is built around rational understanding. There was always one right answer: We were sure we knew what we thought we knew. For over a decade now, business has been referred to as being in a state of permanent white water.[7] Similar conditions prevail around the globe. Nothing seems predictable. What we had known

---

7. Peter B. Vaill, *Managing as a Performing Art: New Ideas for a World of Chaotic Change* (San Francisco, CA: Jossey-Bass, 1989).

rationally just isn't working anymore. By the time a theory is developed and tested, it is out of date. What worked last year, last month, or even last week may not work today. If we are to survive, we must give up the definitive for the flexible. The new approaches talk about "thriving on chaos"[8] and "managing as performing art."[9]

People get scared. How can we lead people through chaos? How can we do management as performing art, if we don't have a script? We're afraid of losing control. There have been some guidelines, some approaches, and some shared experiences. The bottom line to me is that if we are going to lead people under these conditions, we have to accept that they are people and not machines. We have to believe that as people they are as flexible and creative and adaptable as the ever-changing conditions in the business environment. We have to believe they will discover the right answers for each situation as it presents itself. We have to have faith—faith in them and faith in ourselves. We have to trust them, they have to trust us, and . . . we have to trust ourselves. We have to be open, intuitive, inspiring, aspiring, and all those things that are rooted in our essential spirits. We may have to come to know what we didn't know we knew.

DISCOVERING WHAT YOU DON'T KNOW YOU KNOW

Most of my time in organizations is spent helping individual leaders or groups of leaders discover what they didn't know they knew, and what they didn't know that they didn't know (those things that they believed to be true that are false.) The conscious mind has the ability to process about seven pieces of information per minute. The unconscious mind can process three hundred thousand pieces in the same amount of time. Most of this vast library of information is carried around in the unconscious, that part that "we don't know," or the right brain, the nonlinear, nonverbal part of our brains. At any given moment we are exposed to two billion pieces of information. All of this information gives me a lot to work with in helping groups discover what they didn't know.

When people have information they have not brought to consciousness, the right questions or sequence of questions helps them to discover pertinent data in their mental storehouses. Perhaps they have a hunch but haven't been able to verbalize it.

---

8. Tom Peters, *Thriving on Chaos: Handbook for a Management Revolution* (San Francisco, CA: Perennial Library/Harper & Row, 1987).

9. See note 7 above.

The right brain sees things in pictures but since it isn't verbal, it can't generate words; so sometimes we have an intuition that we can't put into words. We are constantly filtering those two billion pieces of data to which we are exposed in order to cull important information from them. Because of our differing life experiences, however, what is meaningful to me may not be meaningful to you. By guiding a process where we get pieces of a picture from everyone in a group, we are able to discover together things that none of us can access on our own. When we experience confusion over a conflict in what our brain believes it knows, the right sequence of questions can bring clarity to the issue.

Experiments with people who have had their brain hemispheres separated show that when our verbal left brain says something that contradicts our right brain's perception or our inner knowing, we make a physical gesture that indicates the conflict. For instance, when people are told that a knife is a fork and then asked to name the implement, their left brain and mouth said, "Fork," but they would shake their heads in a "No" gesture. When we experience confusion, we usually need to dig deeper for more possibilities. It is my belief that many stress-related illnesses have their origins in just such cognitive dissonance. We find ourselves acting out of congruity with our inner wisdom, and the only way our spirit has to let us know is through physical irritation, illness, or pain.

We clearly have different ways of knowing that have been either undervalued or denigrated in most of our organizations. Antonio Damasio, a neurologist who has researched the impact that emotions have on what we know, has said: "Decisions based solely on rational reflection without the participation of emotional elements lead to bad consequences. In other words, your feelings can help you do the right thing. . . . The mind is neither localized in a particular area nor completely separate from the brain but actually emerges from the convergence of many different subsystems. Emotions are the mind's way of monitoring what's going on between the organism and its environment, a 'readout' of the body state."[10]

Deepak Chopra tells the story of meeting the founder and former CEO of Sony Corporation, a man who built an empire and made billions of dollars in his lifetime. He told Chopra that he depended on his heart to guide his decisions. According to Chopra, he would take his decisions home with him and study his heart's and his body's reaction before choosing a course of action.[11]

---

10. Valerie Brown, "Science: We Feel Therefore We Are, Too: Neurologist Antonio Damasio Lectures at the Hult," *Eugene* (OR) *Weekly*, 28 September 1995, p. 13.

11. Deepak Chopra, "The Seven Spiritual Laws of Success," public television special, 18 March 1996, UNC-TV.

COMING TO KNOW "WHAT WE DO NOT KNOW"

Many of the leaders whom I work with profess to be confused about or to experience conflict over knowing what to do in a given situation. I often ask them, "If you did know, what would you know?" In time they unfailingly come up with an answer. Then I probe more. "Are there other possibilities?" I ask. Again more possibilities are discovered. Often there are still possibilities that I know about that haven't come forth, so I push even more. "I think there are even more possibilities. Can you think of others?" They are virtually always able to discover more. All of the answers they are sharing with me are ones that just a few minutes before they didn't know they knew. Such groups often find many more possibilities that they have never before examined.

In one company I worked with two groups of employees, each comprised of people from various levels in the organization. In both groups the same problem emerged as an issue. A time-consuming monthly task could have been assigned to either one of the groups; much friction surfaced monthly over which group was responsible for the chore, and the two groups were at an uncomfortable impasse. The only resolution appeared to be to assign it to one of the groups and then listen to them complain or ask for more help. Because the issue emerged in dialogue in each group, we were able to ask many questions and soon discovered that there were many unexamined factors that contributed to how time-consuming the job actually was. Naive questions asked by people in unaffected departments shed significant light on additional possibilities for approaching the task.

Each group went in a different direction so that two completely different sets of possibilities could be closely examined and different resolutions tested. Among the resolutions being considered, none fell into the category of "either Group A does it or Group B does it." After dialogue opened the issue, it became apparent that the either/or approach was an oversimplification that led to looking at symptoms rather than the problem. In fact a complex set of problems touched various departments. Our explorations resulted in a company-wide inquiry to continue to discover what the workers know that they didn't know they knew.

DISCOVERING YOU DON'T KNOW
YOU DON'T KNOW

Just as I work with leaders to help them realize or "know" what they didn't realize they already knew, I also often help these same leaders discover that things they believed to be true were, in fact, false, or what they didn't know they didn't know. Whenever someone is particularly forceful about the need to take certain actions, such an attitude is often a good sign to me that this information contradicts their inner knowing; their forcefulness is often the left brain's way of getting its way. I say to them, "What if the opposite were true?" There are a lot of opposites in most situations, and without fail, the opposite that the person comes up with immediately is the one that is an unlikely stretch. Again I probe for other possible opposites so that people begin to discover the errors of their certainty.

For instance, a business in a college town experienced declining profits, "certainly" related to falling college enrollments. When I asked them to consider that the opposite may be true, the knee-jerk response was, "You mean that our profits should be going *up* because of dropping enrollments?" Well, I suppose that is a possibility, but it is not one I had in mind. After exploring the domain of opposites a while longer, the executive group discovered that their lagging profits were as likely to be a product of their ignoring the competition and their customers as they were of dropping enrollments. If this group of managers had continued operating on the assumption that all their problems were related to enrollment, they would be in a defensive, victim role until the number of students began to increase. After discovering what they didn't know they didn't know, they were in a much better position to make aggressive operational changes to increase their profits.

As groups struggle with the challenge of building workplaces that are more nurturing to the whole people who work in them, an issue that frequently arises is "What do we do about all these laws that won't let us treat people the way we would like to?" The "What if the opposite were true?" question often results in a first-tier answer like, "You mean we shouldn't obey the law?" I always tell them that is not a course I would encourage, and I challenge them to seek other "opposites." Without fail, they discover many ways to satisfy the requirements of most laws, ways more spirit-respecting than are approaches traditionally taught in employment law seminars designed by people who want to promote attitudes of fear between employers and employees.

BUILDING WALLS TO KEEP FROM KNOWING

For many people security rests on finite rules and their predictability: when we do *A*, *B* occurs. When we know this, we know we can survive doing *A* most of the time. *A* may limit us, but at least it is predictable. For those on the Path of Fear, doing things by the rules and producing predictable results are standard operating procedures. To continue to appear rational means that they must eliminate anything that challenges the assumptions upon which *A* is based; if the assumptions are wrong, *A* may be wrong. If *A* is wrong, then what we knew about what we should do may be wrong, and our rules may be wrong. If our rules are wrong, what can we do? So it is on the Path of Fear, as we enter chaos and confusion.

Rather than develop the courage to examine what we know we don't know and what we don't know we don't know, as may happen on the Path of Courage, those on the Path of Fear have a set of ready responses they use to prevent discovery of any new knowing. Among the responses that I've encountered most frequently—responses that build barriers against joining a forum for generating new learning—are:

- "In the real world. . . ."
- "That's not realistic!" or "Be realistic!"
- "It would violate our policy."
- "You don't understand. Things are different in the. . . ." [Fill in the blank. I've heard them all: public sector, private sector, manufacturing sector, service sector or in health care, education, high tech].
- "Our schedules are too busy to take that much time."
- "My calendar is booked until. . . ."
- "It's not in the budget."
- "It's not in this year's action plan or MBOs."
- "We couldn't include everyone. We have to be able to respond to our customers."
- "We don't have time to sit around and contemplate our navels. We've got a business to run."
- "We've never done it that way."
- "We did it that way once, and it didn't work."
- "ABC Company did it that way and look what happened to them."
- "We couldn't. . . ."

These responses not only block change, they make it seem as though they reflect a unanimity by using "we" rather than "I." There are countless other ways we stop the discovery of what we don't know we know and what we don't know we don't know when we are on the Path of Fear. On the Path of Courage, there is an answer to every one of these barriers to knowing. When the Path of Courage is taken, new and different ways of doing things are almost always discovered; but because they are new, there are no rules for them, and predictability is limited. On the Path of Courage each new venture is an opportunity to learn and grow. When we question what we know, we continue to develop a higher standard of objectivity; we come closer and closer to discovering the truth. If we are to become the dynamic people and organizations we have the potential to be, we must be vulnerable to the truth.

OUR ONLY SECURITY

What we learned in graduate school of management ten years or even two years ago is outdated in today's climate; in fact, what we learned last month may no longer be useful. Acquisitional knowing is not what we need in the middle of permanent white water. Analysis paralysis is the last thing that we need in the middle of the rapids of the business river. What we need is knowing that we already possess. It is knowing that requires us to unlearn how we have believed things to be in order to discover how they truly are. To know, we need to challenge all our old assumptions and unlearn that all that is real is rational, linear, causal, and quantifiable. Spiritual knowing is real. It is not rational or quantifiable; it can't be taken apart to see how it works. It is a way of being. We are either open to spiritual knowing, or we are not.

My husband once delivered remarks to help launch an organizational change retreat that would explore new directions for the future of his organization. I was struck by an Eric Hoffer quotation he used, and I have used it since then.

> "In a time of drastic change, it is the *learners* who inherit the future. The *learned* find themselves equipped to live only in a world that no longer exists" [italics added].

Why do some of us cling so desperately to the need to be *learned* when being stuck in rational knowing equips us only for a world that no longer exists? It is my belief that the obstacles to openness and flexibility lie deep within our personal development.

A majority of the people I work with have built reputations and careers based on what they know, the authorities and statistics they can cite, and the examples they can share. They are the learned; everything they know is anchored in the past and based on unchallenged assumptions. But when they forsake being learned, they have no distinctions that support their self-importance. When I ask them to think in terms of having the questions instead of the answers, they discover there is little that separates those at the top of the organizations from those at the bottom. They hang onto their learnedness—a source of power, prestige, and often high salaries—for dear life; without it, they fear they are expendable.

Our ability to deal with the unpredictable, to feel at ease with chaos and confusion, and to let go of control to gain flexibility and resilience lies in having questions, not answers. This ability lies in leading learning, not being learned, like the learned who are so attached to their learnedness that they can't or won't see the shift that is occurring. To be comfortable with knowing that we don't now know what will be needed to respond to operational challenges next year, next month, or even next week requires trust, faith, and courage. These are things of the spirit, not the stuff of business theory. Spirit is not turned on and off like a faucet. We either have spirit, or we don't. We can't leave it at home or at the office. We can't draw lines and segment our lives. If we are spiritual, we are deeply connected to a system—integrated completely into it on many levels. Spirituality provides us with the intricate interconnectedness to respond to challenges and the faith to know we will know what we need to know when the time arrives.

TOOLS FOR BEING ON THE PATH OF COURAGE

- We carry within us incredible wisdom we don't know we possess.
- To make room for new knowing, we must unlearn what we have believed to be true.
- Much that we have believed we knew is false.
- Questions invite a higher standard of truth. The only way to discover truth or access information we have not known is by asking questions that challenge the perceptions or assumptions upon which our beliefs have been based.
- It is our responsibility to remove barriers to knowing.

EXPLORING THE PATH OF COURAGE

(1) The next time you are confused about something, are agonizing over what to do, or are feeling you "just don't know," ask yourself, "If you did know, what would you know?" Then be aware of what your inner wisdom tells you. You may even want to try this with a friend or co-worker. See how often you and others really do know when you make yourself available to your inner knowing. How often do you discover that what you know actually contradicts what your brain believes? Can you see that this fact creates your "confusion"?

(2) The next time you feel very strongly about something, ask yourself, "What if the opposite were true?" and then try to think of as many different opposites as you can. Assume that each of these actually is true. Does your inner knowing provide you with new insights that contradict those things about which you were absolutely certain?

Chapter 9

Being Self-Reliant Is Neither Self nor Reliant

Tom, a true entrepreneur, is nearing fifty. He has started or transformed several successful businesses. He's a real "can-do" guy, who loves challenge and competition. You only have to insinuate that something is impossible to throw down the gauntlet to him. He quickly sets out to prove that you are wrong. Tom has been making things happen for a long time now. He's very imaginative and comes up with excellent ideas. He does research, analyzes what needs to happen to ensure success, develops a plan, and then does whatever it takes to make sure the plan happens. Almost without fail it does.

Because it was his plan, others have depended on him to provide any additional information, changes, or decisions. They hadn't been involved enough in the planning to understand his thinking, much less to add their own. So even though he has worked long hours, whenever he's gone for a few days or even hours, bottlenecks occur and productivity falls while people wait for him to return with critical information or new instructions.

Tom is a self-reliant person, recognized as a successful businessman. Tom also has stomach problems and headaches, and he works long hours almost seven days a week. Whenever there are problems with his plan, he takes it back, fixes it, and tells those around him what they must do to adjust. He has a hard time motivating people even to do things that deliver personal benefits to them. Although he is a genuinely nice man, many people are afraid of him. Until recently, Tom couldn't go on vacation; even taking a long weekend was a challenge. As he approached the half-century mark, he began to resent not being able to get away. Yet, he knew that every time he left, disaster occurred. No one else could do what he did. He was essential . . . or so he thought.

HOW DO WE GET THERE?

Like Tom and many other business owners, I spent most of my life being self-reliant. When I was around three years old, events in my life began to conspire to overtake my Wonder Child and send my spirit into exile. I discovered about that time that I couldn't depend upon those around me. I was afraid and developed self-reliance as a coping strategy to help me survive on the Path of Fear. As I became better and better at being self-reliant, I moved from being dependent on others, to not needing others to take care of me, to not wanting others to take care of me. Finally I was not able to let others help me, not even those who loved me and wanted to help. I stole from others the privilege of providing loving support as I proved "I can do it myself, thank you!" to the world. Like most self-reliants, I became a human island: I moved through life being near others without ever letting them get close enough to really touch my heart.

For much of my life, I thought this self-reliant strategy was a good one. In order to be self-reliant, I developed highly tuned analytical skills and focused on doing. Although it was far from a conscious process, I learned to figure out and assess all possibilities within my comfort zone. Then I had determined which was the safest, which was the one I'd be assured of being able to control so I wouldn't need help from others. I learned to figure out which possibility would make me look really good so that I would get lots of positive feedback and so that people would give me positions of control in the future. That way I could ensure being in a position to influence courses of action in ways that were safe for me. It became a self-perpetuating cycle: the more often I was in positions of control and could influence the safe course of action, the more often I was given positions of control in the future. The problem was that I didn't know what I was doing.

The escalating demands of trying to stay in control of every activity of life ties self-reliants to their doing: analyze, plan, limit input from others, limit options, frame decisions as black and white, plan, analyze, force outcomes, control assumptions, control conditions, control others, and attempt to motivate others to do what you want them to do. Self-reliants live on the Path of Fear. Because the problem we name is the problem we solve, self-reliants make sure to name the problem they can solve. They use their fear-driven ways of doing. Self-reliants are experts at putting up barriers against knowing what they do not know in case they face a problem that they cannot solve in their traditional way of doing things.

Self-reliants are afraid to have faith in the abilities of others. They are afraid of unplanned outcomes and of new ways of doing things which may make them appear incompetent. Countering the emergence of spiritual leadership, they are afraid to keep options open and fear they may not be able to cope with new ones. They are afraid of leading a group through chaos and ambiguity. They are clearly afraid of the energy, passion, and unpredictability that emerges when spirit is released into the organization. Although he was not specifically addressing the self-reliant personality as I am describing it, John Maxwell summarized the characteristics quite simply:

> "Many intelligent adults are restrained in thoughts, actions and results. They never move further than the boundaries of their self-imposed limitations."[1]

Leaders on the Path of Courage know that in the world at the doorstep of the twenty-first century they need to be open and flexible and to encourage ambiguity. Leaders on the Path of Courage are in touch with their spirits and are confident in their being; they know that in communication with others and when they are vulnerable to the truth, they find better answers. They are more in touch with the marketplace and the operational environment and can turn any situation into a win. It isn't just in the activities of their lives that self-reliants lose. When we live under the illusion of controlling things, we want to eliminate any conditions leading to loss of control—either for ourselves or for others. When we give up control, situations arise that require us to respond spontaneously and from our spirits. Self-reliants insist on a separation between heart and emotions and the workplace; they usually claim, "It isn't businesslike or professional." They ignore blatant data, such as a tear in someone's eye or a lump in their own throats. Over time they build an impenetrable wall around themselves.

SELF-RELIANCE IS A RUSE

Eventually I discovered that self-reliants are neither self nor reliant: self-reliance is a ruse. Our Self is the essential part of us; it is unique and

---

1. John Maxwell in Glenn Van Ekeren, *Speaker's Sourcebook II: Quotes, Stories, and Anecdotes for Every Occasion* (Englewood Cliffs, NJ: Prentice Hall, 1994).

deeply connected to the spirit. It is that place where we are spontaneous, creative, flexible, open, learning, and confident that we will produce a positive outcome whatever happens. The Self lives on the Path of Courage and is deeply connected with others. It seeks to be in community. The self-reliant strategy is anything but spontaneous, creative, flexible, open, learning, or confident. It is a protective posture, driven by the need for predictability, safety, and control. It is enabled by learned behaviors, mechanical responses, and linear, analytical thinking.

The *self* in self-reliance is more about ego than Self. Ego is the part of us that thinks we can independently make things happen simply by exercising our minds and our will. Ego rejects our spiritual knowing and intuition. Continuous feedback is essential to feed the self-reliant's ego and to provide more information to analyze. Ego-gratifying feedback enables the self-reliant to fine-tune analytical skills and the ability to deliver even more predictably in the future. The ego drives this strategy wherein recognition and approval are critical, and ownership of ideas salves our egos. Our commitment is to our egos, and we focus on how events affect us personally rather than on what is the best for either our own spirits or for the organization.

Tom got feedback about "his" accomplishments which fed his ego and ignored the contributions of many other people. His unconscious way of conspiring always to be needed was to showcase his ability to fix a crisis. His ego never allowed him to ask the critical question, "Why are there always crises?" He chose to ignore the fact that his self-reliance often created or significantly contributed to having a small problem become a crisis in the first place. He also chose to ignore that if he'd involved more people in the process, they could have resolved problems before a crisis could occur.

Ego-driven self-reliance doesn't understand the self's desire to be deeply connected with others and to seek community by sharing feelings, thoughts, experiences, and learning as we work together with shared purpose and meaning. It had been more important to me and to the Toms of the world to get ego strokes than to share connection and community. We keep the secret side of us which dwells on the Path of Fear deep inside. More often than not, we don't even know that side as we autopilot along driven by self-reliance.

The reliant part of the self-reliant strategy doesn't work either. It may have worked once, but in the organizational environment of permanent white water, chaos, and ambiguity, self-reliance isn't at all reliable. In a climate in which conditions change dramatically by the year, month, and even the day, a modus operandi driven by analysis of conditions and data from the past and predictable, mechanical courses of action inevitably limits our responsiveness, our flexibility, our spontaneity, and our creativity while making us less and less available to what wants to happen.

Myra owned a small business with great potential. Any time one of her employees brought forth a new idea for expansion, she'd either agree to look into it or would have a reason why it wouldn't work. Because her self-reliance overloaded her schedule and at the same time required her to personally do a very thorough analysis, by the time she was ready to try something new, another business had often already moved into the market doing the same thing. Still more often, ideas just didn't get investigated and died of neglect along with the morale of the person who had made the suggestion.

This fear-driven disconnect has incredible consequences on us and on others. Our spirits and our emotions don't like being locked up any more than those of others do. If we are unable to *be* ourselves and to *be* with others, if we are unable to let others *be* with us, pressure eventually builds and erupts. We get sick. Tom had stomach problems and headaches. I had digestive tract problems and insomnia. In view of the escalating cost of medical coverage and the need to contain medical expenses, the fallibility of the self-reliant strategy from a dollars-and-cents perspective ought to be apparent.

As I began to reconnect with my spirit in exile, it seemed to me that while I appeared to be self-reliant, I was just the opposite. I was highly dependent upon others, not to take care of me, but to be needed and liked and approved of. Then I knew I was all right. When we live from a spiritually connected place we know we are all right without outside help; our power is spirit generated and comes from within us. No one can make us be all right or not all right. In my self-reliant mode, I gave my power away because I was afraid—that I wouldn't be able to deal confidently and competently with whatever life presented to me for learning. I constantly needed approval from others because I was disconnected from my own internal guidance system, just as I was disconnected from the people about me.

SELF-RELIANTS CAN'T WIN

Although I appeared to be quite successful to the world, my fear of disapproval, of not getting things right, and of appearing incompetent or slow was so great that if even one detail wasn't right or one person disapproved, I screened out all the positive outcomes and focused on how I could prevent the negative one from recurring. I recall having orchestrated a very large, successful, county-wide event for which I took responsibility not only for planning but also for presenting. Both the event and the presentation got rave reviews, but the next morning, instead of nurturing myself with all the positive feedback, I was in my office obsessing on why 10 percent more people showed up than I had planned.

I am reminded of an experiment that I heard about some time ago. In the experiment, newborn kittens were placed in a room in which there were only horizontal planes. After several months, they were introduced into a room that had only vertical planes. The cats, unaccustomed to the vertical objects, treated their existence as meaningless data. They repeatedly walked into the vertical objects, as if they were not there.

It seems to me that self-reliants are much like these cats. We are so accustomed to focusing on the negative, analyzing it, and on planning to prevent anything that may require help from others that we won't allow ourselves to experience the positive events and relationships in our lives. We don't know how to process those data, so we refuse to accept them. These very data allow us to safely interact and collaborate with others.

Self-reliants live in an exhausting, high-stress world. As conditions become more and more complex, the need to continually analyze, predict, and control places increasing demands on the person's ability to determine all the inter-related courses of action. As chaos and ambiguity increase, self-reliants revert to protective rule-making and manipulation; they create a world in which they can "safely" operate. At the same time, they are forced to be isolated from spirit-connected activities that bring purpose, meaning, life, and energy to work. Creativity is stifled by the fear of risk-taking and the need to always produce results that satisfy approval needs—including the need for self-approval.

Over time, the self-reliants' need to control progressively limits their options to the safe but mundane and uninspired. In the late twentieth century, people who consistently produce mundane and uninspired work are placing themselves in an increasingly tenuous position. Self-reliants, whose purpose in adopting the strategy in the first place was to always be able to take care of themselves, create the very situation they want to avoid. As their approach to work becomes more and more antiquated, they become less valuable to their organizations, until they ultimately become a liability.

FINDING A NEW WAY

Some time ago, Tom began to realize something had to change. Although he thought it had served him well most of the time, Tom was ready to admit that his self-reliance was no longer enough. As his company grew, he found it harder and harder to know what was happening. He seemed to be needed everywhere. He discovered that people withheld important information from him because he seemed to know everything that was important. Sometimes they withheld information because they had come to believe their input wasn't important. They also knew that he didn't like to have others discover things he had missed. He got angry when he felt his self-reliance was in jeopardy. Self-reliance was robbing his company of life and energy and had robbed him of any personal life. So he began seeking.

He began to explore quality programs that used teams. Because of his self-reliance, he decided that he didn't need any help making a transition. Tom expected that because he was self-reliant and able to figure things out on his own, his employees should be able to do that as well. Training was inadequate. Several false starts ended in Tom's wresting back control when the going got tough. Tom was teaching the employees that he, not they, was still in the crisis-control position. Since they had come to believe that he would always rescue them, they had no stake in making things run well. Some even thought it made Tom feel good to be able to pull things out in the crunch. Yet Tom just couldn't understand why people weren't motivated to make decisions about their own work.

Finally Tom drew a line in the sand. He was tired of all that responsibility. He was just tired. He had come to realize that not only had he not provided adequate training for the teams, but he had not provided sufficient training for himself either. He also began to realize that his self-reliance was creating his own nightmare. He slowly and painfully began to see how operating from this perspective was leading the company to poor decisions in almost every operational area.

The last straw seemed to come on a day when a group decision-making process ended up lauding Fred for doing something Tom had been ready to fire him for doing. For months we had been encouraging the production team members to consult with their team members, to make sure to involve and communicate with everyone involved, to make decisions on their own, and to demonstrate commitment. When Fred did all of those and made a decision Tom didn't like, Tom was ready to fire him. Dialogue about what had actually occurred and what we wanted to model led him to make a one hundred eighty-degree shift in his thinking. He came to realize that Fred had acted correctly. He also discovered that if he had fired Fred, he would have sent a message to everyone on the production team, "Do what we've been asking you to do, and you'll get hammered. Better take the safe and silent route." It was at that moment that Tom began to understand deeply that depending on himself to do all the thinking simply wasn't working.

PERMANENT WHITE WATER DEMANDS COMMUNITY AND INTERDEPENDENCE

A species of burrowing termite found in South Africa and Australia digs aimlessly in isolation. The moment that a termite bumps up against others of the species, the group begins to create intricate structures, veritable cathedrals, which are the highest structures on earth in proportion to their size. The animals switch from isolation to contact, from self-activity to collective activity, and from ongoing, repetitive activity to learning from one another in order to begin producing meaningful work. The individuals, literally, have no meaning apart from the system.

Self-reliants can carry out individual activity in concert with others, but implicit in the self-reliant strategy is that they never truly become part of the community of collective activity. They never truly commit to being part of the whole. Burrowing aimlessly in isolation becomes more important to the self-reliant than does risking connection with, and implicit vulnerability toward, those in their workplace or any other community, whether of two or two million.

Today's organizations demand connection, community, and commitment. They require us to take risks, to make mistakes, to learn, and to focus on relationships and the community rather than on ourselves. They require us to be self-confident that we can produce positive outcomes, rather than be dependent upon others for approval. They require us to act collectively, spontaneously, and creatively with ever new sets of conditions and information, rather than mechanically and predictably as we have always responded in the past. They require trust: trust in our own ability to respond without analysis paralysis and trust in our community that what we create in connection will be better than what we can create alone. They require us to be completely present, "bumping up against" our co-workers, sharing and enlarging ideas, rather than always standing three steps back and analyzing from the safety of distance and disconnection. They require us to be vulnerable.

Although Tom has been intellectualizing the involvement of others, a lifetime of self-reliance often produces hard-to-break habits. During my period of work with Tom's company, we discovered that the basic assumptions on which his thinking was based were often faulty and caused him to solve a problem that didn't exist while he overlooked the real problem. When a new customer rejected many more products than was usual at Tom's company, Tom assumed that the answer was to increase production time and to pass that additional cost along to the demanding customer. I was skeptical; I know that quality is statistically free. It takes no more time to produce a good product than it does a bad one. Quality products, however, require attention to quality throughout the organization. I encouraged Tom to take this problem to the production team meeting that day.

When Tom presented the problem of increased rejects to the production team, they produced half a dozen other possibilities, including poor-quality packaging materials and poor-quality products that were passed from station to station in the production process. Nobody talked about production time.

Tom was astonished and humbled. He meekly apologized and admitted to the group that although he thought he knew the solution, he obviously didn't even understand the problem. His candor, honesty, and vulnerability encouraged the production workers to be more involved. A few days later shipping clerks, sharing information and learning in community, discovered what they believed to be yet another problem. The way products were positioned in cartons for shipping made them susceptible to damage if the carton happened to be dropped during shipping. When the parts were turned ninety degrees, they were much more resistant to damage.

In Tom's self-reliant days, these important problems wouldn't have been discovered and corrected. Tom would have increased his price, and quality still wouldn't have improved much. Then his customer would have had two reasons to be upset: first, she still had lots of rejects, and second, she was paying more to get the same poor quality! In community with the production team, Tom and his customer were able to avoid this unpleasantness.

SELF-RELIANTS LOSE AT HOME, TOO

I've been battling my self-reliance for several years. From time to time I have come to believe that I'm getting ahead of it when I discover one more area where my self-reliance demon is lurking. I have recognized for a long time that perhaps the most personally damaging manifestation of self-reliance is in close relationships. I continue to amaze myself, however, as I discover more and more examples.

As I attempt to live from my spirit on the Path of Courage, the importance of having intimate relationships where each of us is relating as a real person to another real person increases. I have consciously put away and let slip away superficial relationships. Some people, however, I am unwilling to drop from my life. These relationships provide me with the lessons from "life's school" to keep me working at my spiritual discipline and continuously learning. One of these relationships is with my husband. I used to get angry at his self-reliance in our relationship. In view of my belief that all judgment is based in self-judgment, I decided to do some soul searching. I discovered that he was just mirroring what I'd been doing with him. While I was regularly living on the Path of Courage in most of my life, my relationship with Jim was so important to me that I was returning to the Path of Fear and reverting to my self-reliance with him. I was just too frightened of losing him.

I made decisions about things he should or shouldn't know or would or wouldn't like. Then I either shared or withheld the information, based on what I thought would make him happy. In effect, I made decisions for him and then acted on them without ever including him in the process. I withheld important information about my needs and feelings. Instead of openly sharing my truth, which I feared would create disapproval, I withheld.

Over time, I became resentful when the relationship wasn't fulfilling my needs. I withheld that I needed more alone time; I didn't want him to think I didn't enjoy our time together. I did. I loved our time together, but I needed more alone time for reading, reflection, and meditation. I withheld that I was feeling limited in my work because I had chosen to limit myself to local and regional projects. I knew it was important to him for me to be home. I also wanted to be home, but I wanted to grow in my work.

Now to truly understand the irrationality of the self-reliant process, you must understand that Jim is the most loving, nurturing, and supportive man I know. I cannot imagine how he could have been more encouraging to me in my personal growth and in my experiences of graduate school, starting my business, or writing this book. If I had been rational about it, I would have known that he would want to work with me for our mutual satisfaction and toward our mutual goals.

But the Path of Fear is not rational. Because I was withholding, Jim thought my behavior and feelings were inconsistent and insincere, and they were. Some days I reacted honestly, sharing my true feelings, and other days, my self-reliant controller took over and withheld important but potentially upsetting information. My inconsistency made him afraid of being vulnerable with me; he wasn't sure he could trust me and rightly so. I was withholding important data. My fear of damaging the relationship was leading to self-reliant behavior that damaged the relationship and built barriers when I most wanted intimacy.

Had I acted from my spirit by being vulnerable and openly addressing my concerns, in community we could have explored the truth each of us held. Then by collaborating on a resolution we could have deepened our connection and level of intimacy in the relationship. This healthy, spirit-respecting approach is difficult for the self-reliant: It forces abandonment of agenda control, assumption control, problem-definition, and analysis paralysis. Most important, this approach makes the self-reliant vulnerable to solutions never before tried, for which success cannot be guaranteed. It forces the self-reliant into a stance of risk-taking and learning. It robs the self-reliant of his or her self-reliance. As the nature of relationships, and organizations, shifts, the self-reliant increasingly finds him- or herself using a no-win strategy that is reliable only in creating isolation and eventually separation.

EXPLORING THE TRUTH

Three overlapping spheres, in concert, influence our effectiveness to self-organize in collective communities around a particular task or process. The first sphere is understanding the frame of reference each of us as people, teams, work units, and even whole organizations bring to our work. This frame of reference is influenced by our values, purpose and what brings meaning to life for us. The second sphere is understanding the relationships and linkages of all parts of the system to each other. The third sphere is information. To the extent that we are able to create the conditions that flood our organizations with information, help everyone understand as many of the relationships involved as possible, and keep our options within our respective frames of reference, those within the community inevitably learn how best to configure themselves to the task, process, or problem at hand. In order for this self-organizing activity to emerge, we must ask lots of questions and must question our every act and assumption. We must seek more and more understanding of tasks, processes, inputs, outputs, and relationships, which we have previously taken for granted. We must seek more and more clarity about what is important to us, how we do business, and how we relate to one another personally, as well as how our work relates to that of others.

In organizations and in life, each of us brings a unique perspective, influenced by our personal, educational, and experiential backgrounds and by the role that we play in the system. If we are to generate maximum information and to develop true understanding of the relationships between parts of the system and the frame of reference of the whole and its parts, we must be willing to explore the truth. Each of us has a perception of what the truth is, a perception colored by our unique perspective. Because the truth is always colored by our own personal experiences, it is always partly an illusion, and often we haven't even developed clarity about our illusion.

For our organizations to respond in the best way possible to ever-changing conditions, each of us must be willing to share and explore the truth. To truly explore the truth, we must accept that what each of us knows is only a piece of the truth, and we must be willing to suspend what we believe to be the truth in order to get more dimensions of the truth. When each of us is willing to be vulnerable enough to share what we believe the truth to be, and when we are open enough to accept what others believe to be true as their honest perception of the truth, then we can begin to discover a more complex version of reality.

I often introduce these concepts to groups by comparing the truth-building exercise to the process of printing a colored picture. As a piece of paper moves through different phases of the printing process, it receives one color of ink at a time. First blue, for example, is applied, followed by red, yellow, black, and so on. If we assume that each of us brings one color of ink to the table, then we know it takes all of us to produce a picture that accurately reflects reality.

If we become so attached to our own reality that we are unwilling to see anything but the blue, however, we impede the discovery process. Tom learned this lesson when he allowed more information to flood the production team. Any one of the workers may have been able to point to one problem just as Tom had. In community, each work station brings another perspective, another set of experiences, and another "color" to the discussion; each adds to the complexity of the picture they paint. Finally, a full-color picture of the quality problem emerges; only then are they able to address the complexities of the problem in a way that brings lasting and meaningful change for both them and their customer.

SELF-RELIANCE IMPEDES WORKING IN COMMUNITY

Control is implicit in the self-reliant strategy. Self-reliants often find it difficult to collaborate with others because they only feel confident dealing with "one color" of the truth—the one they know how to control. They argue vehemently that there is only one color and often produce convincing evidence to support their view. The idea of employing inquiry to question what we believe to be true is so foreign to them that even when they enter a formal dialogue process, they find it nearly impossible to sustain an inquiring mind-set. They want to influence discovery, force the process along, and get to an answer so they can begin to figure how to be self-reliant in that new context. Letting go of control is virtually impossible.

To retain control requires us to limit the free flow of information; the self-reliant wants to restrict the options for action to those who we are sure are comfortable. If information moves freely throughout our organizations, others will eventually begin identifying alternative courses of action that are less controllable. The self-reliant strategy prohibits widespread understanding of how the system works as a whole and how activities of each person impact all others within the system; such an approach causes additional possibilities to emerge. Furthermore, real reflection about relationships and linkages within the system may point a finger at self-reliance as an impediment to organizational effectiveness.

Constant questioning and challenging of the way things are done and constant seeking of better understanding of our work and work relationships are required for our organizations to be more responsive. The combination of constant inquiry, coupled with continuously changing conditions in our operational and marketplace environments, creates a tension that requires leaders, wherever they may be in the organization, to invite and sustain confusion and chaos to ensure that the highest level of collective intelligence emerges on any given issue. From a place of self-reliance, which requires controllability, the ability to tolerate confusion, much less intentionally create and sustain it, is unthinkable.

LETTING GO

Several years ago I began sensing that my self-reliant strategy wasn't working. I began to realize that I was capable of accomplishing far more than my self-reliance would allow. I began to feel cramped in the eggshell I'd created as a three-year-old. My life was devoid of creativity, playfulness, spontaneity, faith, and trust. The only purpose in life seemed to be protecting and controlling. Everything I did was superficial, and nothing was really meaningful. Little I did really "made a difference," and when it did, it was only an incremental difference. I realized that my need for self-reliance kept me from being the person I could truly be, kept me from really connecting in relationships that were important to me. I am reminded of the words of John Maxwell:

> "There is no meaning to life except the meaning man gives his life by the unfolding of his powers. To 'maximize our potential,' we must take advantage of the resources available designed to increase our understanding of ourselves, the people around us, and the life we are now involved in. . . . The opportunities life offers help us tap our potential and can be explored when we are equipped with the right tools."[2]

---

2. See note 1 above.

My self-reliance always kept me at arm's length; I was more concerned about approval than about being completely present in the relationship. It stole the present from me as I continually analyzed the past and prepared for the future. It kept me from making myself available for wonderful, spontaneous possibilities as I forced the predictable outcome I could handle. The spiritual part of me, impatient with forty years of exile, became increasingly demanding of attention and space; as I spent time in my spirit, I realized that I hadn't felt truly alive for a long time, if ever. The strategy wasn't a failure just in my personal life. As I read, researched, and learned about what produces effective organizations, it became increasingly clear that self-reliance was a thing of the past. Self-reliance limits our organizational options, and it limits the ability of those around us to grow. Self-reliant behaviors are entrenched in the '50s and '60s management mode, not in the flexibility and resilience demanded of twenty-first century leaders. These behaviors belong to those being downsized out of jobs because of their inability to change.

Tom discovered what I had learned: if I was to work in dynamic organizations, I must choose to lead from my heart, to lead from the Path of Courage. I made the choice. I chose to embrace my fear of the unpredictable and give up my self-reliant strategy. I have chosen to be open to more and more perspectives, even when I must learn things that require me to give up my "safe" position. I chose to let go of control and in its place accept that I am capable of handling whatever presents itself. I have chosen to accept and trust myself, to trust those about me, and to have faith. I have chosen to lead from my heart on the Path of Courage.

TOOLS FOR BEING ON THE PATH OF COURAGE

- We must be all right within ourselves. Dependence upon others for approval disempowers us.
- For us to achieve our personal potential, we must continually push ourselves toward the far edges of our comfort zones.
- When we lead from the heart, we are spontaneous, creative, flexible, and open; we eagerly embrace learning and know that whatever happens produces a positive outcome.
- When we involve others in identifying problems, challenging assumptions, generating possibilities, generating and analyzing data, making decisions and planning strategy, we are able to learn more about what needs to be done than we could learn alone, and we are able to build connection.

- When the only tool we have is a hammer, the whole world looks like a nail. We may have developed blind spots to parts of situations unfamiliar or unpleasant to us. The only way to discover those blind spots is to solicit the perspectives that others hold.
- Like the termites, when we switch from isolation to contact, from self-activity to collective activity, from ongoing, repetitive activity to learning from one another, we begin to produce meaningful work.
- When we make decisions to withhold information about feelings or activities that involve others, we are making decisions for them and acting on those decisions. We rob them of the dignity of having power over their own lives.
- To create the conditions for groups to self-organize to accomplish work in community, we must generate as much information as possible. The information should include as much detail as possible about personal and organizational frames of reference and about both personal relationships and the relationship of different jobs to each other. We do this by creating space for each to share and explore his or her perspective of the truth and to produce collectively a full-color picture that none can produce alone.
- Control is an illusion. Letting go of control is the only sustainable answer.

EXPLORING THE PATH OF COURAGE

(1) Revisit a recent decision you made by consciously challenging your truth. Identify as many assumptions that you made when framing the possibilities as you can. (If you don't list at least ten or twelve, you need to think more.) Now ask yourself for each of them, "What if the opposite were true?" Explore the alternatives you considered in the decision. Ask yourself to come up with two to three times as many possibilities. Then ask yourself what person left out of the decision process may have added another "color" or perspective. Invite the person(s) to help you generate more assumptions and more possibilities. Finally, with all this information before you, ask yourself how your decision-making *process* may have changed. The next time you find yourself slipping into the self-reliant mode, try community instead.

Chapter 10

Being Part of Something Bigger than Ourselves

When we are in our brains and egos, we believe each of us is a discrete entity, separate from others with whom we live and work. When we are in our spirits, we know we are all intricately connected in a web of relationships that makes it impossible for us to take even a single action without affecting the entire connectedness. Our relationships, our families, our companies, our communities, and our world are like a delicately balanced mobile. Touch any part, even slightly, and the whole mobile reacts with movement.

The illusion that management and non-management are separate from each other is a brain-based illusion that keeps us from acknowledging our connectedness. The illusion that our customers, suppliers, and competitors are separate from us is a brain-based illusion that keeps us from acknowledging how many of our own problems we actually create. Believing that "sticking to business" or having a "professional organization" means sticking to tasks and ignoring fraying, splintered, bruised, or neglected relationships is a brain-based illusion that keeps us from acknowledging our connectedness to each other. When we think that we can damage the environment for short-term profits without any long-term costs, we buy an illusion that keeps us from knowing how much it really costs us to make our widgets.

When working in China recently, I was told that the Chinese do not think that Americans are good businesspeople because they don't pay attention to relationships. They tend to be so task- and short-term focused that they want to get right down to business without first building a relationship—the foundation from which to do business. We don't often ask questions about compatibility of interests, values, or philosophy. For most businesses, the only questions that matter are, "Can we make money?" and "Can we get the business?" The result is that we find ourselves in relationships in which our integrity is compromised, our co-workers are damaged, and our products are used for purposes that our values tell us are unethical.

A young businesswoman I know told me a story of an account her company was "courting." The account would be one of her company's largest, and people were going to extremes to accommodate the potential client. The client culture, however, which was rigid, directive, and autocratic, was very different from that of her company, which was participative and nurturing. As a consequence, the way in which each did business was quite different. Even before they were actually clients, executives from the other company were treating employees of my friend's company badly.

Concerned that the work her company would do for the potential client might extract a mental, physical, and emotional price from her co-workers greater than the benefit received from the business, my young friend asked in a staff meeting, "Is this business we *should* be going for?" Because they were focusing only on money issues, most of the room was aghast at the question. No attention was given to how the business relationship was going to work, what the relationship would mean for the people who worked for the vendor and for the culture of the vendor company, in the way of increased absenteeism, turnover, or medical insurance costs.

Our organizations *are* relationships. For better or for worse, we are linked together in dozens of ways. In the past, we have largely ignored the relationships or addressed undeniable frictions on a superficial, cognitive level, with a "No emotion, please. This *is* the office," attitude. Although we have been linked, it has often been an unacknowledged and uncomfortable linkage, which we knew about only because we felt stress on the job, developed ulcers, or occasionally had a fire to extinguish.

Until we are able to consciously acknowledge and address all the relationship issues—personal, professional, and ethical—efforts to build community are strained, organizational effectiveness plummets, and the incidence of stress-related illness and burnout escalates. When we lead from our hearts, we pull our organizations together in a respectful, diverse, but unified community intent upon achieving a common purpose while we nurture ourselves and our many relationships for the long haul. When we lead from spirit, the lines between individuals blur, as do the lines between organizations and even countries. When we lead from spirit, we know that what happens today, this week, and this month integrally affects events next year and ten years from now. When we understand that all things are connected across time and space, we can begin to build community.

CREATING CONNECTION

To build relationships it is important to know what gets in the way of connection. To be connected to others, we must be completely in the relationship: We must bring our true, whole, authentic self, complete with beliefs, values, and emotions, to others with whom we live and work. We risk being vulnerable; instead of mechanically saying, doing, or feeling what we believe we "should" say, do, or feel, we honestly share what we are actually feeling. We risk rejection in order to be accepted for who we *be*, not for what we do or say or for how perfectly we do or say it. We are real people relating to real people, not programmed robots speaking without feeling or spirit.

As I help groups become more aware of the way in which we ask others and ourselves to abandon major parts of ourselves in order to participate in a culture that tries to be strictly cognitive, I initiate dialogue sessions with two sets of revealing questions. Because the emotions carry so much important information, I ask the groups to explore how emotion is treated in their decision-making process.

The First Set of Questions Is:

- How often do we talk about what we are feeling as part of the decision-making process?
- What can we learn by directly addressing these emotions that we can't learn unless they are consciously explored?
- In an environment rich with learning, how would emotions be treated in the decision-making process?

Repeatedly, the dialogues reflect that emotions are rarely, if ever, talked about; when they are, people tend to get impatient with the person who wants to talk about the emotional concern, or they dismiss the concern as unimportant. The groups also discover that emotions give a lot of information about components of a good decision which may have been overlooked; emotions also point toward potential impediments to implementation. When people consciously reflect on the role of emotions, they usually agree that when emotions are expressed, acknowledged, recognized, and honored, they can produce information that can significantly improve the performance of the organization. When we fail to treat emotions as a legitimate source of data, implementation is often fraught with obstacles, including strong reactions from the people who are charged with executing the decision. Often managers appear to be perplexed because people appear to be overreacting. Daniel Goleman, who has spent years researching what he calls our "emotional intelligence," explains: "The thinking brain literally grew out of the emotional brain, making it possible for the emotional brain to hijack the thinking brain during bursts of rage, fear or other emotional alarms."[1]

The second set of instrumental questions, which taps into our deeper needs in our decisions and workplace operations, deals with what we really want. The answers to these questions, whether we verbalize them or not, largely influence the will that people have to carry out the decision once it has been made. These questions are extremely revealing of the extent to which we function without clear intention in both our personal and organization lives. The first question is: How would your decision making differ if you started every conversation that would lead to a decision by first asking, "What do we want from this decision?" I elaborate that "what we want" should include any specific personal or organizational task-related desires but that it should also include any process-related wishes we may have.

Things Groups Usually Discover Include:

- We would know where we are going.
- We'd be more focused.
- There would be more involvement earlier.
- Results would be more useful.
- Less time would be wasted.
- There would be greater buy-in to ensuring the success of the outcome.
- We'd be more focused on our customers and not on what we're trying to do or how we would look.

Perhaps the most revealing outcome of such dialogue is the frequent realization of how intently, even desperately, we can become attached to a specific course of action without even knowing, either personally or collectively, what it is that we want from the outcome. As these

---

1. Daniel Goleman, "The New Thinking on Smarts," adapted from *Emotional Intelligence*, *USA Weekend*, 8–10 September 1995, p. 4.

questions divulge, the level of our individual and collective self-awareness significantly impacts our ability to work together in community toward a shared goal. It is only by being aware about what we want and feel that we can bring those concerns to the decision-making forum in a conscious way that dramatically improves the quality of decisions. Working together collaboratively requires us to be aware of what each participant wants, feels, and thinks so that we can explore that information, discover the critical components for a successful decision, and craft a course of action that addresses these components. Then we are able to work together in community toward those ends.

We come to know that each person in an organization adds richness and dimension and helps deepen our understanding of the truth. We want to make decisions involving as many people as possible, thereby not only getting the most information for the best decision but also building commitment and intention to implementation. The high level of involvement in inclusive organizations implies that processes often move slower in the early stages. There is more questioning of assumptions, data, implications, and commitment. There is more contemplation and reflection, and there is more silence as we consciously deliberate how to best serve our shared purpose and act in concert with our values. We are all connected to the decision, and we are all connected to the outcome.

An executive once told me that she and another manager had undergone the tension of generating more and more information for weeks. It was much different from the way they were accustomed to working. But, she said, the decision they finally made was truly the product of working in community, of building the collective intelligence until they were able to learn a solution that met all perspectives. The resulting decision was much different from what either imagined initially; it was far more creative. Both were excited about the possibilities the decision held, and implementation was moving along quickly; they'd been willing to sustain the ambiguity long enough to come to common ground while the decision was in process.

I don't fully understand the magic of the phenomenon, but knowing who we are individually and being able to express that knowing clearly in "I" statements are integral to leading a group to a way of working and of relating to each other that can only be described as being in community with one another. As members of a group come to know who they are individually and develop enough skill, confidence, and trust to begin speaking for themselves in meetings, the power of being able to create what we want for ourselves both individually and organizationally seems to surface. What seemed impossible when we weren't able to name it suddenly seems not only possible but achievable when we are willing to risk coming to one mind. Once we can name our needs, wants, desires, and hopes, to fail to create them becomes almost unthinkable. The group not only comes to be of one mind but truly owns the power to make change. The power to make change happens one person at a time as each comes to own the power to create a workplace community.

When groups have defined what it means to work together in community, I ask them to identify specific behaviors that are associated with that end. Almost without fail, people share what they think others should do. When my next question is "What are you yourself willing to commit to doing differently to ensure that this relationship occurs?" a shock wave often creates a wake through the room as people shift their thinking from what others should be doing to what they personally are doing. I ask them to create or fail to create what they have said they wanted. I ask them what they will give in order to have what they say they want. When each individual commits to doing what he or she can do individually to make change, change occurs, and it occurs instantaneously.

COMING TO WORK RELATIONSHIPS AS WHOLE BEINGS

If we are to be completely in a relationship, we have to be whole, aware individuals who know what we feel and what we want as well as what we think, and we have to truly want to be in community with others. We have to be full and complete in ourselves. We can't come into the relationship as people who depend upon others to provide approval to make them feel whole. In that case we always focus upon what we can get from the relationship rather than on what we can give. When we focus on the receiving, connection is broken; a neediness about us locks us on the Path of Fear. The focus must be on unconditionally giving to relationships. We must give without the expectation of getting anything back from the relationship. As full human beings, we give simply for the joy of giving from the abundance of our wholeness. Although we cannot give in order to get, what we put out in the world over time is what we get back from it. It does not necessarily come back to us from the person or people that we gave to, but it comes back.

When we come to relationships as whole individuals committed to accepting others in the community for who they are, as they are, we are committing to the relationship rather than to ourselves, without giving up ourselves. We can accept others' feelings and beliefs and know that acceptance doesn't mean agreement. Acceptance means that we respect another's perspective as real to that person without judging that the perspective is good or bad or that the person should or shouldn't feel that way. Because all of our relationships are a reflection of the one we have with ourselves, we must be equally committed to that relationship. When I give up my need for approval from others, I take a giant step toward living on the Path of Courage. If I am full within myself, I can act in integrity with my deeply held beliefs and values, without regard to the popularity of those stands and without regard to what this position may mean for my career. I am open to the beliefs of others and to discovering common ground, but there is a new bottom line. The bottom line is my integrity— acting in accord with what I know is right in my heart.

WHAT WANTS TO HAPPEN

When we work in community, there are times when our spirits insist that we nurture another member of our work or home community. As task-oriented Americans, we are not accustomed to investing this time, although it is an investment that pays dividends. When we force ourselves to stay on task, we not only fail to support the connectedness of the relationships involved, but we dampen our own naturally caring, sharing, accepting, and flexible spirits.

I once visited a staff meeting in which a member of the group came into the room clearly distraught. She had obviously been crying. As the meeting continued, the managers pretended that nothing unusual had occurred; but it was clear from watching that almost every person in the room was concerned about their peer who was in pain. A spirit-connected leader would have recognized that this was not a time to stick to the schedule and the agenda. This was the time to build connection and to nurture one who was in relationship with the rest of the group.

In the early weeks of working on this book, a friend was experiencing a difficult personal time. It had been challenging for me to schedule a few weeks to withdraw from clients, friends, and family so that I could write without distraction. I remember well one particularly agonizing morning. I knew exactly what I wanted to write that day and was eager to get started. At the same time, as I drove into the office, I knew I would pass near her home and wanted to let her know I was concerned about her. The closer I came to the turnoff, the more my dilemma pressed me. I finally decided that the relationship was more important. I didn't stop for long, yet my commitment to the relationship rewarded me all day.

My spirit was lifted by the encouragement I had been able to provide my friend, and my work moved to a different level that day. I wrote faster and more feverishly than ever before, and the words had more meaning to me. A dimension to spirit-respecting leadership that I had previously missed emerged. I learned that when we push ahead with our work agenda without addressing personal needs of those around us, our productivity is reduced. We may go through the motions of doing our job, but either our mind or our emotions or both are distracted and not able to be fully present in the work.

Respect for the deep spiritual needs of others fills us with energy and inspiration to move through our work faster, more creatively, and with a deeper sense of peace than is possible without respecting a spiritual need for connection with others. When I thought I was putting the needs of another before my own, I was wrong. By addressing my spirit's need for connection with others and for giving love, I accomplished more than I could have otherwise.

CLEAN RELATIONSHIPS IMPROVE DECISION MAKING

When we are completely "there" for a co-worker, friend, or loved one, we open ourselves to unplanned gifts of the spirit. They are gifts of connection. I remember one group of managers who were all personally committed to the company's vision but were just not able to accomplish what they wanted without extreme difficulty and stress. When they were finally willing to make the commitment and take the time to clean their relationships of psychological garbage, they began to connect and to work in community with each other.

Now they talk about angers, fears, hurt, and disappointment openly with caring co-workers. They are able to come to interactions with an open mind and a "clean slate," free of judgments colored by past interactions. This connection allows them to analyze all sides of a decision on a completely conscious level, one that is open, caring, supportive, and understanding of everyone on the team. They are now able to move quickly through tasks that had previously been laborious.

Workplace communities are also able to do what Scott Peck has labeled "fighting gracefully."[2] From a place of spirit, where we know we are all connected, there cannot be sides.

What has been labeled conflict is nothing more nor less than different ways of viewing circumstances in a situation. Our family and cultural

---

2. M. Scott Peck, *The Different Drum: Community Making and Peace* (New York: Simon & Schuster, 1987), p. 70.

backgrounds, the amount and kind of education we have, our employment history, major life events, and general worldview (conservative, liberal, pro-business, pro-labor) are among the sources that can color the meaning individuals take from any situation. Because there is so much that our brains routinely filter out, any set of people viewing any incident produces as many versions of what occurred as there are observers. No one perspective is complete or completely accurate or completely inaccurate. Each perspective is different. When we agree to build our collective intelligence by exploring the truth together, what may otherwise be a fight can become an active inquiry into the truth. In times of rapid change, the success we experience in the workplace is largely dependent upon our ability to accept each person's ideas as an important and valid data source. As we add piece upon piece to the picture in community, our differences serve each of us and all of us.

This ability to "fight gracefully" that is such a critical part of working from our spirits is a welcome relief in most workplaces. As a society, we have neither liked conflict nor learned to deal with it gracefully. In most of my client locations, learning how to meet each other respectfully to explore the truth together often generates a backlog of conflict resolution. People who have harbored anger and resentment for years finally have a tool to come together in a way that serves all parties. One small manufacturing site that I taught how to explore the truth together engaged in three such processes in four days after the training session. They addressed issues such as failure to involve all parties in a decision that affected them, passing along poor-quality work, and lagging commitment to the company.

Equally important, closely connected individuals and groups share their hopes and dreams with each other and support people in achieving their dreams without judgment. On a personal level, we offer acceptance, encouragement, support, and enthusiasm. We lend our spiritual support to the person with whom we are connected. In an organization, sharing hopes and dreams often materializes when people feel loved and connected enough to offer an idea that may be judged by some as unrealistic or "giving the shop away." When a group of managers or employees is connected and safe enough with each other to share hopes and dreams, ideas are handled gently and explored with the sense of wonder and risk taking that Bradshaw described as present in our Wonder Child. Sometimes the dreams will be shared, explored, and percolated for years before anything happens to them. Other times, a group discovers many useful ideas that are both realistic and potentially profitable right now.

A manager shared a factory worker's shame and embarrassment when it became apparent that the individual couldn't read. She reflected on how many of life's joys depend on the ability to read: reading a letter from a dear friend or relative, reading to a child, reading an exciting adventure novel. Her connection with that individual gave birth to a dream in which she wished she could wave a magic wand and make sure everyone in her plant could read. The manager's safety and connection with other management team members encouraged her to share her dream. The result was an after-work and lunch-hour reading program. Individuals now learn to read or to improve their reading skills. They have many more opportunities in their personal lives, much higher self-esteem, and increased creativity. They have increased loyalty to the company and are more valuable employees because they can use more sophisticated equipment; more cross-training can occur, and flexibility is greatly enhanced.

It is important to keep relationships clean so as to know how we relate to each other from spirit when things aren't going well. As much as we may wish it, decisions made alone, in small groups, or in community don't always work out perfectly. When we don't get the results we anticipated, working communities avoid blaming by creating a learning laboratory and examining the role everyone played in the decision and implementation. Outcomes that may be different than planned are not judged or treated as failures; they are accepted as gifts of learning. People in the community feel safe about sharing their thoughts, feelings, and perceptions in a non-blaming way and can take risks and initiatives in the future.

Keeping relationships clean builds connection and creates interdependent relationships. We are able to develop healthy attachment and commitment while experiencing freedom to grow and develop in different ways. This environment is love in the purest sense—innocent, childlike love—the kind we knew before we knew we could be hurt.

RELATIONSHIPS FOSTER LEARNING

It is impossible to be in a connected relationship and not be in a state of constant learning and growth. We learn about making commitments and can make mistakes and take risks. We learn to let go of expectations and accept people for who they are, to separate people from what they do or how they do it. We learn what it means to suspend judgment and be open, ready, and receptive to different ideas and ways of doing things; we learn about win-win problem solving and communication. We learn about moving closer and closer to the mark every time we miss it. These lessons are the essence of relationships and community, the substance of healthy organizations, creative organizations, quality organizations, and spirit-respecting organizations. When we are willing to practice conscious and connected relationships with everyone around us, it becomes easier and easier to turn off our automatic reflex of fear, protection, and self-reliance.

We can most certainly go through the motions without experiencing connection. But it is my belief that growing requires making ourselves vulnerable in a committed and connected way. Behavior that is learned builds walls to separate us and to impede working together in a spirited way. Once we develop the ability to relate to people on an authentic level, we never again relate to other human beings in the same way. That thought frightens most of us. It has been easier to be distant than to choose to be fully present and responsible in our relationships. It has been easier to go through the motions of superficiality than to take time and courage to share our hearts and those of others and to learn and grow together. We bring a whole new perspective to accepting mistakes, providing safety, guiding learning, facilitating problem solving, seeking communication, and understanding continuous improvement when we are willing to connect with others. When we are open to receive connection, we are not only touched and changed forever but find more and more connections coming our way.

DISCOVERING COMMUNITY BEYOND THE WORKPLACE

When we connect deeply with a person or two or three on a personal level, our lives are changed forever. When I first experienced deep connectedness, it made me keenly aware of how superficial and empty most of my relationships were. I no longer wanted to live in a superficial world. I wanted deep, intimate relationships, which differed from my old ways. When we commit to creating meaningful relationships and to the learning that those relationships require, we commit to discovery of the self that we bring to it.

As I changed the way I was in relationships, something interesting happened. The connection I created wasn't just a connection to another person. I connected with that spiritual part each of us has that is part of something larger than any of us. From that place, we come to know that every time we act, others are affected. We discover we are not islands but parts of a system. When we act, the system changes. By changing how we are willing to be in relationship, we make space for dynamic change to occur. When we begin to discover exactly what it means to be in community with others, it changes our thinking. When we share a commitment to community, we want to share decision making because we know each of us will be affected. Every time we have the courage to say what we feel and discover that everyone feels the same but is afraid to say it, we enable actions to be taken out of values as well as intellect. Every time we have the courage to say what we feel individually, we serve the values of our community. We are able to create what we want the relationship to be. It takes time, but time working on a relationship is meaningful, valued time. When we work in community, we don't spend time; we invest it. We support each other, we trust, we have faith. The sense of community grows. People are energized and committed to what we are consciously creating. Work becomes a joyful part of life, not something we do while we wait to live. Work is an indispensable component of life.

The sense of community grows. It grows beyond our one-on-one relationships and beyond work. It grows to our churches, clubs, towns, and states. It grows to the nation and to the world. The spirit of each of us helps us to see the world as we would like it to be, and we know that each one of us makes a difference. We share a vision of what might be. We know it takes time, and we commit the time. Each of us becomes a custodian for the care and maintenance of the our community at whatever level. We experience a sense of connection with generations past and future and by our belief and commitment to community, we are able to make a difference for generations to come.

KEEPING THE HOUSE CLEAN

When we choose to live and work in community, we also choose to live and work consciously, intentionally, and accountably in the present. Each of us assumes responsibility for creating the space within ourselves and around us which is clean of old relationship clutter. We are not doing spring housecleaning once a year and letting things pile up again the minute we finish. Keeping our personal house clean means that we address differences and disagreements when they occur, so they don't pile up and generate resentment and bitterness. We speak for ourselves truthfully in the present about what we think, feel, or want right now.

Our roles as leaders are both to create an environment in which good emotional housekeeping practices are the norm and to model that behavior in all that we do. If we feel safe to keep our relationships clean, others feel safe to do the same. If we live with a lot of old emotional junk, we find others doing the same.

Housecleaning means staying current with problem-solving. Some time ago, I heard the former Secretary of Labor Ray Marshall speak on the operating rules established for a bipartisan commission he had co-chaired. An agreement that helped define the character of the committee's work was "No glory-grabbing and no blame-casting." I was so impressed with the eloquent simplicity of this agreement that I have incorporated it into all conflict resolution that I do. It has certainly been a good ground rule for keeping my house clean. If we don't look for someone to blame, and we are not making someone else look inept by grabbing glory for what we have done, then those around us do not have to be defensive about what they do.

Blame-casting, glory-grabbing, and defensiveness are not spirit based. They are not respectful, trusting, or accepting. They are not based upon faith, do not encourage risk-taking, and do not build safety for growth. When we stay in our spirits, we create a safe environment for productive problem-solving. We allow ourselves and others to let go of resentment, guilt, shame, worry, confusion, and cynicism. When we don't deal with problems as they arise, resentment, guilt, shame, worry, hope, confusion, and cynicism build up around us. They are the stuff that we must worry about falling on us when we are not looking.

Barry Keesan, founder and former CEO of the largest publisher of educational computer materials in the United States, says that when he owned the publishing company, it had two purposes: to create happiness in work and to create community. People in the company were valued for their unique contributions. The organization lived two precepts about speech to help accomplish its purposes:

(1) Don't speak of the misdeeds of others. Take your concerns directly to the individual involved.
(2) Do not praise yourself or put others down.

Keesan, who has had an active Zen practice for twenty years, says these simple rules helped his small company grow to be the biggest and best in the industry before he sold it. "Competitors just fell by the wayside."[3]

UNHEALTHY CONFLICT CLUTTERS THE HOUSE

Confronting problems when they occur, many conflicts are prevented. We don't have to jockey for position or try to look good. We don't harbor resentments driving us to get even. We don't have to get locked into one outcome—the one we can control. We can be open and flexible. We are able to see, respect, and explore other possibilities. Conflicts occur in any environment; in fact, conflict can and should be an important part of a

3. Barry Keesan. Conversation with author. Transforming the Soul of Business conference, Hilton Head, South Carolina, February 1995.

healthy decision-making process. Without it, groupthink will seize our thinking processes. When our houses are clean of negativity, we can use differences to help us discover new perspectives. We can focus on current differences of opinion.

I have frequently encountered co-workers who carry around a Pandora's box of old arguments with each other; they know only that they are angry but don't really know why they are angry at the moment. The history of their relationships is such that there is very little cooperation and a high degree of competition. Every encounter quickly becomes a win-lose situation, and each party is determined to win this round. People have become incapable of collaborative decision-making that benefits both parties and the organization. This situation is not breeding ground for a workplace community.

Timely, caring, and *complete* conflict resolution are critical to building community in our organizations. Before I arrive at a client location, conflicts have been handled commonly in one of three ways. The first is what I call the "knock-heads-together" approach. This approach to conflict resolution involves a boss who calls both parties into the office and tells them they have to get along. "Or else" is usually added but rarely defined. The boss is apparently under the illusion that, by sheer will and fear, the conflict will vanish. It doesn't; it may go undercover for a while until a "stimulus event" brings it back to the surface.

Sometimes the conflict turns into a guerrilla war in which the parties quietly undermine each other and throw jabs back and forth. Parties to a guerrilla war are quick to play the blame-casting–glory-grabbing game. The only teamwork possible is among the groups of co-workers who gather forces behind their respective favorites in this internal warfare. The focus of the teamwork becomes war, not the enterprise. This approach is clearly not respecting of the human spirit. It isn't caring, trusting, open, accepting, or connecting. It is driven by nonspiritual qualities: fear, defensiveness, blaming, guilt, shame, resentment, resignation, and even cynicism.

The second approach I frequently encounter is the "separate-quarters" conflict resolution. The boss who chooses this approach recognizes that issues must be resolved for conflict to really be resolved; he or she is more insightful although not truly enlightened. The boss meets separately with each party and tries to uncover the issues. Trying to play the combined role of the perfect communicator and the judge with the wisdom of Solomon, the boss explains to each party the other's issue and gives a proposed solution to the problem.

Communication isn't simple. Anyone who has ever played the party game "Gossip" (sometimes called "Telephone") knows that the story changes with each telling. To complicate the "separate-quarters" resolution strategy, the adversaries aren't even in the same room and can't clarify details such as when, where, why, how, with whom. It usually takes a significant number of exchanges between the parties to get agreement on issues, even when they are face to face. The longer the conflict has been brewing, the longer it takes to get agreement on what the issues are. Anything less than face-to-face discussion simply bandages a symptom; it does not discover and resolve the source problem. The surface wound may mend itself, but the infection boiling away under the surface rages on, often undetected for days or weeks.

In the "separate quarters" approach, the boss is more insightful, but the strategy is still driven by fear: fear that the conflict will escalate; fear that the boss will lose control of the situation; fear of emotion that may surface; fear that the boss won't get it perfectly. Negative judgments and self-judgment are involved. There is a lack of respect, trust, openness, acceptance, and connection by the boss with the parties to the conflict. There is no safety in growth for the manager or the parties. There is no positive belief in humanity.

The third approach is the "ostrich" approach. As implied by the name, this approach involves a boss who believes that if a conflict is ignored it will simply go away. The outcome of this approach resembles the guerrilla warfare approach. Without attention, the conflict continues and usually escalates. Everybody except the boss knows it is going on. (Often the boss knows, too, but prefers to feign ignorance.) An incredible amount of time, money, and energy are wasted to keep the conflict from erupting into full war. Sometimes whole systems and processes are built around the conflict. I have seen convoluted reporting systems develop simply because, as one owner put it, "Some people just do not report to certain other people." The structure makes absolutely no sense and leads to decision making with limited information. Again, this approach doesn't respect or believe in the people involved.

BUILDING SUPPORTIVE RELATIONSHIPS THROUGH CONFLICT RESOLUTION

When we don't address and resolve conflict in a healthy way that respects everyone involved, misplaced anger almost always results. As human beings, when we keep suppressing the emotions around unresolved conflict, pressure builds; over time we become more and more volatile. Eventually a mere spark in the neighborhood of our resentment can set off a raging fire of anger. In retrospect we may even acknowledge that we overreacted, but the problem is that we are not expressing anger about what actually angers us. We are angry about months and years of a bad relationship, a relationship rich in win-lose and one we don't want to lose.

When we want truly to resolve conflicts so that relationships improve and people work together in a mutually spirit-respecting way, we must operate from our spirits. In the workplace community this way of working means:

- We believe in the people involved.
- We believe in ourselves.
- We respect and trust the parties.
- We accept the parties and their perspectives and are open to airing all issues.
- We are patient and know that a conflict that has been costing the organization thousands of dollars in lost time isn't going to be resolved in fifteen minutes or even an hour.

When we as mediators cannot bring these positive beliefs to the conflict resolution arena, we are not able to resolve the conflict in a meaningful way.

It is not uncommon for a conflict that I am helping to resolve to have been brewing for several years. It is also not uncommon for such a conflict to take a full day to resolve. It takes time to separate the issues from the people involved, time to lead the parties through a process by which they begin to focus not on each other but on themselves and their own role in creating and sustaining the conflict. It takes time for them to learn to listen completely to both verbal and nonverbal messages. It takes time to peel away the layers and layers of emotion that have coalesced around the relationship. The parties have to unlearn what they believed about each other before they can begin to build a positive, supportive relationship. I settle for nothing less. Sometimes it takes sheer exhaustion before people are willing to challenge their old beliefs about each other.

Resolving conflict takes courage. It takes heart courage, time, patience, and love. It takes belief in people. When we have the courage to invest the time, patience, and love to establish respectful ground rules and then patiently guide and support each party in the painstaking work of pulling out each and every tangled coat hanger and cleaning it off, we learn and grow. The parties learn and grow. The house is clean in a way that it has never been. The organization begins working together in a way that it never has. Such work is the most rewarding of occupations; it is nothing short of inspiring. To begin with parties who look and act like vast icebergs and to watch my respect, acceptance, patience, and love help melt the layers of ice away warms my heart. To see parties who hated each other a few hours earlier leave my office talking about having lunch together makes my spirit soar. When we lead from the heart, it is possible to keep our houses clean. With a clean house, it is easier for us to sustain a workplace community.

CONNECTION, FAITH, AND TRUST WITHIN ORGANIZATIONS

Before we are connected and before we know what community really means, it is easy to see ourselves as individuals or islands in our workplaces. It is easy to see ourselves struggling for survival against everyone else in a never-ending, win-lose struggle. It is even easier to see ourselves as part of a faction struggling for survival against other factions in a never-ending, win-lose struggle. When we are connected we are able to see that win-lose is impossible. Only through trust, faith, cooperation, and community are we able to see that we must all win for any of us to truly win. Community helps us understand that no one in our connection can lose without all of us losing something.

Connection makes the difference. When we are connected with spirit, we are not pulled down by the past. We know that most negative thoughts come from focusing on the past. We are not crippled by the benefits coming to each of us today, tomorrow, or next week. We are not crippled by the benefits coming to our group today, tomorrow, or next week. We are committed to the community, be it the community of the relationship, the community of our organizations, or the community of the world.

Accepting the accountability that comes with being in community, we shift the way we think and work. We become tribal elders committed to our custodial responsibilities, and we must trade short-term thinking for the long view. We look to the common good and bring inspiration to future generations. We are no longer crippled by deadlines contrived to keep us from really examining the issues. We are no longer limited by what we believe must be accomplished before the next quarter ends or the next congressional or presidential elections occur; these artificial deadlines are contrived to prevent us from working from a place of community in our decision-making. We are flexible, open, and connected. We are community. We are today. We are the future.

TOOLS FOR BEING ON THE PATH OF COURAGE

- We are all part of a seamless whole. It is not possible to harm another person, organization, or thing, including the environment, without eventually bringing harm to ourselves.
- Working from a place of shared purpose and values which guides

our actions, we can create workplace communities that sustain us personally and propel us organizationally.

- Community is enhanced by including more people in decision-making and planning. When we slow our processes and encourage silence and reflection, we build an environment for community and connection to emerge.
- Commitment and intentionality are increased by a sense of community.
- Community and connection are enhanced when we are authentic people dealing with other authentic people. We openly share our feelings, beliefs, concerns, hopes, and dreams. We freely accept the perceptions of others without necessarily agreeing with them. We simply acknowledge their beliefs, feelings, and experiences as their own.
- When we feel a sense of community, we explore differences openly in an accepting and respectful way, not with the desire to change people but with the spirit of learning a new perception of reality.

EXPLORING THE PATH OF COURAGE

(1) Take a few minutes to examine your work relationships thoughtfully. Consider how you treat co-workers compared to how you treat your best friend or your children. Do your work relationships reflect the values you espouse to your children, your family, your friends? Can you identify situations in which you followed a "business code of conduct" rather than your personal values? How did you feel? How might the outcomes have differed if you had followed your personal code of conduct? How often do you find yourself separating from your personal values at work? How does that separation interfere with your working in community with others?

(2) Identify times in which you didn't let your judgment, self-judgment, lack of trust, or thinking about the past and future get in the way of responding. How did you feel about what you shared? How did you help to create a connection that might otherwise have been impeded? How much about what you really feel, believe, or value did you hold back? Did you find yourself feeling hurt, resentful, frustrated, or irritated because the parts of you that you were unwilling to share were not considered?

(3) Identify old relationships that are "dirtying your house": the things that can keep you from being flexible. These things may be old resentments, unresolved conflicts, difficulty letting go of the past or of projects or of both, or other relationship impediments that may keep you from making decisions consciously and openly, decisions based on current and pertinent data. Then identify all of the emotions you can connect with each of these: fear, anger, sadness, disappointment, envy, jealousy, disillusionment. Identify the assumptions colored by these impediments and emotions which you bring to decision making. Now assume the opposite of each of these assumptions is true. How may these impediments create problems for your organization?

(4) What things do you allow to get in the way of creating connection and community? How may your organization be improved by a strong sense of community within it and with the world at large?

(5) How are conflicts resolved in your organization? Identify as many unresolved conflicts as you can, and identify the organizational dysfunctions that have resulted: unusual reporting relationships, guerrilla wars, divisiveness, lack of teamwork. What significant gains can your organization experience if all of these conflicts are resolved?

Chapter 11

Being Present

Sitting across the desk from Ellen, Annette tries to explain her idea for expanding their business. During their talk Ellen has taken three phone calls and frequently glances at the computer's screen on her desk and at her watch. Once she jots a note on a lined pad in front of her. Finally Ellen says she'll think about Annette's idea when she's doing action plans for next year's budget. Ellen is not present with Annette, and she is not in the present. Her mind is on her computer project and her phone calls. She is closing her option to be in the present by operating in the past and future.

When we are present, we are aware and in touch with what is happening at this moment. We are totally conscious and in present time—being where we are and when we are there. When we are concerned about what happens or what happened a week ago or ten years ago, we miss the present. When we drift into the future, we also lose it. We find ourselves worrying about things that have not yet occurred and may never occur, or we find ourselves worrying about things that have already happened and about which we can do nothing. When, like Ellen, we are not present in this moment, we sacrifice the only time about which we can do anything—the only time when we can enact change, the present—to time about which we can do nothing.

CONNECTION REQUIRES BEING PRESENT

When we are not present and when we are not aware, we also lose connection. When we think about something we are going to do or something we should have done differently, we rob our relationships of the connection that allows us to build trust, faith, cooperation, connection, and community. I have had occasion to hear several employees of a friend of mine talk about her leadership. One secretary in her large department describes how different his relationship has been since working with Donna. When he walks into Donna's office to say anything to her—anything, regardless of how inconsequential it may seem to others—Donna focuses completely on him. "It is as if she has nothing else to be concerned about except what I have to say." He says he feels so important that he wants to do anything and everything he can to help their department be the best. Others who work for Donna tell similar stories.

When I talk with Donna, my experience parallels their stories. Although I know she has lots of responsibilities, I feel as if whatever I am speaking about with her is the most important thing in the world to her in that moment. Whatever the topic, this is where Donna can make a difference at this moment, where she can create connection and community. This is where Donna can begin to change the world to be what she wants it to be.

As Donna's secretary and many others can attest, Donna is the exception; she has created connection and community that have unleashed unparalleled synergy in the department since she became the leader. Managers who overlook the importance of being completely present and focusing on whom they are with and what they are doing clearly underestimate the importance of "being present" for accomplishing results. I can remember a time when, as head of a department reporting directly to the president of the company, I found it difficult to grab a few minutes to talk with him about important policy considerations. The consequence was that I didn't feel very important; as the principal officer representing the people in our company, I felt that people weren't very important to our enterprise.

WHEN THE PAST OR THE FUTURE GETS IN THE WAY

When we are not present and aware, we lose. We lose our humanity, and we lose touch with our spirits. Thinking about the past or the future gets in the way; worry and hope about our own thinking (self-judgment) and other people's thinking (judgment) steal the present from us. Thinking about the past or the future keeps us from responding as our hearts and spirits dictate. It robs us of our spontaneity and steals our ability to play with new ideas and new ways of doing things. Thinking about the past pillages our creativity. We can become the victims of little voices inside our heads. "That's not an appropriate way for someone your age to act!" "That's childish!" "When you trusted before, you got hurt." "You can't suggest *that*! They'll laugh you out of the department!" Indignant, right-eous voices chatter away in the background of our consciousness; they pull us away from current time into situations in the past or push us into planning avoidance activities or excuses for the future.

Some time ago, I had the good fortune to attend a conference with a physicist from a major U.S. corporation. He said that some of the most important discoveries have been made when he and others were totally present and just playing around with an idea, not really thinking about it. Later he said that people often ask, "Whatever made you think about putting those two things together?" His answer: He didn't think about putting them together. Had he thought on the basis of knowledge acquired in the past, he would never have put those things together. Being in the present allowed him to tap his playfulness, creativity, and intuition and make a discovery that he would never have made if he had stifled his hunch with thoughts about what he knew to be true.

As I was meditating about writing this passage, I recalled some times in my life when I was wise enough not to think and instead chose to be completely present and to respond to the feelings of the moment. Several different yet similar incidents jumped out of the caverns of my memory. The incidents differed in that the events themselves, their locations, and the people involved differed. They were similar in that in each case I responded in a way I would not have done had I thought about it, and because I was completely present, my lack of concern for the future and my display of humanity endeared me to the people involved. These incidents all created a human connection that a thinking response would never have produced.

DOING WHAT I *SHOULDN'T* DO

I recalled a time when I was fairly young, new to a job, and not well acquainted with other managers. Eric[1] was a man of considerable power and prestige in both the company and the community. I was familiar with his distinguished reputation long before I thought about working for the company. Although I didn't know Eric well, he had always impressed me as being pleasant but reserved. As he walked by my office, I noticed he was looking glum, which was not at all his normal demeanor. I remarked that he looked as if he were having a bad day. He stepped into my office, and tears welled into his eyes. "Betty just had cancer surgery and has only three to six months to live!" he said about his wife of thirty years. If I had

---

1. All proper names are fictional unless permission was obtained before publication. The exceptions are Eric and Betty, both of whom are now deceased.

thought about it, I would have given a consoling response and probably would have offered words of encouragement and hope. I didn't think about it. I put my arm around him and cried with him.

When my voices got hold of me later, they reminded me, "Upwardly mobile women managers *do not* cry at the office." "It is not appropriate to touch co-workers, especially male ones." "Who are *you* to act so familiarly with a man of Eric's stature? You hardly know him!" I was glad I put my arm around him. I was glad I cried. As I sit at my computer twenty years later with tears in my eyes, I am still glad I cried. I would not change anything about that moment. My brain would have told me it was exactly the wrong thing to do. I didn't listen to my brain. I was present and aware. I listened to my heart. I was human and connected. It was the most spiritual of moments. It was loving, caring, sharing, giving, respectful, intuitive, and in complete integrity with the person I am. Thinking about what I had learned in the past or about the impact on my future would have killed the moment.

SAYING WHAT I *SHOULDN'T* SAY

Some years later, I had a different and (eventually) hilarious experience. After several years of working hard and paying my dues in a way that only people in their twenties have the energy or foolishness to do, I finally had the opportunity to visit corporate headquarters. Two or three days into my visit, I was invited to join a vice president and a group of five or six people for dinner. We drove several miles out into the country where an old farmhouse had been turned into a wonderful restaurant.

Although I had met the vice president several times before, this was the first time I was able to "impress" him on a social level (again, as only someone in her or his twenties cares about doing). Fortunately, I hadn't grown up in the sticks and knew the social niceties. The evening was going swimmingly, and I was impressing myself with my wit and charm. As we relaxed a bit after dinner over coffee, a rather large cat suddenly sprang out of nowhere into my lap. I was so shocked that I didn't have time to think. I let out a four-letter word that "ladies" aren't supposed to use. No sooner had I spoken than horror and chagrin were apparently painted all over my face. (My voices were quick to inform me, "Well, that's the end of your future with *this* company!") The rest of the table roared with laughter.

The vice president, in a stroke of graciousness I have rarely witnessed, leaned toward me and said, "My wife and I were here with my mother-in-law last week. The same thing happened to her. She said the same thing!" It seems that the owner's cat had the habit of slipping into the dining room and inviting himself to share coffee with the guests. I have no idea whether the same thing really happened with his mother-in-law or not, but I do know that my spontaneous response and sincere humanity were endearing to him and to the other people in a way that my polite, witty conversation was not. Although this experience was very different from the moment I shared with Eric, both were spiritual moments, spontaneous, intuitive, trusting, risk-taking, and unique. I created a new and empowering experience for myself. I made connection with members of the dinner party on a human level.

RESPONDING WITH CARING IN THE MOMENT

A few years ago a friend who had been having a difficult time called me. She was depressed and in distress and had clearly been crying. "Can I come live with you for awhile?" "Of course!" I responded. "I'll be right over to help you with your things." I hung up the phone and told my husband that Debbie was coming to live with us for awhile. I didn't think about it. I didn't say I'd talk it over with my husband and call back, as would normally have been my pattern. I didn't worry about our very small house with little closet space and one bathroom; I didn't think about our privacy. I just responded from my heart and spirit. It was a spiritual moment, a time of connection, loving, abundance, intuition, trusting, sharing, flexibility, and openness.

The three incidents are different and similar. When I don't think about it and act from my heart and spirit, I do the right thing. My best problem-solving happens when I am not thinking, when I am relaxed, at peace, in the moment, and present to spirit. So often at work we fall into left-brain, rational analysis which takes us from the inner wisdom and the spirit of the present. It is ego and fear-driven reactivity to avoid mistakes of the past or fear that we won't do it as well in the future. When we are in the present and in touch with our hearts and spirits, as I was in each of these cases, they will lead us to act with the intention and in accord with both our humanity and our values.

BEING FULLY PRESENT IN THE PRESENT

Millions of hours are wasted each year in our organizations on CYA[2] memos that rehash how we handled the past or aim to control the future.

---

2. CYA refers to "cover your ass" activities typical of many organizations. These behaviors include justification, explanation, rationalization, and other self-protective activities that often occur in organizations when people believe heads will roll because of their mistakes.

Yet people regularly relate how their best management performances come when they are focused on being completely present in the present. When leaders have self-trust and faith in their ability to handle whatever develops, somehow the answer they need just emerges. One human resources professional whom I know spends a great deal of time negotiating with unions and resolving conflicts in her organization. She relates that her best work happens when she is present, flexible, and able to respond to whatever happens. "When I am totally present and I trust and have faith that what I need will be there, . . . it just comes."

As a less confident facilitator, I used to plan exactly how I wanted events in a training or retreat to go. I knew exactly what we needed to accomplish, and I was intent on making it happen. Often at the end of a day or several days spent working with a group, I would reflect on the session and regret that I had missed learning opportunities that I hadn't planned for but that were obviously needed. I had missed these learning opportunities because I was so intent on creating what I had decided on in advance.

As I became more confident of my ability to handle whatever emerged, I began to let go of my need to control the outcomes and made myself available for what wanted to happen. The results were amazing. I spent much less time preparing and produced far better results. I provided groups with the learning required as their needs emerged. The first time I left a three-day retreat during which we'd accomplished very little of what I'd expected to accomplish, I was exhilarated by the important work that had been done—work I had a hunch was needed but for which I had no tangible evidence of a need. It was work that laid the groundwork for the changes I knew the company needed to achieve its potential. When I had been intent upon controlling outcomes, groups often moved on to secondary work before the primary work was done. As a result the secondary work became far more tedious and far less effective.

Spontaneity is essential in responding to the constantly changing business environment, and true spontaneity is possible only in the present. I am not talking about knee-jerk reactivity but spontaneous responses that are within the organization's vision, values, and guiding principles and that look for the positive possibilities in each event. A woman told me a story about a time when she was walking on some slippery rocks along the Baltic, misstepped, and slid into the water. "The only reasonable thing to do was take off my clothes and go for a swim. So I did!" Organizations "misstep and slide into the water" frequently, but instead of figuring out the best thing to do, they obsess about trying to create the end they had predetermined "should" happen.

The spontaneity and zest of living that my friend displayed is critically missing from our organizations today. As a consequence millions of hours are wasted each year hashing and rehashing, getting additional data, charting statistics, and gathering additional opinions to ensure that decisions are totally rational. Analysis paralysis—planning for tomorrow based on conditions of today or of the past—is rampant. It is impossible to know what conditions tomorrow brings before tomorrow arrives. Yet despite the obsession with the quantifiable, more often than most managers care to admit, the decision boils down to a coin toss or a "going with the gut." The story of the Sony founder (described in Chapter 8), who turned to his heart for decisions, attests that being present to our heart's knowing can be a successful strategy.

I am not saying that rational data are unimportant or that we don't need information to make a decision. I am saying that most organizations spend too much time making decisions, especially decisions about people, based on rational data and analysis. Too much time is spent discussing what we believe is true, on the basis of the past or the data, or both. Too little time is invested in questioning what we do, how we do it, and how it relates to other activities, people, or units. Thinking about the past and the future can get in the way of the best decisions.

Often a spur-of-the-moment gut reaction decision is a literal "godsend." When we trust our intuitions, an essential part of our spirits, they rarely lead us astray. Einstein supposedly once asked, "Why is it I get my best ideas when I'm shaving?" Not unlike Einstein, when we concentrate on something too intently, our thinking gets in the way of our best decision-making. Our spirits know what we do not know—what we cannot know.

PRACTICING BEING PRESENT

For most of us, going mindlessly through the day on autopilot is so habitual that it takes lots of practice to start being truly present. One of the gifts of my physical rehabilitation was learning how to be completely focused on a particular set of movements for a sustained period of time as I learned to move and even breathe differently. I continue the process periodically to assist me in my commitment to becoming more conscious and focused. I believe that anyone can benefit from doing such an exercise (without having to endure the pain!).

Try walking, running, swimming, bicycling, or any physical activity done alone without the distraction of television or music, in a totally conscious and present way. Select one set of movements and for thirty minutes focus completely on that set of movements. For instance, if you choose walking, you may want to focus on how you extend your right leg or the roll of your left foot on the pavement. Be totally focused on that single movement. Notice which muscles you use. Notice how the movement changes when you go up or down a hill. Be aware of either the tiring or the muscles or the strength muscles must possess to maintain their activity for a long time.

The most important part of this exercise is to be aware of how your mind wants to drift, and every time it does, consciously bring it back to the focus point. During the thirty-minute time period, notice how often your mind wants to drift and what it wants to drift toward. When you are finished, take a few minutes to make some notes for yourself about how much of the thirty minutes you were really focused on that one movement. Also make note of what drew you away from your focused consciousness. Was it a barking dog, the ice-cream wagon, a crying baby, a runner or cyclist who passed you, or distraction caused by thoughts of the day you have finished or the one that lies ahead? When you carry out this activity several times a week, you should begin noticing that you become better at focusing on the selected movement; you may want to change the object of focus just for variety.

Another way to practice being present is to focus on transforming a "mindless task" or one that you may dislike into a joyful event. As your mind drifts off to other places, bring it back to the activity. For me, cleaning the bathroom, folding the laundry, and washing the car are good activities for this exercise in increased consciousness. I try to focus on every movement of the activity. How does the sponge feel in my hand? Am I relaxed or is there tension in my movement? Does the clean spot shine noticeably more than the place I haven't got to yet? In order to transform the event into a joyful one, I remind myself how wonderful it will be to take a bath in a sparkling tub, or how much I will appreciate the clean mirror. I seek to be hyperconnected to the activity. When you try this, make some notes that are similar to those at the end of the previous activity. Notice where your mind goes and how often you must pull it back. Are the things that distract you from these activities the same ones that keep you from being fully present with people in work situations?

Another way to practice being present is to sit and repeat a single positive phrase to yourself for twenty to thirty minutes. You may choose, "I am at peace in the world," or "I am committed to leading from the heart," and repeat it over and over. How often does your mind drift from the phrase? How often do you stop completely? Are you completely present to saying the phrase, or does your internal chatterbox or voice of judgment provide a continuous monologue?

Each of these activities can help us become better at being focused and conscious. As we get better, we can begin to shift to being more conscious at work. We start to notice how often the mind drifts off when we talk to someone, and then we notice where attention goes when it does. Are we crafting a response before we have really heard and understood the other person? Do we assume that we know what the person is talking about even before asking clarifying questions? When we start being aware of the drifting, we bring it back. We become aware of the need to ask questions whenever we find ourselves ready to respond without more interaction. We start becoming aware of when we have negative thoughts or judgments.

Exercises in learning to be present can speed our ability to break the autopilot diffusion of attention and are essential to learning to be on the Path of Courage. It is only when we are able to be focused and in the present that we can begin to lead from a position of preparing in the present to respond in the future, rather than being locked.

STOP *PLANNING*

When we plan for the future, we try to project what conditions will be and determine in advance how to act to achieve a future goal that we established some time in the past. When we prepare in the present to respond in the future, we focus on our vision and values and on learning. We focus on identifying a key set of questions that tell us if we are on track. Our vision defines for us what we want to be: the most innovative widget maker in the Northwest, for instance. Our values define how we want to do that:

- By being responsive to customers' needs
- By being empathetic and supportive of our co-workers
- By working as a team
- By continuous group learning and creativity
- By being open, honest, and trusting of our team members, customers, co-workers, suppliers and others with whom we do business

The key questions that may be asked of every decision include:

- Does this decision support our vision of becoming the most innovative widget maker in the Northwest?
- Has everyone involved in the implementation of this decision been involved in this decision?
- What are the assumptions on which this decision is based? Are they accurate?
- What if we were to challenge those assumptions by asking, "What if the opposite were true?" Would a different decision result?

- Does this decision provide the best service for our customers in the long term?
- Does it address immediate concerns and needs?
- Is there a more innovative approach?
- Does this solution reflect our values in the treatment of all concerned?
- Does this decision support teamwork in the future?

When we plan in the present to respond in the future, we are able to let our goals become symbolic. When goals become too rigid, they may limit our achievements or take us in a no longer appropriate direction relative to new data that may have been impossible to project. A mechanical calculator company that refused to respond to the introduction of electronic calculators provides an example of the way inflexible goals can bring a company down. The company refused to accept the fact that its goal of making the best mechanical calculator on the market would not be competitive when other organizations introduced new technology. The Swiss watch industry is another example of inability to flex with current market data, like the introduction of the digital watch.

In contrast, for a time the California raisin industry made more money selling merchandise decorated with pictures of the animated California Raisins than they did selling raisins. I'm sure that the industry never planned to have T-shirts and lunch boxes as a principal revenue source when they embarked upon that clever advertising campaign. Executives were present enough, however, to see the possibilities, and they went for it. They seized a new profit center, one that continues to promote their original product: raisins.

If we prepare in the present to respond in the future, our interest in learning encourages us to suspend our assumptions—to play with them, explore them, and test other possibilities. We are also encouraged to examine ourselves, our prejudices, and our natural personality preferences to identify potential shortcomings as well as strengths, to continuously clarify what we are and what we wish to become so that we can be flexible and adaptive to new conditions.

Had Ellen been present in the present with Annette, she would have sought to understand Annette's idea for expansion. How does it help our company accomplish its purpose? Does it support our values? How does it work? What does it look like? How does it complement what we are already doing? How may it invite new business? How does Annette propose to structure the new division? How long will it take to get it up and running? Who is involved? Does she have plans for testing the idea before committing to it? How can success be measured? What is Annette prepared to do to help develop and implement the idea? Can she have a proposal ready for consideration by the time action plans are developed for next year's budget? Probing questions based in current time encourage us to be creative, to see the possibilities, and to identify what needs to be done in present time in order to prepare for the action-planning season. The questions also show respect and encourage a sense of commitment and ownership for the person who generates the idea. Had she been involved in this proposed dialogue about her idea, Annette would probably have left Ellen's office energized and committed to contributing her efforts to the company. She would have been empowered to move ahead with planning if the idea seemed workable, and she would have discovered for herself whether there were problems.

After working with Ellen for several months, I attended a meeting with her, Annette, and other employees who worked either directly or indirectly for Ellen. We were debriefing the early stages of a leadership development project, and I had asked what was different since the management team had started this work. Someone quickly spoke up and said, "When I talk to Ellen now it feels like she's really there. I used to always feel like she was in another world."

Another employee concurred and added, "Ellen used to ask us for our ideas but she never really seemed to have time to listen, so I just never said anything. Now she seems really accessible and interested. She really listens and asks questions and tries to understand." Ellen now proudly reports at our monthly meetings about projects employees have initiated and undertaken and about how much money the company is saving. She is particularly excited about the new level of personal interaction in conversations with employees who bring ideas to her.

BEING PRESENT KEEPS US IN TOUCH WITH SPIRIT

When we are not present and not aware, we lose our connectedness with others. We lose hope and optimism; they lose hope and optimism. All the things that are spirit are in the present. They can be experienced only in the present. We can love and feel connection only at this moment. We may be able to recall having loved in the past or may dream about loving in the future, but recalling and dreaming aren't the same as loving. Peace, inspiration, aspiration, intuition, and all the life-giving positive qualities that add richness and energy to life are experienced only in the present.

Being present means being in touch with myself and what I am truly *feeling* as well as what I am thinking. It also means being in touch with others and what they are *feeling* as well as what they are thinking. It means integrating our vision, values, and learning so completely that we can trust our ability to handle whatever presents itself. We don't have to be concerned about future ramifications. We take care of the present and trust ourselves to be able to take care of the future when it arrives. Wasting ourselves figuring out how to act in the future is just that: a waste. When we strive to control our future response in advance, we inevitably limit our possibilities. Conditions and requirements change. When we are planning, we cannot know exactly what conditions will be in the future. Preparing to respond in the present to conditions and requirements of the present as they arise is the only hope for business in times of increasing change and permanent white water.

TOOLS FOR BEING ON THE PATH OF COURAGE

- Being completely present in the present is our only way to fully experience our spirits and to build connection with people.
- Being completely present in the present is the only effective means to make decisions in a world of rapid change. Rules and plans conceived in the past often no longer apply in the present.
- Being in the present helps us access our intuition and discover new possibilities.
- Designing guides for our actions—a purpose, vision, values—which guide our decisions in the present prevent overattachment to goals that no longer have meaning.

EXPLORING THE PATH OF COURAGE

(1) Start becoming aware of each time your mind drifts off into the past or the future. How do these time frames that you can do nothing about undermine the quality of your preparations for the future done in the present?

(2) Start becoming aware of each time your mind drifts off into the past or the future when you talk to someone in the organization. Then become aware of when you believe others are drifting off as you talk with them and of when the conversation begins to drift forward or backward. How do you feel when others are not "completely present" in the present with you? How is connection impeded?

(3) Develop a list of questions that you can become conscious of using to engage others in a present-based dialogue about ideas, planning, problems, concerns, or issues.

(4) For thirty days, commit to "practicing being present" (as described on page 167), by doing something daily in which you focus completely on some small aspect of an activity. Make notes immediately after the activity each day. Do you stay focused longer than the day or week before? What thoughts impeded your focus? Do you now notice more quickly the times you are drifting? Do you notice more often when you drift at work more than you noticed before beginning this exercise?

Chapter 12

Coming to Peace with Ourselves

Peace is an essential part of our spirits. When we live and lead on the Path of Courage, we come to know a deep level of peace that pervades our being. We may still be afraid, angry, frustrated, or irritated at events of the day, but guiding us like a rudder is a deep sense of peace that tells us we are on the right track. This peace, which in biblical terms passes all understanding, is generated by a spiritual connection made possible by self-awareness and conscious living.

I was once preparing myself, my home, and my business for a cross-country move. It could have been a hectic period, since I was recovering from a long illness and a related surgery two months earlier. I was catching up on client commitments delayed during the illness while attempting to satisfy last-minute requests for "just one final thing before you go" from established clients. I was orchestrating the business transition with established clients while planning a public relations campaign to launch my business in new areas and while dealing with all the details usually associated with a long-distance move. My calmness in the face of six weeks of chaos astonished me, my friends, and my family. I was able to be present, focused, and confident; my carefree attitude reflected my spiritual connection and my belief that somehow everything would work out all right.

Several times in the past I had been more frenzied about moving across town, without the concerns of catching up after an illness, relocating a business, changing banks and phone and utility companies, and finding a new hairdresser. I truly believe that the secret of my profound sense of peace was spawned by my years of work at coming to peace with myself. I no longer had to have everything done perfectly. I knew that somehow I would get the essentials done and would discover a way to deal with anything that didn't get done. I stayed anchored to my purpose and my core values and developed a short list of questions to anchor me when the details began to mount.

- Does this activity serve my purpose?
- Does it support my values?
- Does it bring me to life and life to me?
- Is the action on the Path of Courage?
- Is the action in any way be driven by fear?
- What is the worst that can happen if something doesn't get done?

The last question was a lifesaver. I discovered that many of the "essentials" were just minor inconveniences in even the worst-case scenario. I didn't really plan my trip, make reservations, or decide how I would get by when I reached my new home. Somehow I arrived on the appointed day. I found a place to stay every night when I was tired; the worst that happened was that I ended up sleeping on the floor one night in my new home without electricity or water. I was able to meet most challenges with bottled water, the local deli, a sleeping bag, and a little creativity. Why have I spent so much of my life being frenzied over "getting it right?" Because I hadn't come to peace with myself. I was not living my life in the present; I was living in the future. I was living for my judgment and for that of others about what I should do. I wanted to be perfect. I wanted approval from the world.

When we bring a deep sense of peace to our chaotic workplaces, the attitude is contagious. (The frenzy is also contagious but has less satisfying results.) When we lead from the heart, we have confidence things will work out. We even realize that new possibilities may actually present themselves if we make ourselves available for what wants to happen. From that place of peace, we are comfortable being creative and may actually discover shortcuts for doing some of the essentials. This spontaneous innovation cannot happen when we are pressing to make things happen according to the book. When we come to peace with ourselves, we build a foundation for a healthier, happier life and workplace.

WHERE IS THE PLACE OF PEACE?

When I am not in my place of peace, I feel it a number of places in my body. Sometimes a headache tells me I'm not there, sometimes an ache between my shoulder blades or in my digestive tract. But when I am in my place of peace, I know where I feel it. It resides right around my navel and is about the size of my fist. When the peace is centered there, it feels as if it is sending waves to the rest of my body. It is as if I'd been in a boat on a stormy lake being vigorously rocked about, and then almost magically the storm stopped and the lake got very still. That stillness engulfs the whole of my being. This sensation was a bit strange when I first noticed it—it was unlike anything I had known before. I was almost uneasy. Having spent the rest of my life in the storm, I didn't know it could be any other way. This peace became my indicator mechanism for when I was on track. When I started feeling stormy again, it was time to do some self-examination and see what was upsetting my peace indicator.

It has been said that our place of peace can be found flowing like a gentle river between the banks of fear and desire. When we fear or desire nothing enough to leave our place of peace, we stay in the river of peace. When my peace indicator tells me I've left that river, the first two questions I ask myself are: What is it that I want enough to make me leave my place of peace? What is it that I fear enough to make me leave my place of peace? Often the two are connected.

For instance, I want my team to do well on this project so that I will get the promotion I want and we will all get the bonus we want. This may cause me to leave the river of peace, but as I examine further, I discover a related fear. I am afraid that if things don't go well, that I won't get the promotion. I am afraid we won't get the bonus that I need to meet some financial obligations. I may even fear that I will lose my job if work goes poorly.

When we begin to bring this process to consciousness, fear and desire are virtually always paired. Letting go of both fear and desire almost always leads us back into peace. It is what the Buddhists call the middle way, the place that we let go of our attachment to particular outcomes, the place where we make ourselves available to what wants to happen.

MAKING PEACE WITH OURSELVES

Many people tell me they'd like to see more trust, faith, and love in the workplace. Then they quickly begin to say why it isn't "realistic." The reasons virtually always have to do with other people. All judgment is based in self-judgment. If I love someone, it is because I see the qualities I like most about myself in that person. You may say, "That is not true! Opposites attract. My spouse could not be more different from me." Yet we cannot recognize qualities we do not know. It may be that we choose not to see those qualities that we love about ourselves in ourselves so we don't recognize them. The qualities may be ones that we have not often used and with which we are clumsy. We may even be ashamed to let them show because they don't fit our image of what we *should* be.

For instance, a friend may be really good about sharing his feelings. If I had grown up in a family where feelings were not openly expressed, I may have learned to ignore my reactions to people and circumstances. As a consequence, it may be extremely difficult for me to know what I am feeling. When I do, I may get teary or emotional as I try to reduce the lump in my throat to words, an embarrassing reaction that I choose to stifle. An awkward reaction like this often indicates a part of me that I have not explored or developed.

When I see the way in which my friend so easily expresses his feelings, my brain may believe that, because I have not developed that part of myself, it does not exist. I may even say, "You're good at that, but that's just not me." My heart knows otherwise. When I see the way in which my friend so easily expresses his feelings, it taps a yearning inside me to be able to experience and express my own feelings openly. When I have been able to do that, maybe only once or twice, or maybe only as a child, I loved that part of me, and I remember it. I love it in him. All love begins with self-love.

If we hate someone, it is because we see in that person the qualities that we hate most about ourselves. For instance, when we decry someone for her total lack of integrity, for her inability to tell the truth, or for her total lack of compunction about lying, it is because we see in that person something we hate most about ourselves. We may resist and say, "That cannot be. I *always* tell the truth!" We cannot recognize those qualities in others that we do not first know in ourselves. Perhaps we do not lie in the way we understand that she lies. Perhaps we refuse to examine the assumptions upon which our "truth" is based. Perhaps we distort reality so we believe that we are telling the truth. We may even withhold important information because we don't want to hurt someone. Perhaps she, too, is doing the same. Perhaps her lack of compunction about lying arises from a belief that she is telling the truth; perhaps when we experience her as lying, we remember how we lie to ourselves when we strive for perfection, when we know that *no one* is perfect.

But perhaps we wrongly identify what it is that we hate about her. Maybe it is not her lying at all, but her sense of righteousness about her statement, which we believe to be untrue. Perhaps she reminds us of our own righteousness displayed so indignantly when we decry this other fallible human being. These reactions may all be parts of ourselves we choose not to acknowledge—parts that we hate. When we hate her, we hate that part of ourselves. All hate begins with self-hate.

If we try to see what our physical bodies look like, we can get a rough, somewhat distorted idea of dimensions by looking down. We focus on things we like or don't like and lose sight of the whole picture. When we truly want to find out what we look like, we look in a mirror. Then we know what we look like—the whole package. Even then we may focus upon parts we like or don't like, but the mirror still gives us a reasonably accurate reflection of ourselves.

So it is with looking inside ourselves. We may have an idea of what we are like by looking at ourselves. Again, there will be distortions; we may ignore some parts and exaggerate others. We lose sight of the whole picture. If we truly want to find out what we are like on the inside, we look in the mirror of other people. We can see only those qualities in others that we know in ourselves.

Love, hate, self-love, self-hate all begin in ourselves. This fact presents a special problem for us on the road to becoming spiritual. Spirituality is that place in each of us where we are all those wonderful qualities I have suggested are part of our spiritual selves. It is a place from which we have complete belief in ourselves and in the rest of humanity. Most of us want others to show us they are worthy of love and trust before we give it. We wait for them to give what must begin within ourselves. If we are not able to see those things in others, it is because we have not experienced them in ourselves.

LOVING OURSELVES

Love ourselves? Accept ourselves? Be kind and peaceful to ourselves? Starting our spirituality with loving ourselves is difficult. There we stand alone and naked with no one to blame or to lean on. Until we love ourselves, we always depend on others to love us, to give us approval, and to give us positive feedback. We are forever drawn from our spiritual center by the desire to please others or by the fear of not pleasing them.

What does it mean to love myself? Loving myself means I ask nothing of myself that I would like to think I wouldn't ask of a loved one, however I recognize that I am not always as loving of my loved ones as I would like. Sometimes I'm not as loving of them as I am of strangers. Scott Peck talks about love in terms of the will to grow spiritually.[1] That is clearly a

---

1. M. Scott Peck, M.D., *The Road Less Traveled: A New Psychology of Love, Traditional Values and Spiritual Growth* (New York: Touchstone/Simon & Schuster, 1978), pp. 81ff.

component of self-love, but for me, there is more. As well as the will to grow and develop, loving also involves balance and an element of preservation or maintenance.

A number of writers speak of the need for developing various aspects of life. One of my favorite ideas is Stephen Covey's concept of sharpening the saw. Covey identifies four basic dimensions of our human nature: the physical, the spiritual, the mental, and the social-emotional. He explains that without regularly spending time developing each of these dimensions, a person becomes like the woodcutter who must work harder and harder to cut less and less because he or she hasn't taken time to keep the tools in top condition.[2] Gary Hirschberg, CEO of the popular Stonyfield Farms, says his assistant has come to recognize when he is not leading from his center. "She tells me to go play tennis."

I learned years ago that I don't do my best work when I am not balanced. The first things that go on my schedule are my workout times, time for meditation, and one or two nurturing social engagements each week. (Nurturing social engagements don't include those parties in which all of the conversation is superficial. They involve the people with whom I bare my soul and share my hopes, dreams, fears, and frustrations.) Appointments get scheduled around these inviolables. I sometimes change a workout time to another time of the day to accommodate client needs, but I virtually never cancel these appointments.

Our physical bodies need regular care and maintenance. They need nourishing food, partaken in a relaxed atmosphere, to fuel them. They need regular stretching and aerobic exercise to ensure flexibility and a strong heart, and they need physical strengthening. Taking regular breaks, lunch hours, weekends, and vacations gives us the perspective and stimulation we need to work smarter rather than working harder and harder in the same way. Rest and rejuvenation of the body, mind, and spirit provide the balance for our work lives.

Our lives are also enriched by daily spiritual practice. Such a practice can take many forms, including those already described in this book as part of reflective practice. Spiritual exercise may involve prayer or reading a holy book or a daily meditation guide. Others may find interaction with others is important to their spiritual practice and may choose church study groups or less formal gathering of friends to share whatever brings meaning and purpose to their lives. Some may find playing a musical instrument, painting, or sculpting brings them in touch with their spirits. These and many other possibilities help connect us on a regular basis with that

---

2. Stephen R. Covey, *The Seven Habits of Highly Effective People: Powerful Lessons in Personal Change* (New York: Fireside/Simon & Schuster, 1989), pp. 287ff.

part of us that is universal. Inevitably our belief in ourselves and the fellowship of humankind are renewed.

I believe this "sharpening the saw" is an important component of self-love. Developing the body, mind, and spirit works best for me. When the social and emotional are more than just *doing*, they are part of the spiritual. The labels we use are not important. What is important is that when we love ourselves, we make time for the development, preservation, and nourishment of all aspects of our lives. Attention to one or two of the dimensions is insufficient to develop true balance. Anyone who has ever driven a car with a flat tire knows that unless all four tires are in good shape, the ride is neither efficient nor enjoyable! People wouldn't ride around in a car with two flats, but they may think nothing of developing one or two aspects of life to the exclusion of others. They use time or other commitments as excuses (not reasons) for why they aren't more balanced. When we love ourselves, we cherish these as gifts of balance that we give to our beloved—ourselves.

Yet something is still missing from this definition of love. John Sanford offers more insight in *Invisible Partners*:

> "Real love begins only when one person comes to know another for who he or she really is as a human being, and begins to like and care for that human being."[3]

This quote adds the missing piece for me. Too often we have superhuman expectations for ourselves. We think we can give and give endlessly to others without refueling and recharging ourselves. We expect perfection. We hardly tolerate mistakes. We bear responsibility and guilt for things far from our control, as if we had some superhuman all-seeing, all-knowing vision and power to make all things turn out right.

When we live from spirit, it is much easier to accept ourselves as living, breathing, human beings and with all the needs and wants of human beings. We come to respect and like our own humanness. We really care for the human beings that we are, just as we are. We take time to get to know the human being we are without illusions and we begin to like and care for that human. These attitudes reflect real self-love. This is the love we build into spirit-respecting workplaces—love that takes the time to really know other human beings as individuals and not as members of a monolithic category, like employees, supervisors, secretaries, or union. Spirit-respecting love takes time to know other human beings and likes and cares for the human being.

---

3. John A. Sanford, *Invisible Partners* (New York: Paulist Press, 1980), pp. 19–20.

All of the qualities that characterize spirituality begin in ourselves: trust, faith, openness, abundance, acceptance, caring, sharing, intuition, inspiration, aspiration, and wonder all begin in each of us. For us to see them in others, we must see them first within ourselves. Whenever we look to others as excuses for not living from spirit, we should instead look first in the mirror. What we experience in the world is merely a reflection of what we are inside.

JOY AND PEACE REQUIRE ACCEPTANCE

Joy and peace are essential parts of spirit, and yet they are different from other spiritual qualities. To experience peace and joy requires that we be willing to accept them and to make room for them in our lives. Peace and joy are choices. To experience peace and joy, we choose to find meaning, purpose, and satisfaction from whatever we are doing at this moment. Joy and peace are unconditional. They cannot be dependent on getting something, having something, or being with someone. If we are driven by fear or desire for things that we do not have, we won't have room in our lives for peace and joy. Joy and peace are in the present, and they are always available to us when we choose them.

Viktor Frankl, a psychiatrist, philosopher, and writer, wrote about his life in Nazi concentration camps, much of it spent doing hard manual labor.

> "Everything can be taken away from a man but one thing, the last of the human freedoms—to choose one's attitude in any given set of circumstances, to choose one's way. . . . The way in which a man accepts his fate, and all the suffering it entails . . . gives him ample opportunity—even in the most difficult circumstances—to add a deeper meaning to his life."[4]

Even in the daily terror of a Nazi concentration camp, Frankl found meaning by choosing how to view his circumstances. Yet today millions of people, living in relatively grand and benevolent circumstances, have bleak lives with little hope, peace, or joy; they have chosen not to invite those qualities of being into their lives.

Before I discovered my spirit, I could reflect about how pleased I'd been with certain events or circumstances or how much I'd enjoyed a par-

---

4. Viktor E. Frankl, *Man's Search for Meaning* (revised and updated; New York: Pocket Books/Simon & Schuster, 1959).

ticular time, place, or event. When I had been there, I hadn't been having joy or happiness. I had been either into the past or the future. I had been into perfection, others' judgment, self-judgment, or righteousness. I had been too busy *doing* to feel joy.

Spirit has helped me to experience joy in circumstances that earlier I never would have considered joyful. The happiness I knew when I was dependent on other people, circumstances, and events for happiness is different from joy. The feelings didn't come from my spirit. Spiritual joy is much different from needing other people or things or events to make me happy. Spiritual joy emanates from inside me.

When I grieve over the death of someone close to me, I may feel bad about feeling sad. Yet grieving is normal and healthy; it prepares us to go on in the world after a loss. Sadness, loss, and emotional pain are normal feelings during grieving. It is normal to experience fear about how life will be without a special person in our lives. So I choose to be joyful about acceptance of my grieving although I am not joyful about the loss. I am joyful about being able to be conscious of my sadness, my loss, and my pain, about choosing to nurture my healing soul with special music, candles, and a bubble bath. I am joyful that I was choosing to nurture myself with prayer and meditation to help myself connect with my spirit where I know all things turn out perfectly. I am joyful when I realize that the change probably serves a spiritual end that is important to me. This joy cannot happen through other people and events. It comes only from spirit.

I used to project joy into the future. When I got a promotion or a raise, when I finished remodeling the house, when I graduated from college, when I was admitted to graduate school, when I finished graduate school, when I got my business going, when I got the house decorated, when I lost ten pounds, when I got a new car . . . then I would be happy. Then I would have joy and peace. I used to try to put other conditions on achieving joy and peace. If the neighbor would stop being a jerk, if the boss would treat me as if I had a brain, if the woman ahead of me at the store would stop fooling around, or if the car in front of me would go a little faster, then I would be happy.

Conditions take us out of the present. Joy and peace are not qualities of the past or the future. Joy and peace are choices: We decide to choose peace and joy in this moment—in what we are doing or in what we experience. When I choose to experience the woman in front of me at the store as a thoughtful, giving person because she is shopping for two other people, my irritation at her separate piles of groceries and payments melts away. I can experience joy and respect in her thoughtfulness and giving. When we change our own experience, it gets us out of the negative past. It gets us out of our heads and into our hearts. We don't need anyone else to do anything. We don't need something to change. We have joy, and with joy in the present, we find peace.

When we have complete belief in ourselves, we can have it in the rest of humanity as well. "Maybe myself, but the rest of humanity?" you ask. What about those who commit rape, murder, pillaging? What about those who endure disease, poverty, homelessness, and starvation? How can we have complete belief? If we focus on those things, that is what we see, and we will probably be afraid. What we focus on determines what we miss. We miss the fact that most of the world isn't raping, murdering, pillaging, poor, homeless, sick, and hungry. With that view of the world, we never have the courage to change our workplaces. In fact, we never have courage to lead. If we haven't experienced people in our families, our communities, our workplaces, our country, or the world as being worthy of our faith, is there perhaps a part of us that we don't believe in? When we don't have faith in ourselves, what do we teach those around us about the faith we have in them? Mohandas K. Gandhi told us "We must be the change we wish to see in the world."[5] We have to become what we want to attract. We have to exercise personal leadership where we are, when we are, and in what we are doing. All belief starts with self-belief. All love begins with self-love. Peace and joy come when I let go of fear and desire and accept what is.

MAKING FRIENDS WITH THE DARK SIDE

All that we have to accept about ourselves isn't love and beauty. In each of us there is a dark side. Fear. Righteousness. Judgment. Perfectionism. Resentment. Confusion. Regret. Blaming. Guilt. Cynicism. Worry. Control mania. Arrogance. Victimhood. Greed. Just as all the good things we see in others are a reflection of those positive qualities in us, all the things that we dislike about others are reflections of those qualities in ourselves. All of them are part of me. All of them are part of each of us. We can recognize those qualities in others only in the mirrored reflection of ourselves.

The Wonder Child had a full range of behavioral possibilities. Just as "positive" possibilities were repressed, so were ones that we view as "negatives." They were repressed but are always very much a part of us. They drive reactions. They drive fear, fear of being found out. Someone may discover we have an ugly quality. We may even discover we have an ugly quality in our dark side.

5. Mohandas K. Gandhi, in Glenn Van Ekeren, *Speaker's Sourcebook II: Quotes, Stories, and Anecdotes for Every Occasion* (Englewood Cliffs, NJ: Prentice Hall, 1994).

The dark side unconsciously drives us to plot, calculate, and control so that our dark secret remains a secret. We develop strategies to keep others from discovering. Some of the ways in which I've hidden the real me from others have been perfectionism, self-reliance, resentment, worry, greed, and definitely control mania. (It took me a long time to accept that perfectionism, self-reliance, and control were not positive qualities.) These are all fear-driven strategies that take us from our place of peace and keep us on the Path of Fear. They separate us and keep us from risking doing our best job. I could see the negative impact of these strategies when others used them. The reason I was able to see these in others was because they were very much a part of me. As I began to accept the concept that all judgment is based in self-judgment, I was able to see even more strategies in myself that I'd previously only recognized in others.

Finally, I typed up a list of qualities that I had observed others using to hide behind, including ones that I was *sure* were not a part of me. I put one copy on my desk at the office and the other on the medicine cabinet at home, and I watched in wonder. Over the course of the next ten to fourteen days, I caught myself doing them all to a greater or lesser extent. What a shocking discovery.

ACCEPTING THE DARK SIDE OPENS THE POSSIBILITY OF CHANGE

As I accepted those qualities in myself, I began seeing all of them in virtually everyone I knew, to a greater or lesser extent. This could have led me into real cynicism. It didn't because I was learning ways to undermine the strategies. I gave up my judgment that the dark side was bad. Without judgment, the qualities weren't good or bad: they just were. Whether I saw them in me or in others, when I could accept them without judgment, they became behaviors I could look at, and I could look at the consequences of the behaviors. I could choose to accept the consequences or change the behaviors. Without exception, I chose to change them because when I continued them I found they promoted a negative worldview that kept me away from my spirit and from connecting with other people. I discovered that by consciously choosing to do just the opposite, I was able to reverse my experience in almost every situation. Whenever I fell into cynicism, I chose to have faith. As I became more comfortable with being myself more of the time, faith came more easily.

Faith was rewarded. I soon learned to catch myself slipping into the strategies. I became quite familiar with them. I also discovered that it was fairly easy to undermine them. As soon as I started becoming resentful or seeing myself as a victim, I would take ownership of my role in creating the situation about which I was resentful. I was shocked to discover that I did have a role in events about which I'd previously seen myself as absolutely blameless. Almost instantaneously, resentment melted away. The same thing happened with other strategies. As soon as I was able to recognize a strategy in myself, I was able to look it squarely in the face on a conscious level instead of reacting unconsciously. I was not always able to prevent the strategy from occurring but was usually able to recognize it fairly quickly, adjust my course, and move on in a positive way.

I had experienced the good fortune of creating a business that exploded within a month after I started. Although I had been doing much the same work for employers, doing it as a consultant was different. My insecurity about my inexperience as a consultant shifted my perfectionism and control mania into overdrive. If I made a mistake, people might think I didn't know what I was doing. To appear as if I were perfect meant I had to know exactly what the outcomes would be before I did anything. I worked many more hours than I billed so that I could completely ensure perfection and control. I also took jobs that didn't interest me because I knew that I could do them perfectly.

After a year of working sixty-plus hours per week, hardly seeing my husband and friends, and being bored stiff, I realized that what I was creating was what I feared most. I wanted to be creative and do leading edge work, but I was so exhausted that I wasn't creative. I was so controlled and controlling that I didn't try anything new. I made sure that people always got their money's worth (that was a basic value) but at the expense of balance in my life and passion in my work. This attitude violated some other basic values.

When I was able to recognize that perfectionism and control-mania were strategies for hiding self-doubt and fear about my ability to handle the outcomes, I was able to stop the behavior. Instead of focusing on being perfect and controlling uninteresting jobs, I developed self-confidence and faith that I could do what was interesting and energizing to me. As I took on more and more jobs and worked fewer and fewer hours, I discovered that the outcomes that emerged were often far more important and productive than the ones I would have forced in my perfectionist and controlling days.

LEARNING TO LIVE IN A CONSCIOUS WAY

When I was denying this dark side of me, it was still very much a part of me. I could see it in others. Others could see it in me. When I realized that we all carry all of these qualities, I could accept the dark side as part of being human. Instead of being a part of me that I was ashamed of because it wasn't part of my preferred image, I was able to accept those parts of me. I was able to make friends with the dark side. I grew to accept that the dark side was trying to get my attention. It was trying to tell me I needed to do something different. A funny thing began to happen. The more conscious and accepting I became of the dark side's presence, the less frequently it appeared in my life.

I was learning to live in a conscious way. As long as I would not acknowledge the dark side of myself, I was constantly running from it, and I was getting worn out from running harder and faster with an increasingly heavy burden. Freedom came from acknowledging my whole range of possibilities—"good" and "bad." When I really acknowledged my humanness, I could stop running. I could stop in my tracks and turn and look my dark side right in the face. I didn't have to be afraid of the unknown that was chasing me. I knew what was back there. Everyone else had it too, so I could stop hiding my frailties. I could relax.

Once I acknowledged that the dark side was part of me, I discovered what I could do to change my experience of it. I was no longer driving without options. I had choice. I could continue to try to hide the dark side of me, or I could choose to accept my dark side as part of being human like every other person. Once I made friends with my dark side, I could choose how I wanted to experience it. That was simply not possible until I could accept that part of myself. Increasingly, the emergence of my imperfections was treated with a shrug and an "Oh, well. . . ." Oh, well, I am human. Surprise! Surprise!

Making friends with my dark side made my life a lot easier. Acceptance begins with self-acceptance. When I accept myself just as I am without masks or hiding strategies, I draw closer to my spirit. Instead of wasting all that energy hiding and driving, I have new energy to devote to things that are important to me. I have spirit. I have started my own personal Spirit Cycle with energy-producing activities that recharge my batteries continuously and bring vitality to my life.

THE DARK SIDE IN ORGANIZATIONS

The dark side emerges frequently in organizations. Scarcity thinking gives rise to turf battles and blaming. Self-doubt and control mania prevent risk-taking and creativity and inhibit the safety and learning so essential to the continuous-improvement process. Lack of trust, faith, openness, and acceptance generates confining supervision and incomplete exploration of ideas. Lack of respect, trust, openness, and connection becomes fertile soil for sexual and racial harassment.

In *The Fifth Discipline*, Peter Senge describes "the myth of the management team" as one of the seven learning disabilities that organizations embody:

> All too often, teams in business tend to spend their time fighting for turf, avoiding anything that will make them look bad personally, and pretending that everyone is behind the team's collective strategy—maintaining the *appearance* of a cohesive team. To keep up the image, they seek to squelch disagreement; people with serious reservations avoid stating them publicly, and joint decisions are watered-down compromises reflecting what everyone can live with, or else reflecting one person's view foisted on the group. If there is disagreement, it's usually expressed in a manner that lays blame, polarizes opinion, and fails to reveal the underlying differences in assumptions and experience in a way that the team as a whole could learn.[6]

The "myth of the management team" is one of the qualities of the dark side that I frequently encounter. People who support a decision out of fear in a meeting immediately go out and begin building support for their view that the adopted course of action will fail. Other times important issues just aren't brought up out of fear of how others will react to the information. Often people ensure that the adopted course of action will fail. Fear among managers and executives is a rampant driving force that is rarely addressed. Co-dependence, or behavior that enables dysfunctional management, is the rule rather than the exception; it allows unbridled anger, rage, and competition to flourish, but on an under-the-table level.

When the dark side isn't understood or accepted, it becomes a reactive driving force. It generates divisiveness instead of collaboration and cooperation. It drives fear instead of openness and flexibility. When it is accepted and understood, people can make friends with it. They can learn to recognize it. They can learn how to talk about it. They can learn how to undermine it. But none of this can happen until they accept it. It is only when people are willing to accept that a dark quality, like cynicism, is part of their organization that they can learn what causes it and learn how to debilitate and dismantle it. When cynicism begins to emerge in the organization, they know that it is time to keep commitments and have faith.

---

6. Peter M. Senge, *The Fifth Discipline: The Art and Practice of the Learning Organization* (New York: Currency/Doubleday, 1990), p. 24.

The dark side is the opposite of spirit in organizations. If we want our organizations to be more respecting of the spirit of people and if we want our organizations to have more spirit, then the organizations must also know that the other side exists as well. They must know that it exists in every organization. The qualities that undermine the elements of the dark side are the elements of spirit. The more spiritual both we and our organizations become, the less frequently the dark side occurs. We stop spending time and energy running and hiding from it. We have more attention, energy, and creativity for addressing competitors and regulations, and for changing technology. When we lead from our spirits, we are able to acknowledge the part of ourselves that we do not like. We make friends with the dark side. We get closer to our spirits. Our organizations discover spirit.

Whether leading from our spirits means being open to self-love, joy and peace, or the dark side of ourselves, it is essential for us to be self-aware. If we are not aware of the ways in which we abuse ourselves, how can we be conscious of what impact we are having on others? And how can we respect the spirits of those in our workplace community unless we know what impact our actions have upon them? By the same token, if our self-awareness is so low that we cannot recognize the dark side in ourselves, how can we have patience, love, and compassion for our co-workers? When we develop a level of self-awareness that lets us be at peace with ourselves, then we can become instruments for bringing peace to our workplaces.

TOOLS FOR BEING ON THE PATH OF COURAGE

- Peace runs within us like a gentle river between the banks of fear and desire. Asking ourselves these two questions will help us discover what is taking us from our place of peace: What do I desire enough to take me from my place of peace? What do I fear enough to take me from my place of peace?
- All judgment is based in self-judgment. We cannot see either positive or negative qualities in others except as they are reflected in our own being.
- It is essential for us to learn to love ourselves in order for us to provide courageous, spirit-respecting leadership to others.
- Loving ourselves and each other includes the willingness to grow spiritually; providing for our body, mind, and spiritual needs; and coming to know, like, and care about the real human being in each of us.
- We can choose to experience any set of circumstances or any event in a variety of ways. We can choose to bring peace and joy into our lives simply by deciding that is how we will experience our lives.

- When we come to accept that each of us has a dark side, we can begin to consciously diminish the impact of those qualities in our lives. Until we bring them to consciousness, they keep us on the Path of Fear, driving and exhausting us and creating dysfunctions in our personal and organizational lives.
- It is only by accepting the existence of the dark side in organizations that we can begin to consciously change the behaviors it generates and build a spirit-respecting workplace community.

EXPLORING THE PATH OF COURAGE

(1) Be aware the next time you are agitated, nervous, confused, or uneasy. Consciously explore what is taking you from your place of peace. Ask these questions: What do I fear enough to leave my place of peace? What do I desire enough to leave my place of peace? Are you attached to outcomes that are more important than being at peace? Should you release your attachment to those outcomes, and make yourself available for what wants to happen?

(2) Make a list of friends and acquaintances you like and respect. After each name list the qualities about each that you admire. Identify times in which you have seen those qualities in yourself.

(3) Make a list of acquaintances that you find irritating. Identify those qualities that annoy you about that person. Now identify a recent time in which you have seen those qualities in yourself.

(4) Review the activities of your past week. Does this record indicate that you have loved yourself enough to bring balance and wholeness to your life? Have you spent time in physical, mental, spiritual, and social or emotional activities, or activities that balance body, mind, and spirit?

(5) Are you waiting for joy, or are you putting conditions on joy that make it possible only in a space of time in which you cannot exist (the past or the future)? Take some time to identify the things that you have to be joyful about at this moment. As you go through the next three days, consciously focus on recognizing the joy that is currently in your life.

(6) Does "the myth of the management team" exist in your workplace? Identify those "dark side" qualities in your organization.

Chapter 13

Avoiding Fear Creates What We Fear the Most

Companies that focus only on making money will do things which will undermine the things that support making money . . . that will actually prevent making money.

   . . . PETER B. VAILL, *"Leading-Managing in Permanent White Water"*[1]

Theresa owns a small business and professes confusion about whether to grow the business. Growth requires that the enterprise borrow money and extend both the organization's and Theresa's financial risk, and there is no guarantee that consumer demand will continue to grow. Although the company cannot currently keep up with consumer demand, stabilizing would allow it to pay off current debt and ensure that the company is always in a strong seller's market. When she has the courage to admit it, Theresa knows that an undercapitalized venture is doomed to failure. When a company cannot meet consumer demand, competition inevitably surfaces. When the competition is able to meet demand with a quality product in a timely fashion, consumer loyalty soon shifts to the organiza-

---

1. Peter B. Vaill, "Leading-Managing in Permanent White Water," keynote address for Rediscovering the Soul in Business: Managing for Profit and the Human Spirit, Boise State University, Boise, ID, 23 September 1995.

tion that can provide customers with the product they want *when* they want it. Theresa fears a business failure caused by too much debt. What she fails to see is that inaction creates exactly what she fears, but by a different route: The business will fail because consumer demand declines as the company's inability to deliver continues.

Many believe that all human behavior is motivated by either fear or desire. As I have said earlier, I believe that fear and desire are almost always related. With almost every fear, there is an implied desire. Attached to virtually every desire is an associated fear. The associated fear may be as simple as being afraid we won't get what we desire, but it is there nonetheless. I believe that until we name the associated fear and make peace with it, we never achieve what we desire in a sustainable way. The unspoken fear always undermines our resolve, causes our commitment to wane, and generates excuses for why we haven't been able to achieve what we say we want.

Often when it is unnamed, fear actually causes us to create what we fear. As Vaill said, we take actions that actually undermine our ability to get what we want. Until it is named, the unspoken fear produces a sense of urgency and desperation that can drive us even when we don't know we have fear. Because fear and desire are so integrally linked, however, we could just as easily say that driven desires prevent us from getting what we want; the drivenness of the desire comes from fear we won't get it. The truth is that overattachment to any end, whether it is getting what we desire or avoiding what we fear, takes us from a place of spirit where we live consciously and are able to open ourselves to new possibilities. Either fear or desire can cause us to leave our "river of peace."

BEING AFRAID

A colleague once discussed Christ's admonition to the two Marys at the time of his resurrection. Christ said, "Be not afraid."[2] My colleague explained, "He doesn't say, 'Don't have fear.' He says 'Don't *be* your fear.' " Because so much of what I guide people through in organizations is fear and fear-driven responses, that conversation has become pivotal in framing what our relationship with fear should be. I know what doesn't work: to ignore fear, to pretend it doesn't exist, or to figuratively run from it. My colleague seemed to have hit on something that made sense to me. I know that on the Path of Courage, people regularly accept fear and move

---

2. Matthew 28:10 (King James Version).

on in spite of it. When people do that, they aren't *be*ing their fear. They are being *with* their fear.

When we are being our fear, we are driven by it but rarely even know it exists. We unconsciously create crutches to protect us from it. Perfectionism, judgment, righteousness, confusion, resentment, and cynicism drive many of us. The driving fear is unacknowledged and unconscious. It pushes and pulls us and insulates us from our feelings and from the feelings of those around us. It chokes life of meaning, purpose, and love. Most of us don't know much about this unacknowledged fear. I know it takes so much energy to fight that I used to be tired all the time. I know it generates stress and burnout. I know that when I insulate myself from fear, I also insulate myself from life's positive, energizing emotions as well. I was living on an emotional "flat line." Fear was literally sapping me of my energy, my creativity, and my zest for living. Fear insulated me from my spirit and all the positive feelings it generates.

Life on the Path of Fear keeps many of us in organizations sapped of energy, creativity, and the joy of work. We resist change, even when we know the new way is better for us individually and organizationally. We develop comfort with the status quo because we know it is a place from which we can survive. Even if the new way seems better, we simply don't know how we will survive. We don't know the rules of the game. We don't know what we should and should not do.

Rather than choose the Path of Courage and go toward our fear and the new ways, most of us resist our fear until we have no energy left to fight it and must surrender. Although we would like approval, avoiding the disapproval of others is integral to most of us on the Path of Fear. We cling to old ways partially because our mode of survival is acceptable to those around us—our bosses, customers, clients, and even family members. The way we have come to know what we need to do in order to avoid disapproval is by living by strict rules that we believe ensure we won't encounter disapproval.

When we are honest with ourselves, we know that life doesn't come with a rule book. There are legal rules or laws, but these restrict a relatively small portion of our lives. The *shoulds* of life imply that there are rules about almost everything we say and do. We come to believe that we or others must do certain things in a certain way because that is what the rules say. If there is no rule book, where do we get the idea? Most of my life I have been quite sure that there are rules and that it is very important to know them and follow them *exactly*. Without rules, how can I ensure that I won't do something I shouldn't? Without rules, how can I know what I must do to be perfect? Without rules, how can I be righteous when I am right or resentful when others act in ways I believe they should not? Without rules to measure myself by, how can I know that I am good enough?

DEVELOPING THE RULE BOOK

Most of us assembled our sets of rules in two ways. First, when we were young children, we picked up many of these notions by observing what appeared to be unacceptable at home or school and then composing a rule to guide us in doing the opposite in the future. When we did the unacceptable, the big people in our lives were not happy with us, and they let us know it. We felt bad and didn't want to be disapproved of, so we made up a rule to live by. The second way we get rules is more obvious. They are told to us. Some may include the rules of society at large—the laws of our city or state. Some may be associated with our geographic region, our national or cultural heritage, or our religion.

I have given significant thought to my rules and their sources. As you read my reflections on my rules, perhaps you recognize some parallels in your life. For example, at the age of three, I was drawn to the pretty yellow flowers in my front yard. I knew my mother liked flowers, and I decided that I would pick some and give them to her. I was excited when I presented them to her. When I gave her these beautiful flowers, she wrinkled up her face and said, "Those are dandelions!" I agreed they were dandy! Then, she threw them away and told me they were weeds. I didn't understand. First she said they were dandy. Then she said they were weeds and threw them away. I didn't know about weeds. I did know that when I brought my mother something to make her happy, she made an ugly face, threw my present away, and told me not to do it again.

So I made up a rule. Because I didn't know about weeds and dandelions, the rule must be something I could understand. I understood that I love my mom, and when I tried to show her, it made her unhappy. My new rules were:

- **I should not show my feelings.**
- **I should not do nice things for people to let them know I love them.**

People tell us other rules.

- **When company is coming, we must work very hard so the house is perfect. We must get the dust bunnies from under the bed and sofa and make sure the tops of all the door casings are clean.**

This rule is very important. If we don't have everything clean, our company will think that we are bad people, and they won't like us. I didn't understand this rule. Our company never looked under the bed or on top of the door casings. But, my mother got very upset when the house was not perfect, especially when my grandmother or my aunts came to visit.

When we went to school, we learned more useful rules. For instance, whenever someone made the teacher unhappy, the person got sent to the principal's office. We didn't know what happened there, but it must have been terrible. Just the threat of going to see the principal made people do anything the teacher said. I peeked in as I walked by on the way to buy supplies. The principal actually looked nice, not mean. He wore a suit and tie. The office actually looked quite nice, like a living room, only different. I developed a rule for that, too:

- **Don't trust men in suits with fancy offices. Even when they look nice, they will do bad things to me.**

So as most of us go through early life, we assemble rules to help us get along better and better. The rules usually work for a while. But after years of not showing my feelings, being perfect so that people love me, and not trusting men in suits with fancy offices, I found that the rules weren't working as well as they did when I was young. Sometimes they worked, but sometimes they didn't. Men in suits in fancy offices seemed trustworthy. I actually liked many of them. Some of them recognized my talent and dedication and gave me promotions.

FACING THE FALLACY OF OUR RULES

A woman who worked for me told someone else that I was cold and uncaring. How could that be? I liked her very much. I was quite concerned about her son who was sick a lot. In fact, she was my favorite employee. Well, of course, I couldn't *show* my feelings. That was against the rules, but she should have just known. Then other rules began to fail me. One of the problems was that they were *my* rules. As I got older and had more experiences, I discovered that everybody didn't have the same rules. In fact, I began to think that some people didn't have any rules at all. But if I didn't have any rules, how would I know what I was supposed to do? And if I didn't know what I was supposed to do, how could I be perfect? And, if I couldn't be perfect, how could I ensure I'd always be wanted and needed?

Several years ago, at the end of my first counseling visit, my counselor gave me an assignment for the next week.

"I want you to spend ten minutes each day just *being*," she said.

"Being what?" I responded.

"Just *being*," she responded.

"What am I supposed to do?" I inquired, not getting it. I needed to know the rules for this assignment so that I could do it perfectly.

"What you're supposed to do is *nothing* for ten minutes each day."

"Nothing? You mean like sit and read a book or listen to music?" I inquired further, still trying to find out what I was supposed to *do*.

"No. Nothing. I would like for you to spend ten minutes each day doing nothing," she replied.

"Nothing?! I'm too busy a person to do nothing." I replied. After more discussion, I said, "I'll try!"

I knew, of course, that I would not. How could I waste over an hour a week when I should be *doing* all those other things? If I were to have value, I had to have something to show for it—something I'd done or physical evidence of my contribution. That was a rule. At least, it had been a rule.

LIBERATION FROM RULES

The things I *should* be doing, of course, were the product of my rules. More important than that, doing things kept me insulated from the conscious part of me that would have let me discover that there were no rules. It took a long time before I could simply sit and listen to my inner wisdom. When I listened, I discovered incredible things.

One of the first things I discovered was that rules stop things from happening. As they become etched on our companies and institutions, they make change increasingly difficult. Change occurs when we challenge our assumptions and open ourselves to new possibilities. Continuous change and improvement are essential to remaining responsive to today's ever-changing business climate and to discovering new approaches to old problems. They require new ways of defining what we do which allow us to recreate our businesses regularly. Rules keep us from challenging our assumptions and learning that we may be doing the wrong thing or doing the right thing the wrong way.

As I listened, another thing that I discovered was that rarely, if ever, was there one right answer. I had spent excessive amounts of time trying to discover the right solution to all kinds of professional and personal challenges, only to discover that there could be many right solutions—all right, only different. Each one produced a different right outcome. It has been said that "Often the opposite of an undeniable truth is another undeniable truth." What a mind-boggling concept that would have been for me a few years ago!

When I listened to a speech on decision-making delivered by a prominent and highly respected businessman in our town, he was quite definite as he advised the audience that all they had to do was "look at the FACTS" and the "right answer" would be apparent. He used the word *facts* a lot and emphasized it strongly each time. It became apparent that this man believed in facts and right answers. He believed that his view of the world *was* the world. The possibility of other right answers escaped him. The prospect of a mistake that delivered unplanned gifts was clearly not an option.

RULES FOCUS ON THE NEGATIVE

Rules emerge from the past and focus on negative possibilities. Rules are designed to protect us from any negatives the future may hold. We don't make rules about positive experiences. My rule about not showing feelings was based on the negative experience of having my dandelions rejected, not the positive experience of having my father be delighted when I ran to him and hugged him to show him how happy I was to see him.

Creating protective rules forces us to focus our attention on the negatives of life. They keep us in the past. Looking into the future becomes like driving a car forward, except that instead of looking through the windshield, we are always looking in the rearview mirror. Even though we are physically moving forward in time and space, all our responses are based on what went on behind us. What we focus on determines what we miss. When we focus only on the negatives, the number of positive possibilities appear to be fewer and fewer. The world looks like a pretty scary place. We develop more and more rules to help us control situations and stay safe.

Once we know about them, we have choices about rules. We can be bound by them or liberated from them. What we experience is what we choose to experience. We can be mortified by an outcome, or we can be energized by the learning it represents. The only thing that changes is the choice we make about what we experience. Thomas Edison tried 1,800 different ways to make a light bulb before he found the one that worked, and he considered each of his trials to be a success because he had discovered another way *not* to build a light bulb. Our lives would be much different today if he had chosen to view his first or his five-hundredth trial as a failure and had made up a rule about not trying the electric light bulb again. It is only because he was willing to accept mistakes as successes that we have the light bulb and all that it has made possible in our lives.

When we discover that *failure* is a meaning that we have chosen to assign to a given event or set of events, we can let go of our need to control outcomes and how others would feel about us. Once we discover each of us is the only person who can determine how we will experience an event, we can begin to let go of our need to control. Once we discover that no matter what we do, someone will more than likely have some negative judgment about it, we can let go of internal rules that tell us what to do or not do. We are able to stop *doing* and start *being.*

Rules drive most of our lives. We feel we have to please others. We live for others and not for what nurtures us and feeds our spirits. When we are willing to accept that there are no rules, we can stop being driven to spend every minute doing things, trying to make things perfect (a futile exercise under the best of circumstances). We quit spending so much time doing things to give physical evidence of our worth that we have time to sit back and enjoy what we have created. Only when we are willing to let go of the rules and the expectations that we have for ourselves and others can we begin to relate with other human beings on a level more meaningful than rules allow.

WORKPLACE RULES CAN UNDERMINE COMPETITIVENESS

Most of the rules in the workplace are just as ludicrous as those by which I used to run my life. They are based on assumptions that are untrue or only partially true. Like personal rules, workplace rules tie the hands of managers and employees, smother spirit and creativity, and sap us of energy. They leave most of the workforce waiting for Friday to begin living instead of experiencing work as bringing energy and joy into our lives. It has become a rule for most of us that joy and work aren't compatible, and we don't challenge our assumptions.

I know an individual who started a business around a long-time hobby of his. Now he says that he no longer enjoys his hobby because it has become work. He hasn't challenged the assumption that joy and work, passion and work, or pleasure and work can't go together. Work should bring joy, passion and pleasure to our lives. It should tap our spirits and give us a productive outlet for our creativity. Work should provide us an arena in which we can develop and achieve our potential rather than confine or anesthetize our minds and creativity. If my friend focused on his creative ability to discover a way to use his pleasure to earn a living, he could know joy in his work. Instead, he is focusing on assumptions about work that aren't necessarily true. The rule that "Work can't be fun!" doesn't really exist!

Rules assume there is right and wrong. The truth is that there is rarely, if ever, one right answer. There are different choices in every workplace situation. None are perfectly right or completely wrong; they are only different. There is the potential for failure in every possibility. If we wait to be 100 percent certain that what our organizations are going to do presents no potential failure, either someone else has probably already done it, or we are using thinking based upon assumptions that are so comfortable they have outlived their usefulness. Risk-taking competitors pass us by so quickly that we won't even realize we have been passed.

Some time ago, I was called in to work with a company that was having considerable difficulty with customer service and with getting new products to market on time. At that time they were in the fortunate position of having a market niche with virtually no competition. Working with employees throughout the company, we developed a set of proposals for improving the flow of work. These proposals required some fairly significant changes in how people operated but would cost the company very little. The owners weren't sure the suggestions would work. Things might get worse, so they chose to continue to operate "the way we always have"; no market forces were pushing them to change. My best guess, and it is only a guess, is that somewhere there was a quiet competitor moving for their niche. By the time this company wakes up to the cost of doing nothing, their ship may be sinking.

The old standby rule of "If it ain't broke, don't fix it!" is another rule that doesn't work any more. Like many other rules, it is based on an erroneous assumption—that getting by is good enough. In these intensely competitive times of continual change, being comfortable with the status quo is tantamount to corporate suicide. Doing nothing must be viewed as a possibility that carries with it the potential for failure. Companies on the move are not even satisfied with revamping. They know they must continually reinvent their businesses to survive. Even though they are rarely written down, rules about making mistakes are widespread in our workplaces, and they are some of the most crippling rules I see. Even in organizations that profess to accept mistakes, there is often a culture that undermines risk-taking. Leaders in organizations can develop a culture that determines what mistakes mean for the company, just as we can in our personal lives. After we make ourselves available for what wants to happen, we often find that mistakes become corporate gifts we could not have planned. Post-it Notes and Velcro were both mistakes that were turned into significant profit centers.

The "finding fault and assessing blame" road has a very different outcome. It is based in fear. Our fear-driven inner voices dig into their defensive posture. "When I find the culprit, I will make an example of him or her." "I don't want this kind of thing to happen again." "When I am in control, these things don't happen. We need to tighten the reins." Whether we say things like this or just carry such attitudes, the impact is the same: Risk-taking screeches to a halt. New ideas are quietly swallowed. The boss's ideas are supported without challenge. The boss appears to be in control, but no one ever tells the boss about the company's blind spots. No one challenges assumptions or provides additional information to the boss. Groupthink prevails. Paralyzed by possible consequences when we choose the fault-finding-and-blaming road, no one does anything.

WHY LIVE BY THESE RULES, ANYWAY?

When we are *being* our fear, we need crutches to lean on to ensure us we will survive and protect what we've come to believe must be protected. Our rules enable a set of strategies which we use to psychologically delude ourselves into thinking we are secure. Perfectionism, self-judgment, judgment of others, righteousness, cynicism, and resentment are all fostered by our rules. They are so much a part of us on the Path of Fear that we are not even conscious of them, yet they have locked our behaviors into permanent, unquestioned autopilot.

Self-judgment appears in our lives as an almost continuous critique of our behavior. Appearing as what has been called by different writers by names such as the Voice of Judgment or the Chatterbox, it starts first thing in the morning and is with us all day. When we get on the scales, the voice tells us, "Should have skipped that dessert last night." Even as we fall to sleep at night we hear, "You really should have been more firm about making John stick to his monthly budget. . . ."

Judgment of others is an important part of this network of enabling strategies like self-judgment. Those strategies are the mechanisms we use to stay in our egos and detached from the real human in us and others. "I could have done it better" is the implicit message as we criticize and find fault with others. On some level we seem to believe that if we are able to do it better, we are always going to be needed and valued. We come to believe we will be indispensable. Countless managers, however, are downsized from jobs in which they thought they were indispensable, and these people would argue that no one is ever completely secure.

When we actively engage in judging others and suggesting that "I could have done it better," most of us miss the point. That point is about working in community. Any two of us could do most jobs better than any one of us. Each of us brings different gifts, talents, perspectives, and life experiences, and we almost always produce a better result in community than by choosing to solo the job. Either judgment of others or self-judgment completely misses this point.

We want to know we are not expendable, and we want others to know it as well. On the Path of Fear, we communicate in a way that lets others know we put ourselves on a pedestal. Sometimes fear surfaces as righteousness, as a comment in conversation that lets everyone know "I know more," "I have a better understanding," or "I have knowledge of more recent research." Sometimes fear surfaces as we call on our credentials or the credentials of our source. Righteousness sometimes surfaces as a statement so imperative that we hope anyone would feel foolish questioning the truth of it. From this place of judgment, everything is black and white. This outlook doesn't produce an atmosphere of openness and flexibility about work improvement or working in community.

Sometimes the communication of judgment is less direct. Perfectionism is an important part of the fear game too. It makes being righteous much easier if we are perfect, but it is an exhausting part of the game. Perfectionism was one of my favorite fear places. I had to work twice as long and twice as hard as others. I did more research. I was better prepared. I rehearsed ad infinitum. I even practiced "spontaneous" responses and quips, and I knew the rules. There were no gray areas. I was going to be perfect. Of course, when we live with the illusion of perfection, any critique is devastating. We psychologically beat up on ourselves and feel guilt, shame, and embarrassment. These nonspiritual experiences of ourselves feed our self-judgment and we generate more rules.

MY WAKE-UP CALL

After a couple of years of warning signals that had hinted that my strategy was faulty, my wake-up call came: perfectionism, judgment, and righteousness didn't work. If they didn't work, how would I operate? Those were the only rules I knew. Even if they didn't work well, I knew them. I'd been working with Dave's company for about six months. We were doing a feedback exercise but were one person short, so I sat in with Dave. The exercise was for one person to give feedback to another for two minutes. At least a minute and a half had to be positive, and the rest had to be a negative expression of the speaker's experience. I reveled in Dave's positive comments. When the negative feedback came, I could hardly believe my ears. "Your work here has been excellent. You are very professional. I've been impressed with your knowledge and thoroughness. I don't know why," he hesitated before continuing, "I just don't trust you." He hesitated again before adding, "You just seem too perfect."

Being a good team player, I accepted the feedback and thanked Dave. On the surface I was a gracious recipient. Inside I was crumbling and devastated. My voices, armed with a generous dose of righteousness, had a heyday with that. I'd never done *anything* in my life that wasn't 100 percent honest. How could he possibly distrust me? I didn't even walk the margins. I played straight and narrow. I could think of lots of things I'd done in my life that demonstrated my trustworthiness. In my righteousness I was missing the point; it took several hours, maybe even a day, before the light came on. It was my *perfection* that caused Dave to distrust me!

Since that red-letter day, the irony of the situation has often struck me as funny. I regularly preached the evils of the perfection model to employers who wanted to institute quality and continuous improvement programs. "Accept mistakes. Use them for learning. Take risks," I would say. Yet the very model by which I lived and worked was just the opposite. Since Dave gave me that gift, my work has improved considerably, and I've grown much more relaxed.

CREATING WHAT WE FEAR

Fear led me to create what I wanted to avoid! I wanted acceptance, respect, trust, and love. I had created distrust and separation. No one is perfect. If I put forth the image of perfection, Dave was absolutely right to distrust it. Yet how many people do just that to themselves? They expect and project perfection in order to get approval, and what they get is distance and disapproval. If we project perfection, how safe can people feel around us? If we project perfection, how can others identify and connect with us? Unless they are enlightened enough to see that our perfection, judgment and righteousness are personal problems, people around us are bound to feel they just can't measure up.

Perfectionism and righteousness become our armor—what we use to protect ourselves from rejection. There's only one problem: it doesn't work. The more we try to convince others and ourselves that we are perfect, the more transparent our guises become. Like other armor, this armor is stiff, inflexible, and keeps us from getting close to people. We create what we fear. We fear we won't be loved and accepted. We create armor that ensures we *won't* be loved and accepted. No one can get close enough. When we are disconnected from others, we lose contact with our emotions, our hearts, and our souls. If we cannot be connected to the whole human race as a flawed human being just like everybody else, we cut ourselves off from others and ourselves.

Bill Rosenzweig, co-founder of the Republic of Tea and co-author of the book by the same name, shared with me how his attitude around perfection has changed over the years. "I used to be a real perfectionist. When I started this business, I embraced that there would be mistakes made. . . . You can almost define your success in business by how well you learn from mistakes and leave them behind. We make lots of mistakes . . . , but hopefully only once."[3]

Perfectionism, judgment, and righteousness aren't the only ways in which we arm ourselves against things and people we fear. Confusion, resentment, and cynicism frequently surface as ways in which we protect ourselves from a world in which we perceive danger in being who we really are. If we are pretending to be confused about the right course of action, we can avoid looking our fear in the face and moving toward it. "But what if I *am* confused?" you may ask. My experience has been that there is rarely a time when we don't know, in our hearts, what the right course of action is. Often we are afraid to do what we know is right, so confusion allows us a hiding place. Welcome to the Path of Fear!

Our chapter opened with Theresa, who was afraid to risk business failure and feigned confusion about whether to borrow money for expansion to meet customer needs. She wasn't confused. She knew what she needed to do. She was afraid but wouldn't name her fear. Because she wouldn't name the fear, she couldn't examine it to see if her inaction was creating what she feared. She couldn't even explore the fear to determine whether or not it was rational. She just kept being confused and not acting. She was unable to see that her inaction was an action. She was choosing to undercapitalize the business but chose on autopilot instead of consciously.

Cynicism and resentment are also ways we arm ourselves against our fear. Cynicism and resentment are ways in which we deny our own accountability in the events of our lives. If there is something that undermines us, then we are freed of making the hard choices and mustering the courage to make things happen. When we play the victim role that cynicism and resentment imply, we hide from our accountability in creating our own situations. As Theresa's case demonstrates so graphically, inac-

---

3. Bill Rosenzweig, conversation with Kay Gilley, Hilton Head Island, SC, February 1995.

tion is a decision, and it is usually a decision which will lead us to create what we fear. On the Path of Courage, we are conscious and intentional, and we are accountable for the consequences of both our actions and our inactions. Perfectionism, judgment, righteousness, confusion, cynicism, and resentment are ways we disconnect from others, from our emotions, and from our courage—scarcely a productive way to address our fears.

When we are at one with our spirits, insulation and armor are neither possible nor desirable. We know that people, including us, are imperfect. We know people have fears. In our spirits, we are loved for the person we truly are, as we are, not for what we do, how we do it, who we know, what credentials we have or how perfect we are. We are accepted just as we are. And, that attitude is what we attract. Bill Rosenzweig is convinced that the leader sets the tone for what the company attracts. "The founder puts out a spiritual message. You will attract like-minded people—people who possess both business savvy and spiritual aspects."

Rosenzweig notes that 70 percent of his company's employees are women as are most of his key managers. He says, "We didn't set out to have either a spiritual company or a company full of women. We started with a seed of our own values, and the more clearly the owner can articulate those values, the more easily the seed can take hold and grow." When we hide behind our armor, we attract others insulated behind armor. Connection is impossible. We fear lack of connection, and our fear creates lack of connection. When we, like Rosenzweig, choose to plant the seeds of spirit we find that we attract people of spirit and courage for whom working in connection and community is not only possible but essential.

OTHER WAYS IT HAPPENS

This self-defeating cycle perpetuates itself. Emily seems disconnected from her people, and I wonder with her whether she is afraid of something that keeps her from developing connection. She confesses to me that she is concerned that her fast-growing company will fail and many people will be out of work. She doesn't want them to know because she is afraid they may doubt the company's viability and quit. What has happened is that her lack of connection with people makes them distrust her. They fear that she will fire them, so they look for other jobs where there is more safety. She is afraid to be open with her employees for fear they will quit. By being disconnected from them, she creates what she fears: they quit anyway.

I have worked with employers who decry the unions. They believe a union is always out to get all it can from the company. "Why can't we work together?" they ask. Yet as they ask the question, they are creating the very thing they fear—lack of teamwork—in a hundred ways that shows the union membership that it is not trusted. Instead of trust, abundance, openness, and flexibility of teamwork, management brings distrust. A team without trust between the coach and the players isn't headed for the World Series or the Super Bowl.

I have worked with employers who say they want to encourage employees to participate in group problem-solving so that quality is improved. They fear that if quality doesn't improve, the company will lose market share. Yet when mistakes or problems are identified, the managers obsess on knowing who did it, whose idea it was, and why someone didn't stop it. They focus on the past. They judge. They expect perfection. They focus on finding fault. The consequence is that people don't participate, quality doesn't improve, and market share declines. The managers create exactly what they fear. Finding fault is based on perfection-thinking and righteousness, and it is based in the past. These fear-based qualities create what the employer fears the most.

SAFETY IS ALSO AN ILLUSION

If we wait until something is absolutely safe, we do nothing. Safety in decision-making is only an illusion. The safety that most organizations seek in rules can be accomplished more simply by accountability, accepting the organization's role in creating its problems, and practicing prudence and good judgment achieved by organizational learning. When I discussed my thesis for this book over dinner with a client, she agreed that she would like to live with a positive belief in humanity. "But," she said, "I deal with the public. This is such a litigious society, I have to protect myself and my business from potential legal problems." She shared an example to make her point. Many would agree with her.

Upon probing, my friend admitted that her organization had stretched its own rules beyond what prudence and good judgment dictate to accommodate a particularly bothersome member of the public. Now she is trying to protect her organization from "the public." Yet, if her company had exercised prudence and good judgment, the problem with the public would never have arisen.

Instead of being accountable about her organization's role in creating its own problems, she complained about the litigious nature of our society and tried to construct more rules to protect her from the public. She misses the company's learning in the incident. Here is a clear example of how we create exactly what we fear by the very actions contrived to prevent the feared event. What she fears is that the public will take advantage of the company and cost it money. She creates more rules focused on the public, when prudent enforcement of the ones she has would prevent the problem she fears. She neglects accountability and training in the company. When a similar problem arises, the employees probably respond in the same way. The *public* that she fears (who are really a few isolated representatives of the public) again takes advantage of her.

There are companies that take the opposite tack with the public. *Inc.* magazine's 1993 Entrepreneur of the Year honors went to Robert Nourse, president and CEO of the Bombay Company. Nourse's company offers an unconditional guarantee to its customers. "The best time to capture customers for life . . . is when they need a refund. We'll take the thing back with no hassle, no questions, no guff about 'Where's the receipt?' The cost of that is peanuts compared with what you gain in customer loyalty."[4]

Nordstrom's apparel stores also have a history of "No questions asked!" return policy. Yes, the public takes advantage of them occasionally; they once took back two automobile tires, items they don't even sell. Yes, someone in management could grouse about the public's taking advantage of them. That is one choice. Nordstrom's received hundreds of thousands of dollars of free advertising—advertising that Nordstrom's never could have bought—as newspapers across the country added the tire story to the self-perpetuating Nordstrom legend. Absorbing the refund cost of the tires as an investment in positive public relations seems to be the choice Nordstrom made.

SAFETY FROM EMPLOYEES IS NO LESS AN ILLUSION

I have seen the illusion of safety used time and again by employers in their dealings with employees. Employers who have tight personnel policy manuals legally contrived to protect them from their employees wring their hands because someone slipped through the cracks. They have policies on everything. At the same time they feel trapped into keeping a troublesome employee, their rigid employee manual builds a culture of confinement and fear which prevents the organization from achieving its creative and competitive potential. Upon further probing, I find almost without fail that the employee who slipped through the cracks was merely an object of the lack of prudence and judgment on the part of the company's management.

---

4. "Survival of the Smartest," *Inc.*, December 1993, pp. 78–79.

"Did you give the employee feedback about poor performance?"

"No."

"Did you do the normal employee evaluation at the end of the probationary period?"

"Well, no, it was our busy season."

"Did you discuss the employee's attendance problems?"

"Well, no, we were waiting to see if a pattern developed."

"So did you do anything that let the employee know that the behavior was unacceptable."

"No, but we were going to. . . ."

This situation happens again and again. The company doesn't need more rules for the employees; it needs more training and more accountability for supervisors and managers. Normal prudence and good judgment coupled with group learning would have accomplished what needed to be accomplished.

Many times managers neglect giving employees feedback that they perceive to be negative because they don't want employees to feel bad. The consequence is that, instead of addressing problems when they are small and just beginning to emerge, they procrastinate until the employee seems to be hopeless. When we create an environment in which feedback is always top-down and is given only as part of a disciplinary process that can lead to dismissal, employees are conditioned to associate all feedback with dire consequences. As a result, getting feedback becomes a negative experience even when the content is not intended to be negative.

When I work with companies, I encourage them to think in terms of disciple-ing, instead of discipline. The word *disciple* means "learner, pupil." I help leaders learn to disciple their employees. The act of discipling is different from the way managers have traditionally taught or trained employees when they share their wisdom with those who would learn. When we disciple, we guide individuals to discover what we want them to know. We help them learn to think through a problem or situation so that people inevitably feel good about what they have been able to figure out on their own. The leader is happy that important information has been related to the individual, and the employee is happier with his or her work. The next time an employee encounters the same or a similar situation, she or he doesn't have to come back to the manager; the thought process has already been learned.

Often when we create rules we choose not to invest the time or develop the skills to help people learn on their own, and at the same time we don't want to address the problems that eventually result when we do not make the extra effort. When we give people a rule about how to do something rather than help them learn how to do it themselves, we increasingly limit their possibilities and make them more and more dependent upon us. At the same time, we put ourselves in the position of being the bearers of bad news whenever people break our rules. We dampen their spirits and our own.

We again find our actions creating a situation that is exactly what we wanted to avoid. We want people to perform in a desirable fashion without our having to intervene continually, but we ask them to check their brains and their spirits at the door and follow our rules. As rules accumulate, it is almost impossible to learn them all. Even when we do, we discover there are always situations that aren't covered. People accustomed to having a rule for everything become paralyzed and cease independent thinking. They become more and more dependent upon the manager for everything.

During the diagnostic stage of a project with a client organization, I sat in on a two-hour employee meeting. Ninety minutes of the two hours was devoted to getting clarification upon how a work rule should be interpreted in a particular situation. The discussion was one of the most ludicrous that I have ever experienced. The really important question was never addressed. Both workers and managers had become so rule-focused that no one asked, "What difference does it make?" From all that I was able to ascertain, it would have made absolutely no difference which of several possibilities was chosen. Yet the resolution of the meeting was to decide on a rule and discipline employees for breaking it!

The illusion that rules create safety or control or productivity is just that, an illusion. Rules are meaningless in creating safety by themselves. Rules *can* produce negative employee and public perceptions that hurt our businesses more than they help.

> "The fewer rules the better. Rules reduce freedom and responsibility. Enforcement of rules . . . diminishes spontaneity and absorbs group energy. . . . When the leader does not impose rules, the group discovers its own goodness."[5]

Rules disarm an employee's ability to think, solve problems, improve, and give quick, effective service. If a company has the reputation of having

---

5. John Heider, *The Tao of Leadership: Leadership Strategies for a New Age* (New York: Bantam/ New Age Books, 1985), p. 113.

rules that allow it to fire people willy-nilly, is it going to be able to attract the best employees from other companies? Will the company suffer over the long run? If a company has a reputation of giving poor service and making it hard to return merchandise, are customers going to flock to it or to the more customer-friendly competitor? You know the answers!

LEARNING TO LIVE WITH THE WORST-CASE SCENARIO

Fear is going to be there; if we are to grow and learn as individuals and as organizations, it is essential to accept its presence. On the Path of Courage, leaders consciously acknowledge fear as a warning sign for what it is: a caution sign, not a stop sign. When we are able to look at fear consciously, we can talk about whether our fear is rational. When the fear is rational, we can exercise the caution and prudence merited by the situation; when we are in denial of fear, we often cannot act prudently. Acknowledging fear also allows us to examine possible outcomes and to discuss how we can turn each scenario into a winning situation. When we are able to accept the worst-case scenario, we develop new confidence that whatever outcome develops, both we and our organization will gain from it. We can let go of efforts to force outcomes and be open to discovery of new meaning from other outcomes.

Fear is always with us whether we acknowledge it or not. On the Path of Courage, we can choose how we will be in relationship to it. We can choose to learn to be with fear and to let go of fear-driven control that limits our possibilities. We know that when we choose to dig in with more and more "protective" control strategies, we often create exactly what we fear. Whether or not things go as we hope, when we are prepared to learn from any outcome, we and our organizations are always winners.

For instance, significant evidence suggests that if we give away control and seek more participation, we produce better products or services at lower costs and in a more timely manner. Yet we may fear giving away control and seeking more participation because we fear people may take advantage of us. They may steal from us. They may be lazy and not perform their jobs well. These are always possibilities. Just for the sake of argument, let's assume that this scenario occurs. What are the "terrible" outcomes that might happen to us? Let's examine some of the possibilities.

One possibility is that the company will die, and we will lose our jobs, almost always our ultimate underlying fear in workplace decisions. The managers may discover that money has bought happiness and friends, but when the "friends" evaporate, the managers may discover they don't want the kinds of friends that money bought them. They start over again with fire in their bellies that only wanting can cause, and they start with the family, friends, and support system that money can't buy. That is one possibility: our "worst case scenario."

Another likely possibility is that chaos will result. In fact, if we are to have an organization that runs well, we even want to sustain the tension of chaos until we can learn all that the chaos has to teach us. Some people may quit because they are not comfortable with ambiguity, openness, acceptance, and accountability. We accept that we as a company, and they as individuals, are happier if they work somewhere else, somewhere that is predictable and where there is no risk-taking and growth. After a chaotic period, a new order emerges. The company is lean; people who didn't care about the company and its dreams and values have been identified, and many are no longer with us. The new order is more open. Information is shared, mistakes are analyzed, learning occurs. Oddly enough, this situation that we fear is probably the best of many possibilities for which we can hope. We live in chaotic times organizationally, and developing a comfort with chaos gives us an edge. Chaos is critical to the continual re-creation that we must do to respond to constantly changing conditions in the business environment.

There is one more possibility. There is the possibility that we submit to our fears and don't increase participation. Chances are that choosing this scenario means that the organization is already spiritually dead. It lacks the responsiveness and energy to grow and learn and respond to new business challenges. It will probably die, and the death will be blamed on foreign competition or regulation or environmentalists or any of a number of scapegoats that we look for when we don't have the courage to be with our fear.

YET ONE MORE PARADOX

When we live from the Path of Fear, things seem quite simple. There are ways we do things and ways we don't. We do what we judge is a good job, keep people happy, and deliver predictables. When we embark upon the Path of Courage, we discover one of the things we didn't know when we were on the Path of Fear. We didn't know the world is a complex place. A big part of that complexity is the introduction of dozens of paradoxes into what we thought was a simple world. We've already visited the faith paradox. We don't have faith until we are in touch with spirit, and we can't be in touch with spirit until we have faith.

Fear presents us with another such paradox. When we are on the Path of Fear, most of us don't know it. We don't think we are afraid, and most of us would strongly resist the suggestion. On the Path of Fear, we find acceptable labels for perfectionism, judgment, cynicism, and the like. These labels assuage our need to feel we aren't afraid. Perfectionism becomes competence and conscientiousness. Judgment may be labeled "good analytical skills" or a host of other guises. Cynicism becomes "just being realistic."

For us to lead from the Path of Courage, one of the first things we have to do is admit we have fear. Bringing our fears into consciousness allows us to look at and make peace with them. We can stop *being* our fear and start being with our fear. Instead of living and leading from strategies that take us away from our fears, we become conscious of them and learn to move toward them. We are able to reap the benefits of rational fears as we discover how we prepare to meet them. At the same time, we are able to develop a rational process for keeping our irrational fears from stopping us and for coming to peace with them.

The first of two fear paradoxes then is that the more we become aware of our fears, the less they dominate our lives and the less they stop us from growing, trying new things, and learning. So it seems the more we feel our fears, the less they influence our behavior. The second paradox of fear is when we are afraid—when we are *being* our fear—we create what we fear the most. We actually make the thing happen that we are attempting to avoid.

ACCEPTING ACCOUNTABILITY AND DETERMINING OUR EXPERIENCE

There really is no *safety* in the sense that we would like to think of it. Rules certainly don't build safety. Pretending that we are ostriches and that the fear will go away if we can't see it certainly doesn't generate safety. The only way we can create something rightly called *safety* is when we accept accountability and determine our own experience beyond the confines of good and bad. There are no rules about the right or wrong way to view your people or the public. There are companies trying a variety of postures toward both groups. Some operate from a position of fear: There are enemies out there who will get us. Those companies fail to develop internal accountability and learning to protect themselves from a small percentage of people who may become problems. As they seek more and more rules, they become increasingly rigid. Responding to a changing business environment becomes more and more difficult and time consuming. The flexibility and resilience needed to respond to change becomes nearly impossible.

Other companies choose to focus on the overwhelming bulk of humanity who want to do a good job and can be trusted. They focus on building connection, being accountable, and encouraging learning. They may encounter a few who attempt to take advantage of them along the way, but because they learn from every outcome, they are never victims. They may lose a few dollars, and they consider it the price they pay for learning. They use that learning to build flexibility and resilience. They use that learning to discover more about accountability. They use that learning to propel them forward in the permanent white water of business.

The choice is: How do we want to experience our businesses? Do we want to expect the worst or the best from people? For me, there is no choice. Fear-based rules keep us focused on the negative possibilities. They emerge either from an event we chose to experience negatively in the past, or more likely from something that we heard had happened to another company. Most confining company rules are based upon fear of a possible problem with a minuscule portion of the employee population or the public; yet the rules confine everyone. When we write fear-based rules for our organizations, we do not write from a place of spirit or of belief in humanity. We write from a place of fear where there is no way to be safe because we choose to see threat in every event.

The Chinese language character for *crisis* combines two other characters: one for opportunity and one for threat. This certainly reflects my experience that in every crisis, both possibilities are present. Fear-based rules simply keep us focused on the threat and cause us to miss opportunities and limit our own options more and more.

When we live consciously, the possibility of "protective" rules, either for us personally or for our organizations, grows more and more ridiculous. There is no safety in rules. There are only illusions. The more we believe in those illusions and the rules we create to support them, the more ridiculous our attempts to comply with them seem. From accountability, acceptance of our organization's role in creating problems and practicing prudence and good judgment come flexibility and openness. From flexibility and openness, we can accomplish all things. From rules, we can only limit our possibilities. The choice is ours to make.

TOOLS FOR BEING ON THE PATH OF COURAGE

- Fear is always with us. We can choose to acknowledge and accept our fears, or we can ignore them and gradually become our fear.

- There are two paradoxes of fear. When we are being our fear, we usually don't know we are afraid. When we are afraid, we create what we fear the most. When we are on the Path of Courage, we are conscious of our fears, and we are able to benefit from them and move ahead in spite of them. We are able to be *with* our fear without *being* our fear.
- On the Path of Courage, we choose to let go of fear-driven strategies: perfectionism, judgment, self-judgment, righteousness, confusion, cynicism, and resentment.
- There are no "safe" courses in life. Anything we do has the potential for pain, mistakes, outcomes we hadn't planned, and disapproval from some people. Anything we do also has the potential for learning, growth, and approval from others.
- If we wait for something to be absolutely safe, we never do anything.
- We attract to us what we are.
- The only safety lies in being accountable, choosing how we will be in relationship to fear, and choosing to determine what our experience will be.

EXPLORING THE PATH OF COURAGE

(1) Identify two or three things that you fear personally or organizationally. Then identify your coping strategies. Carry the progression of events from your strategies to several likely conclusions. Did your strategies create what you feared?

(2) What are some of your personal "rules"? What are the *shoulds* of your life? Start being aware of every time you use the word *should* (or *should not*) and ask yourself, "Why?" Next determine what you fear or desire. Have you created rules that don't work because you are too attached to a particular outcome? Walk yourself through several different scenarios of not doing something your *shoulds* tell you to do. Identify at least one positive outcome from each scenario, including the worst case. When you make peace with the worst-case scenario, does that change your relationship to your rule?

Part 3

Buying the Ticket

Chapter 14

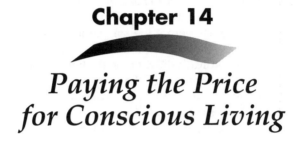

Paying the Price for Conscious Living

The business of expanding your consciousness is not an option. Either you are expandable or you are expendable.

. . . ROBERT SCHULLER[1]

In the early '70s most businesspeople and, for that matter, many Americans, thought we had to choose between price and quality. As more and more foreign products came to our markets, consumers discovered they didn't have to tolerate automobiles with door handles that fell off the first week or kitchen appliances that quit working what seemed like minutes after the warranty expired. Manufacturers across the country have slowly come to know that quality is free. It doesn't cost more to produce a high-quality product than it does a poor one.

Although it doesn't cost more to produce a quality product, there is a price to pay. Manufacturers don't magically wave a wand over their factories and instantly begin producing quality parts. The price that must be paid is increased training of workers, reduced hierarchical decision-making, diffused problem-solving, improved communication, expanded attention to

---

1. Robert Schuller, in Glenn Van Ekeren, *Speaker's Sourcebook, II: Quotes, Stories, and Anecdotes for Every Occasion* (Englewood Cliffs, NJ: Prentice Hall, 1994).

statistical variability, and dramatically altered ideas about how things are and have to be. It is a price businesspeople have become ever more willing to pay to remain viable in the United States and competitive in international markets. Those who have been successful now thrive in the world market-place; those who haven't, continue to wallow in "if only" thinking. They look for excuses and for others to blame for their own troubles.

There has been a price those businesses have had to pay, a price paid in willingness to change. Those who have done it have found that it was a small price to pay. In fact, after the change is made, most realize they were paying a much higher price before their metamorphosis, in loss of sales, customer and employee goodwill, and high accident, absence, and scrap materials rates. The costs didn't show up on the books in a way that linked the costly outcomes to the conditions that generated them.

So it is with building spirit-respecting organizations. We have been paying the price for not respecting the spirits of people in companies, but until now we haven't really linked costly outcomes to what we have or haven't been doing. We have seen medical costs and burnout soar while morale, creativity, and energy lagged. Traditionally we have chosen to address these concerns with quick fixes like cost-containment programs or incentive programs for ideas rather than to look for the systemic causes.

Just as the manufacturer cannot wave a magic wand over a factory to improve quality, we can no more wave a wand and magically produce a spirit-respecting workplace than we can wave one over ourselves and begin living from spirit. To build organizations in which people and spirit thrive, we must pay a price. Just as the price for quality seems relatively small, the price for living consciously from spirit eventually appears to be modest. But there is a price to pay.

WHAT IS THE COST?

The ability to lead and live from spirit is the result of choosing to live con-sciously. Being committed to living consciously in a society that largely muddles through on autopilot isn't easy. There is a price to pay for choos-ing to live consciously, and sometimes it is a hefty price tag. A friend of mine prefers to say that living consciously requires us to be more charitable. Unlike the grudging donation made from obligation, true charitable giving comes from the heart. (In fact, *love* is a definition for "charity.") We still pay, he says, but it is charitable because we willingly choose to pay, and it feels good all over when we do. Whatever term is used, there is a price to be paid.

We were all born with spirits and the ability to live from that place. A group of friends recently discussed our belief that we knew all the basics we needed to live from spirit by the time we were twelve years old. So why does it take years to recover spirit, and why does it come with a hefty price tag? If we are born with it, shouldn't it be free?

Our Wonder Child was born with spirit, and living from spirit is free . . . at birth. We were free before all the insulating devices, walls, armor, roadblocks, coping strategies, and countless other impediments were constructed. Even though our group thought we had the basics by twelve, we unanimously agreed that sometime not much later we had all lost touch with those core qualities and positive beliefs.

The price to be paid for returning to the Wonder Child spirit is the price of personal restoration, like restoring an old house to its original condition. Old additions must be removed, and countless layers of paint must be scraped off the woodwork. Even more layers of wallpaper must be steamed off the walls, doors must be eliminated, and many later improvements must be removed. After each project, refuse must be to be hauled away. Part of the cost of regaining our spirits is a refuse removal charge for the years of accumulated refuse that we have stuffed between ourselves and spirit. Each piece of refuse has to be painstakingly removed, one by one, to make space for spirit to emerge into consciousness as a vital, energy-giving part of daily life. We can't lead from spirit until we live from spirit.

The price tag for our spirits isn't a fixed price, dollars-and-cents arrangement for which we can go to the bank and get a loan. It's more like an open-ended, variable-rate installment plan, with no early pay-off privileges. The duration of the loan is our lifetime. The payments vary from day to day and week to week; they depend on how much learning we have to do and how quickly we choose to give up the insulation we have used as protection.

Usually, the closer we get to our spirits, the higher the price; that is when we are removing assumptions that have framed our whole world. Other times we are able to remove several layers easily at a low cost. Even if we are willing to pay the price all at once to get it over with, we cannot: We have to do the personal work to remove each and every layer one at a time. We cannot even start to come closer to spirit until we make the commitment to pay the bill. We have to be willing to say, "I choose to start being different in my business, in my community, and in my life. I can no longer view life as having discrete parts. I want to see my life as a continuous whole, and I am willing to pay the price."

The price we pay for "refuse removal" is a personal one. We cannot write a check for payments and have someone else carry all our refuse away in a bag or can. As with any restoration project, there are choices that we must make if we are to move forward through the project. Along the way are choices to get rid of thinking, behaviors, and attitudes that don't work for us anymore. We must also pay in courage and commitment to stick with our choices to end destructive habits and relationships that are incompatible with the new direction we choose. Choices about what part of the old to leave behind are coupled with choices about new thinking, behaviors, and attitudes compatible with the life we choose for the future. The price we must pay for spirit is choice, commitment, and courage.

We pay the price by giving up a lot that has become comfortable to us on the Path of Fear; the burden inevitably weighs us down and holds us back on our journey. The toll fees that we pay for access to the Path of Courage are the things we must forsake:

- Living in the past and for the future
- Living from habit and in autopilot mode
- Making excuses for not being accountable for what we create
- Needing or wanting the approval of others
- Thinking negatively
- Thinking and acting like a victim
- Blaming others for the way in which we have chosen to experience events and people
- Blaming ourselves for not being perfect, for not knowing, seeing, believing, or acting
- Feeling resentment, resignation, cynicism, and worry
- Having judgment, self-judgment, perfectionism, and righteousness
- Guilt, anger, hate, bigotry, and jealousy
- Giving to other things and people the power to create our happiness
- Using labels and categories
- Being self-reliant and needing to do things on our own
- Having to know the rules
- Believing in one right answer, one correct way to do things, or one correct outcome
- Needing to control
- Needing to have our brains know what will happen and how things will end
- Needing to find safety in familiar, controllable circumstances
- Being driven by fear
- Being paralyzed and unable to act out of fear
- Being on the Path of Fear

These are the things of demolition and refuse disposal. Giving up the things that don't work anymore parallels the unlearning process. This process is what makes room for new ways of being. A great deal more effort is demanded for demolition and refuse removal than for new construction costs. With all the negativity gone, the new pieces arrive and fall into place relatively effortlessly. Remember: This is how we came into the world. This is what is natural. Even though it has become habitual and quite comfortable, most autopilot behavior is not natural. The demolition just makes space for an original part of us to emerge.

After we've paid for refuse removal, we must also pay for reconstruction. The price we pay for knowing a new path, a new way of being, is simply recognizing that we have choices and then choosing new thinking, behaviors, and attitudes compatible with spirit. Some of those choices may be neither popular nor comfortable for ourselves and others around us. The choices spirit demands are:

- Choosing the Path of Courage
- Choosing to live in the present
- Choosing a positive belief in humanity
- Choosing to commit, accepting no excuses, and producing only results
- Choosing to love and be lovable
- Choosing to be peaceful, kind, caring, respectful, trusting, giving, accepting, inspiring, and aspiring
- Choosing abundance, openness, expansiveness, and flexibility
- Choosing connection rather than separation
- Choosing to create my own joy and happiness in whatever I am doing, *when* I am doing it
- Choosing creativity, intuition, wonder and risk-taking
- Choosing learning and continuous improvement
- Choosing faith
- Choosing to live in integrity with my new choices
- Choosing safety in what I am rather than in what I do
- Choosing courage to be with my fears

The price is choosing these new ways of being, committing to make them happen, accepting no excuses, producing only results, and displaying the courage to carry through for the long term.

This price can be a high one at times, especially when we go solo and choose to *be* on our own and not as a part of a larger organizational-transformation project. When we choose to *be* and others are in a doing mode, we must be patient, committed, and courageous enough to stay the course, despite knowing that others will attempt to lure us back to the Path of Fear. When we choose to be vulnerable when others are not, we risk rejection, judgment, ridicule, and perceived loss of respect. When we are willing to talk about what we are afraid of while others who are detached from their feelings pretend there is nothing to fear, we may be engaging in one of the highest levels of organizational risk-taking. It is critically important to remember that to lead from spirit, we must give up our need for the approval of others. This is the price we pay for choosing the Path of Courage.

I have known people who choose to go solo on the Path of Courage in an organization and lose their jobs; they are no longer perceived to have the "right stuff." One man I know lost his job as chief financial officer because he was committed to asking the hard questions that others preferred to ignore. He brought values and ethics into the financial decision-making arena. It did not take him long to find another position in a consulting firm that valued his approach, but in our society being fired from a job, however noble the reason, still carries with it a considerable social stigma.

I know several people who felt they had to voluntarily leave jobs that forced them to do things that did not reflect their values. One person felt the customers were not being dealt with honestly. Another was involved in what she considered a financial scam. For anyone who chooses to go solo on the Path of Courage, the price may very well end up being the job. You recall that I made the choice as a businessperson to no longer do certain work or work for certain organizations. This choice was risky and brought me some uncomfortable times when I relied on faith that somehow things would work out. They always have, but nonetheless I paid a price as I looked nervously at my dwindling resources. Just asking what for me are the defining existential questions makes the path I choose clear over and over again.

- Why am I here?
- What is my purpose?
- What brings meaning to my life?
- What brings me to life?

When I ask these questions, the directional signs to the Path of Courage are clearly marked. But I suspect that if I live to be a hundred, I will always be tempted from time to time to take the Path of Fear.

WHAT PRICE A SPIRIT-RESPECTING ORGANIZATION?

When our businesses choose to lead from the Path of Courage and build a spirit-respecting workplace, there are also prices to pay as well as rewards to reap. We choose to:

- Give up being driven by events and accept being guided by our vision and values
- Give up money today to invest in our guiding principles for the future
- Give up valuing people only for what they do and value them for who they are and what they bring to our consciousness as well
- Give up win-lose and work toward win-win
- Give up "doing it the way we've always done it" and accept creativity
- Give up doing it alone and be part of a team
- Give up our negative belief in our people and accept our role in creating circumstances and outcomes
- Give up being organizational victims and accept that we can create what we want our organization to be
- Give up blaming and glory-grabbing and accept accountability
- Give up our need to control people and outcomes and empower others
- Give up our fear of spirit, entrepreneurship, and leadership at all levels and be willing to nurture these qualities instead
- Give up fighting the white water and be *in* it; have trust and faith that our skills will carry us to an outcome we see as positive
- Give up our belief that the world is black and white and accept that it is various shades of gray
- Give up living for the short term, and exercise the courage to focus on the long run
- Give up what is known and familiar and exercise the courage to explore the unknown

This is the price that we pay for a spirit-respecting organization. This is the price that we pay to discover the spirit that is present in all of our people, in all of our organizations. This is the price that we pay for flexibility, resilience, creativity, quality, energy, and vitality in our companies. It is the price that we must pay with no early pay-off privileges. The duration of the loan is the life of the organization.

THE COURAGE TO ENDURE

The path of spiritual growth is long, arduous, and never-ending. It requires patience and persistence. It requires a learning model: We are *never* perfect. Regardless of how evolved our development may be, we always make mistakes. There is always more to learn. We often fall short of what we hope for ourselves. It takes courage to accept our imperfections.

No one else is perfect either. Regardless of how evolved a friend or co-worker may be, he or she always makes mistakes, has more to learn, and often falls short of hopes and goals. We probably even taught some people about being non-spiritual before we began living from spirit. It takes patience and courage for us to accept others as imperfect and to still respond to them from spirit—especially those who are doing what we taught them. They remind us of our dark side, and we remember to continually make friends with the dark side. There are always those, insulated from spirit, who try to take advantage of those who choose the Path of Courage. But it is impossible to take advantage of a person on a spiritual path; a gift of learning is always found in whatever happens. Those on the Path of Courage always choose to grow and come closer to their spiritual center.

We accept that we and others are imperfect. We accept that there are those who do not respond to us in a spiritual way. Spirit is the source of the courage to endure, to respond with love and caring. We know that those who are disconnected from spirit have great fear and lack the strength of spirit and conviction to preserve themselves. Therefore, we respond with care and loving, over and over again. It takes courage, compassion, and patience to respond from the spirit again and again, yet we choose to do it. Can we do anything less?

Does this mean we let ourselves become doormats? No! We have the courage to respond with love and caring. If I am an employer and someone steals from me, I respond with love and caring. I may choose to fire the employee, but I do so from a place of love and caring. Firing someone from a place of love and caring means that I separate the person from the unacceptable behavior. The employee isn't a bad person. He or she has committed an act that violates our values and is unacceptable in our trusting culture. The courageous act of firing in a loving way may be the act that starts the employee's own development. It may provide a much-needed wake-up call. (I have known people who, months or years later, point to being fired as one of the best gifts they have ever received. Few of them thought so when it happened.)

Every parent at some time, denies a child a privilege or makes a child do something unpleasant that contributes to the child's growth. Such acts are love when done in a loving way; these acts take courage. Many respond with "tough love" toward a loved one who is an alcoholic or is drug addicted. They say, "I love you, and you can't live here anymore. You are a good person, and you are damaging me and the rest of the family." Such a deed takes courage.

To lead in this way in a fallible world requires self-acceptance and more courage. We may even find ourselves tolerant of negative acts from others when we see that we can be the source of such acts. Living from spirit is quintessentially human, and humans are not perfect. Mistakes are ways of learning, our mistakes and those of others. When we make a mistake, we obviously have more learning and growing to do. It is a lifelong process. When we have the courage to celebrate the beginner in each of us every day each time we fall and learn we are closer to our spiritual core. Living from our spiritual core isn't about being perfect; it is about choosing a spiritual path, practice, and discipline, a discipline of continuous learning and growth. Living from spirit is accepting our fallible selves and growing.

As we begin to live in our new way, we may be what we would like to be only 10 percent of the time. We are all similar in the refuse removal stage. We are still unlearning and making space for new behaviors and attitudes. It takes courage and faith to endure and to keep learning and growing. It may seem that we never get "there," and it takes courage and faith not to throw in the towel and give up. We won't ever be "there" all of the time. Spiritual growth isn't a destination but a journey. It isn't a task to *do* but a lifelong process. In our goal-driven society, to choose a path with full knowledge that we will never achieve our goal takes courage.

PAYING THE PRICE OR CHARITABLE GIVING?

Leading from the heart means operating on a conscious, spiritual level as much of the time as possible, until the process becomes like breathing. Spirit is breathing, inhaling the breath of life to ourselves, our friends, our family, our co-workers, our organizations, and our world. When we are spiritual, we have complete belief in ourselves and in humanity. We have courage to walk where others have not walked. We have faith that whatever we do is a gift for us and for others, even if it is just a gift of learning. We cannot fail; we can only grow.

The price we pay for discovering our personal and organizational spirits is choice, commitment, and courage. We *choose* spirit and the Path of Courage. We *commit* to finding and living from spirit. We act with heart *courage* to ensure that what we want happens. The price is dear, but our lives and organizations are in the balance. When we pay the price, we are filled with the breath of life, charged with energy, and overflowing with creativity. When we choose not to pay the price, we slowly rob ourselves of life as surely as if we are tightening a noose about our necks.

Perhaps my friend is right to say that leading from the heart is like charitable giving. We don't have to do it, and when we do, it feels good all over. Whether we call it charity or paying the price, when we choose to pay, to do the hard work, to have the courage to look even the scariest things in the face and walk toward them lovingly, we commit to an open-ended, lifelong journey and know that the gift we receive is the gift of life. We pay the price, and it is a small price indeed!

TOOLS FOR BEING ON THE PATH OF COURAGE

- We are all born with spirit and the ability to live on the Path of Courage. Events of our lives added insulating devices: walls, armor, roadblocks, coping strategies, and countless other impediments to life on the Path of Courage. Now a personal restoration process is required. This process begins with "refuse removal" (giving up attitudes, beliefs, or behaviors associated with the Path of Fear) and moves into "reconstruction" (choosing new attitudes, beliefs, and behaviors associated with the Path of Courage).
- The path of spiritual growth is long, arduous, and never-ending. Part of the process includes developing patience with ourselves, persistence on our path, and acceptance of our mistakes.
- Leading from the heart does not mean that we become doormats. Learning to separate an unacceptable behavior from the person who does the behavior allows us to live our values and to respond with love and care while courageously taking whatever action is necessary to address a situation.

EXPLORING THE PATH OF COURAGE

(1)   Do a personal inventory of the attitudes, beliefs, and values that you espouse. Now identify recent behaviors that reflect these espoused attitudes, beliefs, and values. Then identify specific recent behaviors that did not reflect them. Where are the gaps? What undermines your commitment? What would it look like if you were living in accord with your values all the time and were in complete integrity? What would it take for you to truly commit—accept no excuses, produce only results—to living and working in complete integrity all the time?

(2)   Survey the list of attitudes, behaviors, and beliefs on the list for "refuse removal" (p. 218). Choose one that you believe would improve your life dramatically if you released it. Develop intentionality around letting go of it. Make an *A* list of things that will happen in your life when you let go of this item. Make a *B* list of things that won't be happening that

are happening now. These lists will become measuring sticks for your progress. Make a C list of situations, people, and places likely to trip you up and send you back onto the Path of Fear. Write down a specific strategy beside each item on your C list to assist your resolve when you encounter obstacles. If you know in advance that you will encounter one of your C items, spend a few minutes visualizing yourself using your Path of Courage strategy. For the next thirty days, spend five to ten minutes at the end of the day reviewing your lists and the events of the day. Be consciously grateful to spirit for all the new things (A list) you create in your life by releasing this item. Then review your B list. Be consciously grateful to spirit each day for Path of Fear events that have left your life. When B list items occur during the day, identify new situations or people, and add them to your C list. Be consciously grateful for each of those events or people or both for helping you learn more. Reassess C list items to see whether you need to develop new strategies or adjust ones you previously named. When you do this assessment at the end of thirty days, plan a ritual or celebration to mark your progress. (Remember, there is no perfection, only continuous learning.) Then choose another item to work on for the next thirty days.

Chapter 15

Discovering Leadership at All Levels

See things as you would have them be instead of as they are.

... ROBERT COLLIER[1]

As I was coming into my office building one morning, I met a woman who used to work for a former client of mine. I will call her Susan. Susan looked at me rather sheepishly. "I was just down the hall from your office. I almost came down to see you, but I didn't know. . . ." Her voice trailed off, then started up again. "Well, our last encounter was not the most pleasant, and I wanted you to know I don't hold bad feelings for you." Several months earlier, I had been involved in Susan's involuntary termination from employment. I told her I wished she had been comfortable stopping in, but as I was not in my office, we were obviously supposed to meet in this more casual way.

Susan had been negative about her former organization for a long time. She had chosen not to demonstrate constructive leadership. For at least the year that I had worked with the client, Susan had been the victim

---

1. Robert Collier, in Glenn Van Ekeren, *Speaker's Sourcebook II: Quotes, Stories, and Anecdotes for Every Occasion* (Englewood Cliffs, NJ: Prentice Hall, 1994).

of "if only" thinking. She professed great commitment to the organization and thought it was a great place to work "if only. . . ." (You can fill in many "if onlys." There had been a lot of them for Susan.) It "would do good work for its customers 'if only. . . . ' " "would be a good place to work 'if only. . . .' "

The organization was negative, and Susan had responded to negativity with more negativity and cynicism. She used her ability to influence people in a negative way because she did not see that she could make a positive difference. Her victim thinking trapped her. She didn't have the courage to demonstrate leadership and change the organization, and she didn't have the courage to leave the organization. At the end, she did something that was so blatant that she was certain to be fired, and she was. It is my belief that she unconsciously engineered her firing to enable herself to get out from under the negativity of her employer when she didn't have the courage to do it on a conscious level!

When I bumped into her in my building that day, Susan looked better than I had ever seen her. She was relaxed and glowing and easily looked five years younger than the last time I'd seen her. She had come to realize what a burden she had been carrying for a long time. She had come to realize how she let herself be a victim by not choosing to make a positive difference in her experience or for the organization. Susan had a new job in a new field; she had significantly more responsibility and was earning quite a bit more money in a new field. She had come to realize what a gift her firing had been. She was open and flexible about new possibilities. She was enthused. She was reclaiming her power! Full of wonder, risk-taking, optimism, and resilience, Susan was reclaiming the positive spirit of her Wonder Child.

A year later I had occasion to talk with an associate of Susan's at her second place of business. Combining the skills she had gained in the new business with the passion she had once felt for her former work, Susan had recently became head of an organization similar to the one she had worked in when I first knew her. Her former associate told me she was doing great, loved the job, loved the people she worked with, and felt she was finally achieving her potential.

Many people may experience being fired from a job and being forced to take a job in a different field as a disgrace. Susan chose to experience these things as learning. Anchored once again in her spirit and discovering her natural ability to lead, she used her resilience, optimism, and eagerness to learn to keep her moving forward. She remained flexible about outcomes and chose to accept her firing as a growth step rather than as a failure.

THE ESSENCE OF LEADERSHIP

On the Path of Courage, leadership is seeing "things as you would have them be" and then having the courage to be the change you would create. On the Path of Courage, there is an instant in which the leader comes to know what is possible. With spirit as guide, the leader believes all things are possible, and from spirit the leader knows, "If I can think it, it can happen." Spirit brings the leader peace, inspiration, faith, trust, and complete belief in self and others. On the Path of Courage, leaders know job one is to give birth to an atmosphere in which every person comes to see him- or herself as a leader and is confident in exercising that skill. On the Path of Courage, leadership occurs at all levels and in every part of our organizations. This is what Odwalla's Steltenpohl called "leaderful" organizations.[2]

On the Path of Fear, people look for exceptions and excuses instead of possibility: "*I* believe in the spirit of people, my co-workers, my friends, and my family. If only I could get everybody to think this way, this would be a great world." Victims of "if only" thinking aren't leaders anywhere in their organizations. Instead of leading change, they look for reasons why change won't work, and their lack of leadership ensures it won't. They lack the consciousness, the commitment and the courage to even try.

" 'If only' . . . my mother, my husband, my wife, my child, my boss, my secretary, the man in front of me in the checkout line at the grocery store . . . would do something or be something different, then I could do what I want to do." "If only" thinking is victim thinking, not leadership thinking. When we think like this, we believe that we cannot change our own lives, we cannot change our workplaces, and we cannot change our world. We believe we need someone or something else to make the world what we want it to be. Our beliefs become self-fulfilling prophecies.

On the Path of Courage, all that changes. We no longer need to have others change for our experience to change. We choose what we experience, and we create it. From that worldview, we also know that change begins with each of us. We cannot change other people or circumstances, but each of us can change the way we are in relationship with other people or circumstances. And, we can choose to be in relationship to them in a way that creates what we want. We know that we make the difference. It matters not who we are or where we are in the organization. It matters not what our job may be. Leadership begins in each of us. Leadership comes from spirit and courage, and it occurs at all levels in the organization.

Leadership begins with one person—one person who believes he or she can make a difference. It begins with one person who has faith. It can

---

2. See note 4, Chapter 2.

start anywhere. It begins with unconditional acceptance of our ability to make change. Someone else doesn't need to change for our experience to change. It begins with being in the present and giving up the past and all of our negative thoughts that are part of the past. Negative thoughts get in the way of believing we each make a difference. Negative thoughts breed cynicism and disillusionment. Negative thoughts create expectations of perfection the first time we do something. Negative thoughts bind us to the need to know how things turn out. Negative thoughts bind us to the outcome the rational mind thinks is necessary.

The leader chooses to give up control. The leader chooses to give up rules that tell us what we can or can't accomplish or what we should or shouldn't do. The leader chooses to give up attachment to a specific outcome in exchange for making change in a positive direction and accepting the outcome as the source of ongoing learning and improvement.

The essence of leadership lies in the *being* that a person brings to what he or she does. The being that is the essence of leadership is characterized by three qualities:

- The ability to envision a relationship, company, community, or world the way the leader wants it to be
- The ability to believe that one person—the leader—can make a difference in creating what he or she wants
- The ability to have the consciousness, the commitment, and the courage to see that the envisioned change does occur

Believing we can make a difference—that we can produce a positive outcome—is the source of the courage to make the difference happen. This belief is the essence of leadership. Without leadership qualities, a person can *do* all the things described in leadership books, but leadership does not occur. With the needed qualities, leadership occurs easily and naturally. There is no bag of magic techniques to help us to be leaders. The magic lies in our being.

A person may exercise the controlling power that comes with position or financial resources and still never be a leader. When this failure of leadership occurs, its source almost always lies in the person's need to control. The need to control comes from needing to win in a win-lose game. What such people miss is that win-lose is a game that everybody loses. Their need for control becomes more and more desperate as time progresses, until all perspective is gone from their lives. They bring their fears to reality.

I remember having a conversation with another student in graduate school about the desperate need for control that many managers and business owners have. The student posed the question, "Don't they understand the negative impact that kind of behavior has on the bottom line?"

My response was one I believe I will always remember, perhaps because it is the first time I verbalized many years of experience with managers. "It has been my experience," I said, "that the bottom line is not the bottom line. The real bottom line is whether they have power to control. It is an addiction that drives all they do, and like any other addiction, they have to have it without regard to the cost. If the bottom line suffers, that is a moot point to them. If the company folds, that is secondary to their need for their drug of choice—control."

Recently, I had a similar conversation with a colleague who said she regularly asks managers and business owners explicitly, "Do you want control, or do you want a well-run organization? You can't have both."

Real leaders don't need control. Their source of being gives them a different power, a power that increases as they give it away to others. The term *empowerment* has been tossed around a lot in recent years, but it is my belief that few people can even conceptualize what it means to really empower others. Power presents us with still one more paradox on the Path of Courage. To get more of it, we have to give it away. The more we give it away, the more we get back. When we try to withhold power with controlling measures, we reduce the amount of power we have. The harder we hold on, the less we have.

Leaders not only understand empowerment but live in a way that empowers others wherever they go and whatever they do. What I am describing is leadership that anyone can demonstrate. The only thing standing in the way is choosing it. When we develop consciousness about creating our vision, our commitment to make it happen, and our courage to do whatever it takes to keep our commitment, choosing happens easily. When we choose it, we bring all the optimism and other positive qualities that come from being our spirits.

In her negative company, Susan chose not to be a leader. She chose to be a victim. She could identify changes that she might make, but only to the extent that others needed to change first. She was stuck in "if only" thinking. She did not believe that *she* made a difference. She did not have the courage to choose to make a difference. In discovering flexibility and openness to cope with the aftermath of her firing, Susan discovered her spirit. It is doubtful that she will ever be a victim again. She has discovered the source of leadership: her spirit.

Most people have lots of excuses for not demonstrating leadership. They are exactly that: excuses, not reasons. They will say they are not in the right position, or they don't have enough money. They will say they have too many other responsibilities, or they had a bad experience in childhood that crippled their self-esteem. It is "if only," victim thinking. People who go through life living excuses haven't reclaimed their spirits and the courage that comes with spirit. Some of the most powerful leaders I have known in my life were not in positions of authority. They were people who had vision and knew they made a difference, everywhere they were, whatever they were doing. The stories I am about to relate reveal how three women in positions that may have seemed powerless to others have used their leadership in unlikely ways and places. Each is making a difference.

DEMONSTRATING LEADERSHIP AT ALL LEVELS

Since I have been in my current office building, I have had two different maintenance people, both women who are middle-aged. The first was a victim. I will call her Mary. Although we did not talk much, the impression I always had about Mary was that she felt stuck in a job that was beneath her. Her demeanor was spiteful. My office was always clean, but Mary definitely did not bring her spirit to work with her. Mary always seemed to be miserable.

Wendy maintains my office now. She brings her spirit to work with her each day and demonstrates quiet leadership in all that she does. Although she rarely sees most of us, she is connected to "her people." Wendy always has a personal remark about something she has seen in my office. She notices little things. I am not "Suite 730" to Wendy. I feel I am "Kay, a special person," to Wendy. Even when I do not see her, I have the sense when I walk into my office that it has been tended to lovingly. Wendy has encouraged me at every turn as I have been writing my book, sometimes at strange hours. Wendy brings love to her work. Wendy brings spirit to her work. She makes a difference in the lives of every person on her hall. And, Wendy always seems happy. She experiences the joy that comes from making a difference.

I know nothing of the personal lives of these two women. I do know that Wendy is personally powerful because she *chooses* to be. She *chooses* to make a difference, so she does make a difference. Mary has chosen to be a victim. She has chosen to be powerless. She has chosen *not* to make a difference, and she doesn't make a difference. Wendy seems to be happy and powerful. Mary seems to be miserable and powerless. What a difference their choices have made for them.

The second powerful leader is a young woman who works with juvenile delinquents. Terri is an extremely attractive and feminine woman and in her job deals with some pretty tough kids. She has a reputation for being able to work with youngsters that no one else can handle. Terri once requested an assignment in a rough rural community. She quickly learned that she had her work cut out for her. Terri is patient . . . and tenacious.

In her gentle way, she began making inroads and used her creativity to develop new ways to reach people. She is teaching concepts totally outside the realm their rough-and-tumble experience to the young people she works with. She arranged an anger-management class for those who believed there was no option except a punch or a blow. Countless juvenile counselors across the country have similar jobs. What I believe makes Terri special is her spirit. She looks at each person and sees hope. She brings love, kindness, respect, caring, dedication, trust, and a huge load of faith to every encounter. Terri demonstrates the essence of leadership. She envisions the community the way she would like it to be. She *knows* she makes a difference. She has the heart courage to make a difference. She *does* make a difference.

Every community has stories. Jean is one of my community's stories. Jean has demonstrated the purest form of leadership. She saw a problem. She knew how she wanted the world to be. She believed she made a difference, and she had the courage to make the difference. A former child development teacher, Jean saw the devastation that child abuse brought to families, communities and the future, and she believed in the parents! These were not people who were accustomed to having people believe in them. She looked at the parents and saw people who had, themselves, been abused. She saw people who knew no other way to parent. Jean envisioned a world in which these abusers would get the parenting education and practice that they needed to be the loving parents that she believed they really wanted to be. She was loving, respectful, creative, intuitive, trusting and caring. She treated the families with dignity.

Jean knew she could make a difference, and she had the heart courage to try something new. She didn't let herself get caught up in negative thinking about what was possible. Although she didn't have a background in fund-raising, she learned as she went. She began knocking on doors, stopping people on the street, calling people, and making speeches. She was aspiring, inspiring, dedicated and positive. She had faith, compassion, passion.

In 1983, the Lane County Relief Nursery was born. Housed in a local church, the therapeutic preschool worked with abused children and their parents to teach them to respect the human spirit. The school now employs thirty-five people, including six parent graduates from the program, has an annual operating budget of nearly one million dollars, and has become a model for similar programs across the country.

After ten years of service to the community, the school moved into its first real home. Jean is still at the helm, and she tells incredible, heart-rending stories about the difference the nursery has made. She believes in the parents and in the community. Jean has a vision of what the world can be, and she puts her spirit into making changes occur. Jean lives her spirit. Jean lives leadership. She has heart courage.

A century and a half ago, Henry David Thoreau wrote, "Most men live lives of quiet desperation." At the doorstep of the twenty-first century not much has changed. Millions of people still live "lives of quiet desperation" because they choose not to bring to their lives a positive belief in their ability to make change.

Jean could have looked at child abuse and seen a desperate situation. Terri could have looked at hardened teenage criminals and seen a desperate situation. Wendy could have looked at a job emptying trash and cleaning toilets as a desperate situation. Any one of these three women could be living "lives of quiet desperation."

They don't. They are leaders. Jean looks at child abusers and sees opportunity to make a difference. Terri looks at juvenile delinquents and sees the opportunity to make a difference. Wendy looks at the tenants in an office building and sees the opportunity to make a difference. Jean makes a visible, quantifiable difference. The difference Wendy makes is less visible. Yet one of Wendy's tenants is the Rotary Club that helps fund Jean's program. Two others are neuropsychologists doing therapy and behavioral research. One is writing a book about bringing spirit to work. If the psychologists make a major discovery, or if this book inspires twenty programs like Jean's, who is to say that, over time, as Wendy almost invisibly makes each of our lives better, her quiet leadership may not have far-reaching effects?

CONTINUOUS IMPROVEMENT REQUIRES LEADERSHIP AT ALL LEVELS

In recent years, it has become increasingly apparent that our organizations cannot make the transition required by the fast pace of change in the world today except under one condition: Change must happen throughout every level of the organization almost simultaneously. Personal entrepreneurship and commitment have been mentioned. What these ideas boil down to is that people all know what they want the organization to be; they also know that they personally make a difference in making it happen.

A man who manages a large manufacturing facility told me this story about leadership emerging from within his plant. He had worked and worked to lower the cost of a fairly large budget item associated with shipping. He had almost given up in despair and put the project aside for a while. During the same time and unrelated to this one item, he had begun sharing more information about the facility and its budget with everyone in the plant. Because he had established an environment in which people were comfortable taking on projects and moving them through to completion without permission, he had been unaware that a group of people on the factory floor had fingered the same item as one they wanted to reduce.

Over a period of months, he noticed the costs associated with this item inching down. Eventually the reductions became quite significant. He started asking questions. "What's going on? Why are our costs going down so much?" The answer, of course, was that leadership had emerged on the factory floor: Working in community with their co-workers, the operators had discovered this problem area on their own. Then they began to find ways to cut cost. They eventually reduced the budget item to about one third of its original amount. This is leadership, pure and simple. This plant manager hadn't just handed out financial data, and then voilà! like magic, the operators discovered the cost area and began cutting. He had to start being the change he wanted to see in his plant. As change happened over time, what he had hoped to see really did transpire. This is just one of dozens of stories he can tell about leadership that regularly bubbles up everywhere in the plant.

Executives committed to building a leaderful organization often miss a point suggested by the power paradox. Producing an environment for leadership to emerge at all levels doesn't mean just changing conditions for the workers. It means the traditional leaders must change the way they *be* in relationship to those workers. They must give the power and control away before the power comes back. Many look at the change they want to see in the worker group without stepping back to determine how they, too, must change in the new scenarios.

DEVELOPING INTENTIONALITY

On the Path of Courage, our natural leadership helps us to see the change we want and to know we make the difference, but we cannot simply think how we want conditions to change and expect that change will happen. We cannot stop at changing the conditions for others and expect it to happen. Such approaches are really nonverbalized "if only" thinking. The implication is that if only I wish for it enough, I can change the system without changing me. If only I change everything else, I can create the organization I envision without changing me.

On the Path of Courage, we know that if we want others to be different, everything in the system must change, including us. The executive leader on the Path of Courage knows that making a difference at the executive level requires developing intentionality—the personal and organizational will to make change happen. That is what making a difference at the executive level means.

The first of the three essential qualities of leadership is:

- Leaders envision a relationship, company, community, or world the way they want it to be.

Envisioning the work environment that we want requires more than getting an idea and sharing it. Envisioning is imagining a detailed picture of what it would look like, sound like, and feel like when our vision becomes a reality. We have such clarity of what our vision entails that we know even what is and isn't happening when our vision exists and how we will measure our progress toward getting there. We know what people will be doing and how they talk and relate to each other, and we know what behaviors characteristic of traditional organizations won't be happening in our visionary one. Envisioning is having such a clear picture of your idea that you could list two hundred qualities to anyone who asked about it. When we have that clarity, we are able to move forward and integrate the next quality of leadership:

- Leaders believe they personally can make a difference in creating what they want.

Once we know what we want to create, the executive leader continues to develop intentionality by asking the questions that help us collectively discover what needs to change in the system to enable this new environment to happen. The very first questions are:

- How must I change *how I am in relationship to the system* for this to happen?
- How must I change *how I am in relationship to my work*?
- How must I change *how I am in relationship to those around me*?
- How must I change *how I am in relationship to myself*?

DEVELOPING AN ATTITUDE OF SERVICE

If we want to build a spirit-respecting workplace, the answers to these questions inevitably lead us to a transformation of the role of the executive leader. We shift our thinking from focusing on the product, the task, or the tangible outcome to being in service to those who make the product, perform the task, or produce the tangible outcome. We shift from being responsible for production of one million widgets generating an eight-million-dollar profit to being in service to those who do. We shift our role from sustaining a system to being in service to the vision. That brings us to the third essential quality of leadership:

- Leaders have the consciousness, the commitment, and the courage to see that the change they envision does occur.

Consciousness begins to surface with the process of developing intentionality. When we believe we make the difference, we become mindful of how every single thing we say or do either supports the vision or undermines it. When we develop consciousness or mindfulness, we realize how critical it is to choose to leave autopilot behind and to begin to question each thing we do to determine whether it is an action in service of the vision.

Several months into a shift in consciousness, one of my clients complained good-naturedly to me. "It was a lot easier the old way. We didn't have to think about things; we just did them." I'm sure they thought about them before but not in a way that caused them to understand that every action or inaction is a decision, and it is either a decision to support the vision or a decision to undermine it.

Consciousness, commitment, and courage appear to spring forth almost simultaneously. The very process of developing intentionality and consciousness builds commitment and courage. The more conscious we become of the magnitude of the role each of us plays, the more clear it becomes that we really do make a difference. We don't just make *a* difference; we make *the* difference. When we come to know something we haven't known, something almost magical happens. A leap in our being occurs.

"We cannot not know what we have come to know."

I have watched the process many times, and it is something to behold. At the moment I come to know that I am the one who makes the difference, commitment is born. The old days of "try" are behind, I am now accountable. Because each of us makes *the* difference, I realize that the only reason my vision does not occur is my inaction. I realize the importance of playing my role.

A shift in responsibility ensues. When we shift our view of work to being in service to others and the vision, we stop seeing respons-I-bility as something I do or make happen and come to see response-ability. I begin to ask myself, "How do I shift my service role in this situation so I am responding in service to the vision?" The shift is from one of individual work to working in community and connection with others.

The shift in how we experience responsibility leads us to meet yet one more paradox on the Path of Courage. The work is harder. (We have to think about everything.) The work is easier. (We all share response-ability, working in community and connection, and we experience energy-producing joy as we do.)

Almost as magically as commitment surfaces, courage is born. "You can't ask me not to know what I have come to know." Once I know it, the struggle between our ego and our conscience when we don't act requires more of us than having the courage to act. In the process of developing consciousness and commitment, most of us find spirit. Spirit gives birth to faith, trust, and courage.

SO IF THEY'RE DOING WHAT I DO . . .

When we build a spirit-respecting workplace, somewhere well into the construction, a question begins to haunt those accustomed to being in traditional management roles. Sometimes the question is voiced, sometimes it isn't. Sometimes signs of the question appear in the way the process is or is not supported by a person or two. The question is: "So, if they're doing what I do, then what do I do?" It is a Path of Fear question. It is a question for those who are creating what they fear most.

The answer from the Path of Courage is "Work yourself out of a job," and those who are best at being in service to the vision of spirit-respecting workplaces know that if they do their jobs well, their jobs as they have traditionally known them will evaporate. There are always countless ways, however, to be in service to the vision; those people whose jobs evaporate always find other work waiting for them. Notice I say "other work" and not "another job." This is the work of passion I have talked about. It is "our work." It is the work that sets us on fire. The work usually has a job attached to it, but the work, not the job, is what has become important.

One more time the Path of Courage presents us with a paradox. On the Path of Fear, we try to build security by proving how well we do a job, how much we know, how good our analytical skills are, and how valuable our role is. On the Path of Courage we become more valuable by working ourselves out of a job! The managers who get downsized out of jobs are often those who cling to old ways. Those who are in service to the vision may shift assignments more frequently than is traditional, but they move because their ability to work themselves out of a job has made them valuable. On the Path of Courage, the best way to build job security is to work yourself out of a job.

My approach to the consulting business is exactly what I have described here. I do not want to build a relationship in which my client depends on having me around all the time. I want to build the ability of the organization to do those things internally that they have hired me to do while they learned from me. When I was explaining this to a potential client, he posed this question, "So if I understand you, you're trying to work yourself out of a job, right?" Exactly! And the more often I am able to do that, the better I feel about it.

One of my happiest days as a consultant came when a manager I had worked with about a year earlier called me with the following story. "I had an unusual situation arise, and I just wasn't sure what to do. I talked with the owners about it, and they told me I should feel free to call you if I thought I needed help. So I went back to my office and thought about it. 'If I call Kay, I know what she will do. She will ask me questions, and then I will have the answer.' So, I asked myself the questions, and *I* got the answer." She was most pleased and proud. So was I!

On the Path of Courage, leadership is as natural as breathing. From spirit, we bring the faith, trust, and belief that we can make positive things happen, and making things happen is what we are able to do. Our self-fulfilling prophecies are positive ones. Whether we work at the executive level making space for leadership to bubble up or at the bottom taking our first tentative steps into leadership, on the Path of Courage we discover leadership at all levels.

TOOLS FOR BEING ON THE PATH OF COURAGE

- When we are on the Path of Courage, leadership is natural. With spirit come all the qualities that are essential to leadership.
- Leadership is imagining how you would like things to be, knowing that you make the difference and then having the consciousness, commitment, and courage to *be* the change you would create. Believing that we make the difference and developing consciousness help us discover the courage to make the difference.
- Imagining how we would like things to be and believing we make a difference requires developing a very detailed picture of what we want. Developing intentionality requires us to examine how each of us will be differently in relationship with the system, the work, the people around us, and our self to create the change we dream.

- If we are at the executive level of an organization, leadership entails building an environment in which every person comes to own his or her own leadership abilities and then supporting them in exercising those abilities.
- When the continuous improvement process is working well, everyone in the organization learns how to make it work better. When everyone has plenty of information and understands what needs to happen, leadership does occur at all levels.
- Transforming the role of executive leader to one of being in service to those in the system and to the vision is key to creating a spirit-respecting organization. So is shifting our thinking about responsibility to response-ability.
- There are still more paradoxes on the Path of Courage:

> The power paradox: the way to increase our power is to give it away. The more we give it away, the more we get back; or

> The work is harder. (We have to think about every single thing we do.) The work is easier. (We share response-ability in community and connection with others, and we experience joy in doing that); or

> The way we build job security on the Path of Courage is to work ourselves out of a job.

EXPLORING THE PATH OF COURAGE

(1) Look around your workplace and community and identify people who are demonstrating leadership by making their workplace, community, or world a better place. Do they exhibit the qualities that reflect spirit as it is defined in this book? What do you notice about them personally that makes them different from those who never seem to exhibit leadership?

(2) Now look around your workplace and community and identify situations that you would like to see change. What stops you from demonstrating leadership? If you are someone who regularly takes the lead, examine the possibility of demonstrating leadership in a new form—by encouraging and supporting others to discover their natural leadership abilities. Choose to make a difference by exhibiting pure leadership.

Chapter 16

Sparking the Fire in Us at Work

> Godly enthusiasm is not a fire of our own kindling. . . . If a man, however, has caught fire, let me not quench the Spirit by dampening the ardor of his pure devotion. Enthusiasm is not contrary to reason; it is reason—on fire.
>
> . . . PETER MARSHALL[1]

Work is a spark that bridges a critical gap. It is a gap between two essential places: the spiritual place deep within each of us that is the source of our uniqueness, our creativity, and our courage, and the rational, thinking, and productive world in which we live and where we develop our mental and physical abilities and produce the things needed to survive. Work is the bridge that brings wholeness and balance to life. The spark ignites and sets us on fire with passion for work and for life. When we have paid the price, the workplace we create is one that not only allows but encourages us to be wholly present in our work, passion and all.

WORK IS AN OUTLET FOR OUR CREATIVITY

Work can be energizing, exhilarating, and a place of learning and growth. It can provide an outlet for our creativity. Creativity is, among

---

1. Peter Marshall, in Glenn Van Ekeren, *Speaker's Sourcebook II: Quotes, Stories, and Anecdotes for Every Occasion* (Englewood Cliffs, NJ: Prentice Hall, 1994).

other things, learning. Creativity is learning new ways of looking at old problems and learning new ways to arrange old solutions so that they produce a better result. It is learning to challenge old assumptions and limitations. When my friend's factory workers figured out how to cut shipping costs, creativity was at work. When my client's shipping department discovered that turning parts ninety degrees when they were being packed for shipping significantly reduced rejected parts, creativity was at work. Creativity dictates that we be completely *conscious* of opportunities to learn and improve *everywhere* in our workplaces and our lives.

The uniqueness that each of us brings to the workplace is the fuel for creativity. That uniqueness is part of our Wonder Child and part of our spirit. When employers build spirit-respecting workplaces, they provide the match and tinder for lighting the fire in each of us. People have an unlimited supply of fuel, most of which has been locked away with our spirits, kept safely away from our workplaces. When our uniqueness is respected, our spirits spill forth with creativity. The creative solutions that result have limitless applications throughout the enterprise and can have significant ramifications on the bottom line.

Workplace spirit, creativity, and innovation are contagious. Organizations that have learned to foster creativity and innovation find that when people become conscious of improving everything in the work environment, improvements just continue to happen. One organization I know gives employees a brightly colored, two-inch "GISMOS" button whenever a suggestion for improvement is submitted. GISMOS, an acronym submitted by an employee, stands for Good Innovative Suggestions for Making Operations Simpler.[2] Employees quickly began to see who could accumulate the most buttons. They were displayed everywhere. Manufacturing employees covered jackets with the buttons to proudly show how many creative suggestions each had submitted.

Workplace improvements have become so much a way of life at another employer site that providing suggestions becomes a qualifier in compensation evaluation. For an increase in pay even to be considered, an employee must have made at least thirty suggestions for improvement in the preceding year. In a really creative organization, good ideas become better ideas when connection and community come into play and groups of employees improve upon each other's suggestions. This is spirit at work, and it is a manifestation of spirit difficult to replicate outside of an

---

2. GISMOS—Good Innovative Suggestions for Making Operations Simpler—was an idea submitted by employee Tina Howard for use in the Eugene (Oregon) plant of Trus Joist Macmillan.

organizational setting. Work bridges the gap between the creative part of spirit and the rational, thinking, productive world in which we live.

FANNING THE FLAMES

Work brings community to our lives. Work brings to our lives a sense of being part of something larger than any one of us. Indeed, at work the whole is greater than the sum of its parts. No individual can even begin to do what our workplaces do collectively. Each of us not only has a unique way of doing our own job, but each job is important to the success of the enterprise. Each of us makes a difference. Work is a place where we know we belong and where we know we make a difference. We share a common purpose. The connection that we all feel as we pull together to bring life to our workplaces each day is spirit, spirit at work!

For many years, I worked on a daily newspaper. Perhaps more visibly than in many other industries, the production of a daily newspaper symbolizes this synergistic coming together of people with a common sense of purpose. Ours was an afternoon paper that went to press at 1:10 P.M. each day. All morning there was a hum that accelerated as we drew closer to the noon deadline for getting items in the paper. Although some people had actually begun to work on a given day's issue several days or even weeks in advance, each knew his or her role in getting the paper to press that day. The reporters and advertising salespeople prepared items which subscribers would read in their papers. Others did important tasks, like designing the layout of the paper to find room for everything without any large blank spaces and with coupons arranged not to run back to back.

Still others were charged with taking the layout plan, articles, photographs, and advertisements and pulling the individual physical components together so that the finished product looked like the plan. Other people took finished pages and photographed them. The negatives were printed onto aluminum sheets by means of a darkroom process, and press plates from which the paper would be printed were produced. While their co-workers were preparing the press plates, other pressmen were loading the necessary colors of ink into the appropriate press units and webbing the newsprint paper so that correct pages containing multicolor pictures would run through all the necessary units and ultimately come off the press line assembled in the correct page sequence.

As one o'clock approached each day, the heartbeat of the organization gradually quickened, and by the time the last plate with the first page went to the pressroom everyone shared a collective excitement and relief. At 1:10, the presses very slowly began to turn and gradually gained momentum like a giant mechanical elephant slowly waking from a nap and moving at a faster and faster pace. Within a few minutes, the roar of the presses made it impossible to speak, yet everyone in the team knew that the job wouldn't be done until every subscriber had a paper waiting on the doorstep. Pressmen continuously made adjustments in the flow of ink and the tension of the paper web. At the end of the press line, two dozen workers ensured that papers would contain all the appropriate advertising inserts, would be labeled and bound in the correct bundle size for the carrier routes, and then loaded into the correct delivery van for drop-off to the carrier's home.

The final player on this team, the carrier, was a youngster probably ten to fifteen years of age. The carrier's role was to deliver a paper to everyone on his or her route by mid-afternoon. Well, the carrier was *almost* the last person. There was the receptionist in the front lobby who sold copies to people who stopped in to buy issues on the day of publication and for several weeks thereafter. She also took calls from impatient subscribers at 3:32 P.M. when their paper, usually delivered by 3:30, was late.

Everybody in this intricate network of jobs formed a closely working team. No one individual could do the job alone. If any person didn't work with all the others, the job wouldn't be done. Everyone made a difference. The excitement of hearing the presses start caused my heart to race a little each day. I sighed with relief, and we all breathed a little easier each day at 1:10 because subscribers would get their paper on time.

I felt considerable pride in saying I helped bring the newspaper to twenty-eight thousand people today. I felt considerable pride when our paper won an award for a good story or an exceptional advertisement and when we won the First Amendment Award for service in protecting the First Amendment of the U.S. Constitution. I felt special pride when an advertising series to salute long-time employees which I had conceived won statewide recognition and brought honor to the paper for everyone to share. What I felt was spirit, the spirit of teamwork, of working in community with others, of sharing common purposes, of connection, and of trusting all people to do their part. I felt the spirit of making a difference in my workplace community and in my community at large.

The daily newspaper is the place of work which has most visibly displayed this spirit to me, perhaps because of the operation's daily momentum or perhaps because it is my own experience. It can happen in any organization, and I have seen it in many. I remember similar feelings when I'd worked during registration at a state university. Months of planning and scheduling all came together in a few intense days when students started new classes, bought books, and paid fees. I saw it in a regional medical center where a team of highly skilled professionals, supported by a whole hospital system, responded to a helicopter transport of a trauma victim. I saw it in a property management company in a college town when several hundred tenant transitions occurred in the space of a few days at the beginning and again at the end of the school year. I saw it as a network of counselors and social-service support providers worked together to help an abused or neglected child.

In all of these organizations, every person makes a difference. It matters not whether it is the surgeon who performs an emergency open-heart operation or the bookkeeper who never gets near the operating room but ensures that the hospital stays open and the lights are on so that the surgeon has a place to work. Each makes a difference. Each shares in common purpose. Each is a link in the interconnectedness of the enterprise. Each has faith that the others will do their jobs so that as a whole—as a community—we can all do more than any one of us. This process is sharing the spirit of the organization.

WORK IS A SOURCE OF CONNECTION AND RELATIONSHIPS

It is impossible to work in community and common purpose with a team that "breathes together" without developing important relationships. Years after leaving employment at the newspaper described above, I still keep in touch with a number of my co-workers. I consider my most important mentors to have come from that organization. I care about those people. I trust them. I respect them. I have been inspired by them, and I have aspired to more complex and interesting work at least partially because of their belief in me. I am very connected to them long after we stopped working together.

I see this connection wherever I go. In some places, a spirit-respecting employer nurtures the connection. In others, the connection happens in spite of the employer, or it happens as people join forces against the employer. Sometimes it happens when a fraternity of "escapees" coalesces from former employees who suffered together in employment at an organization that didn't respect their spirits. Connection happens in every workplace to some degree, even in spite of the efforts of some employers to quash it. We cannot work together closely in common purpose without sharing a connected spirit.

WORK ISN'T ALL OF LIFE

Work is an integral part of a balanced life. It is an excellent place for achieving our full spiritual potential, both alone and in community with others. It is a place in which we can become charged with energy for the rest of life. It is a place in which we can display leadership at all levels. Work can bring meaning and purpose to our lives and can provide an outlet for what a friend has called "the incredible, godlike quality humans have to create something where nothing existed."

Without work, most of us can keep busy, but our lives may lack that sense of purpose that comes from work. Now work, as I describe it here, does not necessarily have to be employment. It can be any productive outlet. Full-time mothers have a productive outlet in the home which requires creativity, faith, and belief in the ability to produce a positive outcome. One successful professional woman I know considers the most important work she has done to be rearing two confident and competent daughters. Many full-time mothers experience "empty nest syndrome" when the productive outlet of parenting is gone until they discover different outlets for creativity, productivity, connection, and community. Many people who have retired are active in volunteer work, doing important work that otherwise might go undone. They certainly have an important purpose. Each volunteer task contributes to the success of the project proving all work is important work.

I have been blessed with a life that has often brought me in touch with people who are senior citizens, and my experience has been that those who stay healthy and alert have a productive outlet, an ongoing sense of purpose, and a place or places to be in connection and community with others. They keep their spirits alive. I know a person who had retired but was kept so busy volunteering on local and state commissions and advisory boards that I once joked to him that I wasn't sure how the state had run before he retired!

My grandparents actually experienced improved health and well-being after retiring from jobs that did not tap their spirits and moving into activities that brought them that connection. My grandfather, who lived to be almost a hundred, kept a large garden and hunted and fished with friends to provide most of the food for him and my grandmother to supplement their meager pensions.

My grandmother preserved and canned much of what my grandfather grew, caught, or hunted. But this was not the only productive outlet keeping her spirit alive. At retirement my grandmother was finally able to develop her interest in writing and research. She became an authority on local history and other topics of interest to her and gave group presentations well into her eighties. After she developed an interest in a topic, she would read every book on the subject she could find in the library, and then write about her new interest.

Working with passion from the heart keeps us alive. We can live without passion, but neither our minds nor our bodies receive the stimulation they need to be their best. Work is an important part of a balanced life, but it isn't all of life. Our minds, bodies, and spirits are the tools with which we work, and when we don't take care of them, they are not available to achieve their potential in the workplace. After stimulation in other parts of life we bring increased patience, a new perspective, and well-developed ideas to work.

Some companies are beginning to adopt the practice of employee sabbatical leaves, a long-time practice in academic environments. Employees are paid for several weeks during which they don't come to work, but they learn something new, anything in which they have an interest as long as it is new to them. During these periods of active learning, personal creativity and energy are recharged, fostering innovation when employees return to work. Regular exposure to new ideas rekindles us mentally, enhances our growth, and challenges our assumptions about how things are and how they must be.

We also need the personal connection that comes from developing relationships with family and friends away from work. The different roles we play in family, church, community, and volunteer organizations give us new understanding and perspective for the roles we and others play at work. We all thus have the opportunity to demonstrate our leadership skills and to be of service to part of the world beyond ourselves which is yet very much a part of us.

FINDING THE COURAGE TO *BE*

When we choose to lead a spirit-respecting organization, our first job is to learn to *be* a leader. Regardless of where we are in an organization, what our formal role may be or where we are on the organizational chart, there is nothing that a facade can bring to leadership which is not improved by being the people we uniquely are. All of the lessons shared in this book describe the path to a way of being that grows closer and closer to our native selves. This maturing Wonder Child shines brightly with all our natural qualities rather than wearing the masks that our egos may have created to protect us on the Path of Fear.

As we come to accept the Wonder Child in us, we come to realize that openness and trust are impossible when we hide behind a mask, as are freedom, healthy attachments, emotional expression, and loving who we are "for who I am, not what I do." None of these qualities is possible from an ego place.

Our self has rich inner knowing to guide us as we lead, but when we cannot trust our self to be good enough, how can we trust its knowing?

How can we create deep, meaningful, connected relationships when we are afraid to show others who we really are? How can we have a deep, meaningful, connected relationship with our own self when we do not know and love ourselves? How can we be comfortable with ambiguity, chaos, flexibility, and openness, when we depend on arbitrary sets of rules established by people outside of our self? Where will we find courage to walk toward our fear when we don't believe that we have the inner qualities to ensure that we will always be able to produce a positive outcome?

It is easy to forget our uniqueness and become faceless, beingless doers, and it is easy to forget the uniqueness of those about us and to begin to see them as faceless, beingless doers. It is easy to forget the person each of us is inside when we are doing. It is easy to forget the uniqueness and greatness of ourselves and of others when we are doing. It is easy to lose faith.

When we live and lead from spirit, the concerns of everyday doing don't go away. We just learn to be at peace with them. We learn to stop running. We take time to discover and name our fears each day and then to call upon the courage from our spirits to be with our fears. We take time each day for self-love. We nurture our bodies, our minds, and our spirits. Then we are able to go through the day in peace. We need not spend the day in a race to get love from others. We know we are loved with a love that emerges from deep within us. We are filled, and we are safe. Each one of us is at one with our spirits. The choice is one we make each day for the rest of our lives.

When we are filled, we have plenty to give to others. We don't see life from a win-lose perspective; we live from abundance and know we may all win. Wholeness stops the race stemming from the fear that we will not have enough or be enough. We may not recognize the fear, which can seem like an urge to redo something until it is perfect or like a nagging inner voice that haunts us, "Now what will people think if you do *that*?"

When we are not whole in our spirits, we look for love in things, but things never fill us: They are never enough. When we live in fear and scarcity, we are looking to things to fill the hole of not being whole. We feel the hole of nonbeing, and we cannot fill it by doing. Still we try to fill the hole with doing and things. We can never fill the hole in our being or be whole except by choosing to *be*. We choose: We are needy and are always doing and seeking to possess and control more and more outside of our self, or we are abundant and safe. The choice is our own, and we make it every day.

When we are moving toward wholeness, it is easy to admit mistakes. They help us grow. When we are one with our spirits, we are able to catch ourselves. It becomes easier to say, "Stop! Let's play that through again. Let's take advantage of the opportunity to learn." We are not afraid of what people think. We are not afraid to admit that we are not perfect. We are safe in ourselves, and we gain respect, our own respect and the respect of others, from our willingness to grow.

When we choose to *be*, leading from the heart is easy and natural. We are safe and abundant. The choice belongs to each of us, and it is a choice we make every day of our lives. There is no definitive point after which we can just coast. If we are to lead from the heart, we must choose to consciously and continually choose the Path of Courage and rechoose it every day and every moment.

AN END TO *EITHER-OR* THINKING

When we lead from the heart, we model the marriage of rational thinking with spiritual respect. We provide an environment rich in new ways of looking at every aspect of our workplace. We guide the use of rational thinking to support intuitions with facts and details. We guide the integration of everyone's two essential sides to discover possibilities, to foster improvements, to analyze, and to produce. We don't forsake the linear, quantitative, and analytical, and we do not allow it to become the only part of our businesses either. We strive for a perfect marriage of both parts of innate abilities. We look for the enthusiasm that Marshall calls "reason on fire."

This book is *not* intended as a call to dump the rational side of organizations. It is imperative for bringing people's spirit and their own native intuitive processes to full consciousness and respecting that side of ourselves as much as we do our rational, analytical processes. It is a plea for bringing new assumptions—positive and life supporting—to the workplace in every human interaction. It is a petition for safety in learning, for the honoring of mistakes. It is an appeal for openness and flexibility.

Openness and flexibility allow us to replace either-or thinking with both-and possibilities. For too long, we have looked at workplaces as *either* rational, analytical, and productive *or* respectful, self-motivating places to work. We have looked at *either* profitable workplaces *or* ones that were healthy. We have looked at giving the customer *either* quality *or* price. We have been *either* pro-labor *or* pro-management. We have looked at *either* win *or* lose. We have envisioned the workplace world as a set of dichotomies. We had it either one way, or the other. When we challenge these limitations, more and more possibilities present themselves.

Bill George is the CEO of Medtronic, a thirty-six-year-old company that has focused, from its inception, not on profit but on "helping people lead fuller lives."[3] Yet, George proudly reports, the company has been

---

3. "A Company with a Soul," *Business Ethics*, November–December 1993, p. 17.

extremely successful financially as well. "If you had invested $1,000 in Medtronic in 1960, that would be worth $2 million today. . . . That's a pretty good return."[4] Medtronic has a soul, *and* it is profitable.

> "If you read our mission, you can see we serve our customers first. . . . If [employees] feel they really have a worthwhile mission themselves and are a part of carrying out this corporate mission, then the result is that we make a lot of money. But if you do it the other way around by saying, 'We're here to make a lot of money. We'll figure everything else out later,' it doesn't work. You can't sustain it."[5]

Medtronic embodies both-and thinking and refuses to accept that the company's profitability requires the surface of its spirit.

We need workplaces that are rational and analytical and productive and respectful, self-motivating places to work. We need workplaces that are both profitable and healthy. We need to give customers both quality and value. We need businesses that know there is no win-lose. We need organizations that are both pro-labor and pro-management. In the past we have made ourselves and our employees choose between *either* work *or* family. This choice isn't useful; it is a choice that robs us of spirit. We know that it is not only possible but desirable for people to have both work and family. It is not useful to make either ourselves or our employees choose between either work or health. This choice not only robs us of spirit but also robs both the company and the people in it of our most important work tool: our bodies. We have to have both work and health. As leaders from the heart, we have faith and trust that if we have a balance of work, family, and health, our company will be stronger over time.

Either-or choices are rarely useful or productive in the workplace, or anywhere else, because they tend to oversimplify complex issues. Rarely is a choice either black or white. More frequently it is a hundred shades of gray. The leader's role is to keep those around us from simplifying complex issues by reducing them to either-or, to bring more of the whole into light for conscious examination.

I believe with my whole heart and soul that we all have a need to produce something, to be of service, to support ourselves and others, to find something we *do* that brings meaning and purpose to life. And I believe equally in our deep, essential need to be a unique, creative, courageous, spiritual person *while we do what we do*. This is not an either-or situation. We do not have to choose between leading a profitable organization

---

4. See note 3 above, p. 18.

5. See note 3 above.

that produces high-quality, leading-edge products and providing a spirit-respecting place to work anymore than we have to choose between loving our children and doing the laundry. We can do both. We can generate the enthusiasm that "is not contrary to reason: it is reason—on fire."

Increasingly more often companies who operate in a spirit-respecting way are proving that when leaders think in these terms, their organizations are more successful both financially and spiritually than when they emphasize one or the other aspect. They make better widgets, provide better services, respect people more and more, and do it all well. They integrate the wholeness of life into all that they do and move the organization, as individuals and collectively, toward the completion that Johnson says is so essential in our lives.

WE CANNOT DO IT WITHOUT CHANGE

U.S. organizations are managed largely from unacknowledged and unspoken fear. This fear is not conducive to a springing forth of spirit in its full glory to guide the organization and those within it to be their very best. To be our very best commands that we take the Path of Courage. To be our very best requires us to try new things that we don't know will be successful because we've never tried them before. It demands moving forward when we know we are on the right course even though we may not know exactly what lies ahead. Being our very best invites us to accept risk as a part of life that can energize us rather than paralyze us.

Until leaders are willing to let go of their fear and discover the courage of their hearts, our workplaces will continue to stifle the natural forces that produce energy, vitality, flexibility, resilience, learning, and excellence. Even the most organized Total Quality Management (TQM) program implemented on a foundation of fear is doomed to fail. The sustained energy for flexibility and responsiveness in a world of escalating change will never emerge. This sustained energy cannot be willed, only discovered, and it can be discovered only when we have the courage to seek it with the understanding that we cannot know what form it will take until it emerges. We must have faith that this integral part of us, both individually and collectively, will produce positive ends even when we do not know what those ends will be.

A few years ago I had the opportunity to join a Citizen Ambassador delegation to the People's Republic of China, where the nation is embarking upon a business journey whose results they cannot foresee. They are embarking upon a movement never tried before. There are no rules, only learning and improvement. In a country with the world's fastest growing economy, the leaders grapple with building an infrastructure that sustains growth, economic development, and prosperity and respects the spirit, philosophy, and traditions of the people of China.

During one of our meetings, a young man who had earned a Ph.D. in business from a well-known U.S. university expressed the commitment of businesspeople in China to create an environment that will allow China to compete globally and to produce and sustain a thriving economy while it respects what he called the Oriental heart and philosophy. "What works in the United States will not work here. What works in Japan will not work here. We must listen and create something that is Chinese."

As he spoke, it was clear to me that he didn't know what would emerge as leaders grappled with many issues about business and human resources development. What he did know was that the people wanted to build the economy while maintaining their philosophy. He was totally connected with his spiritual courage, and it allowed him to be comfortable not knowing what would emerge. He was confident that as long as they stayed on course, they would achieve their desired outcomes.

This man is part of a cadre of people who will influence the destiny of China in years to come. He is focused on creating the outcomes that are important to China, and he has the courage to know that, if the outcomes are to be achieved, he cannot know what needs to be done along the way. What needs doing becomes clear one step at a time as the collective business intelligence of the nation increases. If he is frightened by that prospect, he has made peace with his fear and is moving ahead with it. None of the typical signs of fear-driven decision-making are present. There is only openness and receptivity.

When we bring this courage and openness to our work, we can leave mediocrity on the Path of Fear and risk being our best. We can embrace our instincts and intuitions rather than hide them behind the need for quantitative, linear data or what we have come to believe we *should* be doing. We no longer need to ignore what is good for people or for the organizations in the long run because we are afraid of this quarter's results. On the Path of Courage, these intellectual distractions melt away into a sea of peace and calm.

For work to be part of the wholeness of life, there must be change on a core level, down to the depths of our souls. Chaos will come and go and come again. Permanent white water is all about us in business, government, and nonprofit organizations. Nothing is as inevitable as change. If we do not do our part to provide a spirit-respecting organization, the winds of change will thrash us about and leave us uprooted and struggling for our very existence. Driven by fear, we limit our thinking to surviving for this moment, this week, this quarter. We forever run from a storm that is always with us. We are always afraid. When we provide spirit-respecting organizations rather than fighting the winds of change, we are anchored by our spiritual roots. We have the openness, creativity, and courage to greet the storm with flexibility; we know change is always with us and we will continue to learn from it. We occupy a spot of strong, powerful tranquillity amid a sea of turbulence. We stand the test of time over and over and over again.

WHO IS THE WIZARD IN YOUR COMPANY?

In *The Wizard of Oz*, the wizard is really an ordinary man behind a screen. With the help of some special effects, he gets people who come to him to believe in themselves. He helps them believe that they have heart, courage, or whatever quality they desire because he tells them they have it.

Ultimately, our success at leading boils down to our ability to help others have trust and faith in themselves. We can only do that when we, like the Wizard of Oz, believe that we can do it. We can help others believe in their ability to accomplish things only when we believe in our ability to lead them to do it. Courage to lead amid chaos and confusion and continuous change is possible only when we know that all we need resides within us. When we are in the middle of organizational white water, we had better believe that we have the skills, intuition, creativity, spontaneity, and flexibility to guide us through the rapids successfully. We don't have time or resources to constantly be looking outside ourselves, gaining additional training, trying to figure out the most protective strategy, and determining new sets of rules when we are in the middle of a white-water rapid.

When we believe in ourselves and are able to help those around us believe in themselves, we discover that we can create a workplace full of wizards, each en-couraging those around him or her to accomplish whatever is needed at any moment. This magic holds organizations together with creativity, energy, and quality to accomplish the undoable consistently through continuous turbulence. This magic vitalizes people so that they leave work with more energy than when they arrived. This magic allows people to meet challenges head on, courageously and ingeniously. This magic is the spirit of the organization.

When we have courage to be what we truly are in our hearts and our souls and to let go of the ego, we can tap spirit in ourselves, and we can tap it in everyone else. When we have the courage, we can create an environment in which every person becomes a wizard because each believes he or she makes a difference. When we lead from the heart, we can discover spirit in our workplaces everywhere.

Chapter 17

Choosing Courage over Fear

This above all: to thine own self be true, /and it must follow, as the night the day/ thou canst not then be false to any man.

... WILLIAM SHAKESPEARE, *The Tragedy of Hamlet, Prince of Denmark*

For a long time I wondered whether I was writing this book for the rest of the world or just for me. Now I know it doesn't matter. If I was to be true to my self, I had to write the book. I cannot be a leader until I have a healthy and respectful relationship with myself. While writing what my spirit has guided me to write, I have learned about myself and about listening to my own knowing and ignoring the rules of a lifetime. As Polonius advised Laertes in *Hamlet* (1.3.78–80), I have learned about being in relationship with all human beings. I have learned that from compassion all human beings are part of me, and so to be more fully in relationship with me is to be more fully in relationship to all people.

This writing has become a spiritual practice or discipline for me as I wrote and rewrote, learned and learned more, and became better and better at listening. It has taught me to let go of control and of trying to force spirit to my schedule. It has taught me about spiritual surrender, respecting that the book (or whatever we are doing) is done when it is done and no sooner. The spiritual practice of writing this book has taught me the patience that I must have as a leader to stay in the present yet always keep the end in mind. It has helped me know that the diversions, the blocks, and the challenges are the sources of learning a lesson deeply. Practicing the discipline has helped me know that the lessons of the moment eventually take me closer to my goal as long as I had the courage to stay on the path when I didn't know where it would lead me.

As I have respected my spirit with the commitment to see this project through when it seemed just too hard, I came to know deep and sustained peace and joy as I had never experienced them. I have come to know the passion and the enthusiasm to lead others to the Path of Courage. I stand in my little office and feel totally alive and at one with spirit and the world. I say to myself, "I feel rich beyond my imagining!" to serve others in coming to know themselves. I have known the courage and determination to be whole in a world that seems to attempt to limit us at every turn. Whenever we have the courage to surrender to spirit, allow ourselves to be lead, and learn the lessons this entails, we open ourselves to the fullness of life and work—a fullness that inevitably changes our lives.

People beg for leadership. They want someone to awaken them from the trance of disenchantment, despair, and despondency. They want someone to en-courage them to stretch and grow and try new ideas. They want someone to help them see the possibilities they have missed in themselves. They want someone to enable them to feel fire and passion in their work. But they cannot and will not see it in a leader who has not done his or her own work, who has not surrendered to spirit and learned the lesson of a work spiritual discipline.

From the place I have called spirit, our passion and enthusiasm allow us to be leaders because people *want* to follow and not because we contrive to make them do what we think is safe. From this place of being true to our Self we can come to live the integrity of leadership that demands that we be true to others because any other has become us. Spirit is our place of inspiration.

To be leaders who inspire courage, we have to be conscious. We must awaken from the spells that our autopilot modes have cast upon us. When Joe came to know his personal fears, he was able to ask for the help that "jazzed" others in his company to pull together behind a common goal. When Sam came to know that he was accountable for the 50 percent of things he didn't like to do, he could then ask for complete accountability from himself and others.

Only when Tom came to see that his self-reliance limited important input from others did his team begin getting to the core of process problems and doing effective group problem solving. When Ellen was willing to see the demoralizing effect her inability to be present was having on people, she was able to begin to effectively engage people and to start a free flow of ideas that energized employees and opened the company to significant cash savings.

Only when I had the courage to see how destructive my perfectionism and self-reliance were to me and to others could I give them up. Abandoning them allowed me to embrace my creativity and to explore new ways to look at leadership and organizations and to discover how to effect meaningful change.

None of us can find the path to more effective leadership without having the courage to look within and to discover how that most important of relationships—my relationship with myself—impacts every other relationship that we have. I can say for myself and for those whom I work with that coming to peace with ourselves is the hardest work we ever do. It is also the most important work, and it continues to reward us day after day as we learn and grow. That is what spiritual discipline is: it is the practice of learning to come closer and closer to what we want to be. This discipline is necessary to be true to self, so that we cannot fail to be true to others. It is knowing of the heart that allows us to lead from the heart.

This book has been built on the premise that there are two paths in work and in life. The Path of Courage requires incredible courage to commit to look inside, to come to know our own heart, and to develop the will and determination to live consciously from a deep sense of awareness. That deep awareness is of our *being*, and to be true to our core being may mean forsaking the rules of a negative organizational culture.

It takes courage to awaken from our trances, turn off the autopilot, and give up habitual living and working. It takes courage to choose to be mindful about everything we do when mindlessly moving through life demands far less of us. Courage is needed to know that everything in our lives is a choice and to own that we are fully accountable for our lives and our relationships.

When we choose to live consciously, we can choose the workplace we will have, and we can create it. We can choose the relationships we will have, and we can create them. We can choose to be fully human, to bring our selves to work and to life, and to allow work to become an integral part of the wholeness of life. We can choose to allow others to be fully awake and human as well.

Leading from the heart is a leadership of courage. It is marching to the beat of a different drummer—our own internal, spiritual guide—although much of society tells us to become mindless, heartless robots. It is having the temerity to listen to our own inner rumblings ahead of the rules of society that have created a culture of doing and non-being.

Leading from the heart is choosing peace and joy when the rumblings you hear aren't like any you've heard before because they are your own original and creative rumblings. It is choosing to act as General H. Norman Schwarzkopf, the commander of Desert Storm, advises young leadership students to act, "Not so much doing what the policy wants, but doing what you feel is right in your heart and what's right in your mind."[1]

Leading from the heart is choosing to be a learner rather than to be learned. It is choosing to come to our work from a place of not knowing so that collectively we can learn together. It is having the courage to be open, flexible, and dynamic. It choosing to go toward our fears and to risk being great when it is easier to produce the lackluster and predictable. It is choosing to have faith in and to trust ourselves and each other that we can learn together how to make every outcome a "win."

When we are on the Path of Fear, most of us are victims who accept what we believe to be fate in work and life and muddle through. When we step on the Path of Courage, we must leave the excuses behind. On the Path of Courage we know that when we choose to live consciously, purposefully, and with intention, each of us holds the power to create what we want. I ask you, indeed society is pleading with you, to commit to make a difference in our workplaces. I ask you to choose courage over fear in your workplace and in your life. It is a choice, and the choice is yours.

---

1. Peter Bacqué, "School Turns Out Leaders—Young UR Program Is First in the Nation," Sunday *Richmond* (VA) *Times-Dispatch*, Richmond, Virginia, 24 March 1996, p. B5.

BIBLIOGRAPHY

Autry, James A. *Love and Profit: The Art of Caring Leadership*. Chicago: Nightingale-Conant, 1991.

Bacqué, Peter. "School Turns Out Leaders—Young UR Program Is First in the Nation," Sunday *Richmond* (VA) *Times-Dispatch*, 24 March 1996, p. B5.

Berrigan, Philip. *Widen the Prison Gates*. New York: Simon & Schuster, 1973.

Bjornstad, Randi. "She's Kept Relief 'Club' Heart Open." *Eugene* (OR) *Register-Guard*, 30 November 1992.

Blenk, Steve, and Susan Blenk. *Blenk Cards*. Sequim, WA, 1992.

Bradshaw, John. *Homecoming: Reclaiming and Championing Your Inner Child*. New York: Bantam Books, 1990.

Brown, Juanita, and David Isaacs. "Building Corporations as Communities: The Best of Both Worlds." In *Community Building: Renewing Spirit and Learning in Business*, ed. Kazimierz Gozdz. San Francisco, CA: New Leaders Press, 1995, pp. 69–83.

Brown, Valerie. "Science: We Feel Therefore We Are, Too: Neurologist Antonio Damasio Lectures at the Hult." *Eugene* (OR) *Weekly*, 28 September 1995.

Capra, Fritjof. *The Turning Point: Science, Society, and the Rising Culture*. New York: Bantam Books, 1983.

Chopra, Deepak. *The Seven Spiritual Laws of Success: A Practical Guide to the Fulfillment of Your Dreams*. San Rafael, CA: New World Library, 1994.

____. "The Seven Spiritual Laws of Success." Public television special. 18 March 1996. UNC-TV.

Covey, Stephen R. *The Seven Habits of Highly Effective People: Powerful Lessons in Personal Change*. New York: Fireside/Simon & Schuster, 1989.

Finegan, Jay. "Survival of the Smartest." *Inc.*, December 1993, pp. 78–89.

Frankl, Viktor E. *Man's Search for Meaning*. Revised and updated. New York: Pocket Books/Simon & Schuster, 1959.

Goff, J. Larry, and Patricia J. Goff. *Organizational Co-Dependence: Causes and Cures.* Niwot, CO: University Press of Colorado, 1991.

Goleman, Daniel. "The New Thinking on Smarts." Adapted from D. Goleman, *Emotional Intelligence. USA Weekend*, 8–10 September, 1995, pp. 4–6.

Hargreaves, Kay Gilley. "The Human Factor: The Rewards of Creativity." *The Business News* (Eugene, OR), 18 October 1993, p. 4.

Heider, John. *The Tao of Leadership: Leadership Strategies for a New Age.* New York: Bantam/New Age Books, 1985.

"Interview: Bill George: In Care of the Company Soul." *Business Ethics,* November–December 1993, pp. 17–19.

Jeffers, Susan. *Feel the Fear and Do It Anyway.* New York: Fawcett-Columbine, 1987.

Johnson, Robert A. *We.* San Francisco, CA: HarperCollins, 1983.

Johnson, Spencer. *The Precious Present.* New York: Doubleday, 1992.

Kabat-Zinn, Jon. *Wherever You Go There You Are: Mindfulness Meditation in Everyday Life.* Los Angeles, CA: Renaissance, 1994. Audiotape, side 1.

Kabat-Zinn, Jon, and Bill Moyers. "Meditate! . . . for Stress Reduction, Inner Peace . . ." *Psychology Today,* July–August 1993, pp. 37–41.

Kaeter, Margaret. "Mission: Impossible?" *Business Ethics,* January–February, 1995, p. 24–25.

Lucas, George (story), Leigh Brackett and Lawrence Kasdan (screenplay). *The Empire Strikes Back.* 20th Century-Fox Productions, 1984.

Moses, Kenneth. "Shattered Dreams and Growth: A Workshop on Helping and Being Helped." Presented by Resource Networks, Inc., Evanston, IL., Portland, OR, April 1993.

Nachmanovitch, Stephen. *Free Play: The Power of Improvisation in Life and the Arts.* New York: G. P. Putnam's Sons, 1990.

National Public Radio. *Weekend Edition/Sunday.* Robert Ferrante, executive producer, Robert Malesky, show producer. 5 December 1993.

Needleman, Jacob. *Money and the Meaning of Life.* New York: Currency/Doubleday, 1991.

Oakley, Ed, and Doug Krug. *Enlightened Leadership—Getting to the Heart of Change.* Simon & Schuster, 1991.

Orsborn, Carol. *Inner Excellence: Spiritual Principles of Life-Driven Business.* San Rafael, CA: New World, 1992.

Osbon, Diane K., ed. *A Joseph Campbell Companion: Reflections on the Art of Living.* New York: HarperCollins, 1991.

Peck, M. Scott, M. D. *The Road Less Traveled: A New Psychology of Love, Traditional Values and Spiritual Growth.* New York: Touchstone/Simon & Schuster, 1978.

Peters, Tom. *Thriving on Chaos: Handbook for a Management Revolution.* San Francisco, CA: Perennial Library/Harper & Row, 1987.

Rankin, Michael Scott. "Spiritual Entrepreneuring." In *The New Bottom Line: Bringing Heart and Soul to Business,* eds. John Renesch and Bill DeFoore. San Francisco, CA: Leaders Press, 1996.

Ray, Michael, and Rochelle Myers. *Creativity in Business.* New York: Doubleday, 1986.

Richards, Dick. *Artful Work: Awakening Joy, Meaning and Commitment in the Workplace.* San Francisco, CA: Berrett-Kohler, 1995.

Robbins, Anthony. *Personal Power: How to Get What You Really Want: The Power of Focus.* Audiotape. Learning series by Robbins Research International. Produced by Guthy-Renker Corp., Irwindale, CA, 1989.

Rosen, Robert H, with Lisa Berger. *The Healthy Company: Eight Strategies to Develop People, Productivity and Profits.* Los Angeles, CA: Jeremy P. Tarcher, 1991.

Sanford, John A. *Invisible Partners.* New York: Paulist Press., 1980.

Senge, Peter M. *The Fifth Discipline: The Art and Practice of the Learning Organization.* New York: Currency/Doubleday, 1990.

____. "The Leader's New Work: Building Learning Organizations." In *New Traditions in Business: Spirit and Leadership in the 21st Century,* ed. John Renesch. San Francisco, CA: Berrett-Kohler, 1992.

"Survival of the Smartest." *Inc.,* December 1993, pp. 78–79.

Vaill, Peter B. *Managing as a Performing Art: New Ideas for a World of Chaotic Change.* San Francisco, CA: Jossey-Bass, 1989.

____. "Leading-Managing in Permanent White Water." Keynote address for Rediscovering the Soul in Business: Managing for Profit and the Human Spirit. Boise State University. Boise, ID, 23 September 1995.

Van Ekeren, Glenn. *Speaker's Sourcebook II: Quotes, Stories, and Anecdotes for Every Occasion.* Englewood Cliffs, NJ: Prentice Hall, 1994.

Von Bertalanffy, Ludwig. "The Theory of Open Systems in Physics and Biology." *Science* (1950) 3: 23–29.

Von Oech, Roger. *A Whack on the Side of the Head: How You Can Be More Creative.* New York: Warner Books, 1983.

____. *A Kick in the Seat of the Pants: Using Your Explorer, Artist, Judge, and Warrior to Be More Creative.* New York: Harper & Row, 1986.

Websters II: New Riverside University Dictionary. Boston, MA: Riverside/Houghton Mifflin, 1984.

Weisbord, Marvin R. *Productive Workplaces: Organizing and Managing for Dignity, Meaning and Community.* San Francisco, CA: Jossey-Bass, 1990.

Wheatley, Margaret J. *Leadership and the New Science.* San Francisco, CA: Berrett-Kohler, 1992.

INDEX

Kat Gilley, M.S., PHR, brings nearly 30 years experience working in general and human resource management to her current work as a leadership and organizational development consultant, specializing in guiding the development of leaders and what she calls "intentional organizations." She is most interested in writing to "real business people" about current business issues. Her writing, as all of her work, focuses on building organizations that respect people, learn as groups, and produce quality products and services.

Ms. Gilley received her MSIR (Industrial Relations) with a minor in law from the University of Oregon Graduate School of Management, and her PHR (Professional in Human Resources) from the Human Resource Certification Institute in 1991. She resides in Eugene, Oregon and Durham, North Carolina.